Topical Issues in Pain 2

Physiotherapy Pain Association Yearbook

Topical Issues in Pain 2

Biopsychosocial assessment and management
Relationships and pain

Editor

Louis Gifford MCSP BSc MAppSc

Foreword

Paul Watson MCSP BSc MSc

CNS Press Ltd, Kestrel, Swanpool, Falmouth, Cornwall TR11 5BD, UK
    info@cnspress.co.uk
    www.achesandpainsonline.com

First published 2000

ISBN 0 9533423 1 X

British Library Cataloguing in Publication Data:

Physiotherapy Pain Association Yearbook: Topical Issues in Pain 2.
Biopsychosocial assessment and management. Relationships and pain.
Edited by Louis Gifford
Includes bibliographical references and index.
616.047 dc21

Editing JJ Editorial Services
Indexing   Master Indexing
Typesetting Sangar Services Pty Ltd
Printed and bound by Rowe the Printers, Cornwall, UK

Foreword

This is the second in the series of Topical Issues in Pain, the first volume met with resounding praise from reviewers and has proved to be very popular with physiotherapists and other professions. At the time of writing the first volume is being reprinted such is the demand. From the outset, the remit of this series was to bring together information with a sound evidence base and present it in a way that would make it possible for physiotherapists to incorporate that information into clinical practice. I hope that readers will find once again that we have gone some way towards achieving this aim in this volume.

There are four introductory essays from: Louis Gifford, George Peat of Keele University, Heather Muncey, past chair of the PPA, and Jennifer Klaber Moffett and colleagues.

Louis Gifford presents a biological argument against the use of uni-disciplinary/single dimension/single modality reasoning and therapy models for pain management and treatment. We are asked to consider a more widespread multidirectional model for the repercussions of therapies and productive interactions with patients. For example, that in one direction all successful therapies and interactions with patients have at their heart an alteration in the expression of gene activity!

George Peat provides a thought-provoking essay which may prove to be uncomfortable reading for many. He asks the fundamental question: Has there been a real change? Evaluations of pain management programmes have often been criticised as only measuring change on their own terms. Perhaps I can explain this criticism through the following anecdote. In a conversation with a physiotherapist working in pain management I asked what she thought was a useful outcome measure. She told me that her programme found self-efficacy the best outcome measure as it was most responsive to change. Pain management programmes frequently identify changes in self-efficacy and fear avoidance beliefs as goals for the programme. We then assume, because we read it in some of the literature, that there is a close link between self-efficacy and disability; that we need to change one before the other changes. Is this true or are we playing what George Peat has called the substitution game; measuring what we can change rather than what is important? The measurement of outcomes in chronic pain management is particularly difficult in a condition that fluctuates as chronic pain related disability does. We must be clear which changes are sustainable and whether they are cost effective if we are to justify our role in the management of patients with chronic pain. We all need a dose of constructive self-criticism and self-appraisal from time to time and I hope reading this chapter will prompt this in physiotherapy.

The title of Heather Muncey's chapter *The challenge of change in practice* might, on first sight, appear to be odd for inclusion in a book on pain. However, in the biopsychosocial section, Nick Kendall and I suggest that we need to develop a new approach to the assessment and management of patients with painful conditions. This approach, grounded very much in the biopsychosocial model, argues for an expansion of physiotherapy assessment to assess more explicitly the psychosocial factors involved in the development and maintenance of disability. This suggestion may not find favour with all physiotherapy practitioners. Although, in my opinion, there has been considerable change in the way in which physiotherapists approach pain problems, some therapists find it difficult to see the relevance of this approach and may be resistant to change. Heather Muncey's chapter will be of particular relevance to those therapists trying to introduce new ideas in conservative departments.

The fourth introductory essay reproduces a piece of work first published in the British Medical Journal and headed by research physiotherapist, Jennifer Klaber Moffett. This work provides some hard data for the long term effectiveness of a physiotherapy-led exercise programme for sub-acute and recurrent back pains that incorporates cognitive behavioural principles. The 'key messages' highlighted by the authors on page 64 are of great significance to physiotherapy and the work and aims of the Physiotherapy Pain Association.

The biopsychosocial section of the book also looks at the current evidence for the role of psychosocial factors in the transition from acute to chronic incapacity and response to treatment. This is a timely inclusion when there are increased pressures on physiotherapists to develop some form of psychosocial triage in order to enhance outcomes from the management of musculoskeletal pain. The biopsychosocial model demands that the patient is given a full biomedical assessment and the reliability and importance of this is presented by Lisa Roberts (Ch. 1). The role of attitudes to pain in the alteration of its perception is discussed by Jennifer Klaber Moffett (Ch. 5).

Nicholas Kendall and I take on the problem of reviewing the evidence for the use of psychosocial screening and assessment in musculoskeletal pain. Dr Kendall was responsible for the development of the psychosocial risk management strategy in New Zealand which coined the term *Yellow Flags*. The authors suggest a practical way forward for those (not only physiotherapists) involved in managing people with musculoskeletal pain. Although we both recommend the integration of an assessment of psychosocial factors into physiotherapy the reader is cautioned against developing this into yet another poorly researched 'fashion', a phenomenon which is all too frequently observed in physiotherapy.

The section on relationships and pain gives a social focus to the suffering of the patient with chronic pain. Although physiotherapists are not trained specifically to intervene in this area it is important that they understand the social consequences of chronic pain and the way in which these are managed by psychologists and how they can be managed jointly. Issues relating to the relationship between patients and their pain and the potential of the physiotherapist/patient relationship are also addressed by Hazel O'Dowd (Ch. 6) and Toby Newton-John (Ch. 7). In the final chapters of this section Toby Newton-John, Suzanne Brook, Christina Papadopoulos, and Vicki Harding give very practical guides to helping chronic pain sufferers with sexual dysfunction, and women with back pain through pregnancy. Many women are worried about the potential adverse effects of pregnancy on their pain, and this practical approach will be invaluable to physiotherapists working in this field.

I would like to give my personal thanks to all the contributors to this volume. There is an old adage 'If you want a job done well ask a busy man', or in this case *person*. All the contributors are busy people because they are highly respected individuals who are in demand by their own profession and others. I am grateful that they have taken time to contribute to this volume in what is proving to be a very exciting and informative series. I look forward to the next one!

Paul Watson
Physiotherapy Pain Association Chairman 1999-

Preface

This volume is about changes in practice that will benefit patients and clinicians. It is also about our relationships with our patients, and their's with their pain and their families.

With changes in practice there is a necessary extension of traditional thinking into new territories and new skills to be taken on. We need to encourage those who are involved in the early treatment and management of pain to take on new information and new assessment and treatment approaches; the burden of responsibility for chronic pain prevention is with them. In particular, all the chapters in this book underline the recognition that musculoskeletal pain has biomedical and psychosocial components that must be managed within a biopsychosocial framework. There is plenty of practical guidance.

If clinicians better understand the development of chronic pain and disability and the processes that precipitate them, they can take an active and recognised role in prevention and the human and social costs of this major problem can be reduced. A major theme of this volume is that we need to think differently and, above all, that we need to understand and recognise what the traditional biomedical model means and where its values and weaknesses lie. The biomedical, or 'disease' model of pain is a single level construct which may be fine where a problem's cause can be established and which has a remedy available for it. The biomedical model assumes that an individual's complaints should result from a *specific* disease state represented by a focus of disordered biology, the diagnosis of which is confirmed by data from objective tests of physical damage and impairment. Intervention is directed specifically toward correcting the organic dysfunction or the pathology and if this doesn't work the patient, rather than our inadequate understanding, is frequently blamed. Thus, the traditional medical approach adopts a simple dichotomous view: symptoms are either somatogenic (real and potentially fixable) or psychogenic (not real and hence of little or no interest).

Although variations of this view still pervade, supporting evidence is lacking. If we really want to explain and understand pain, pain disability and pain response and prevent them from continuing to be major health care problems, we need to adopt a much more open minded multidimensional approach. We need new broader based models to help us understand chronic pain and incapacity and its development. This is what many in the vanguard of pain management and disability prevention are suggesting.

In the epilogue of his book *The Back Pain Revolution*, 1998, Gordon Waddell, a uniquely enlightened orthopaedic surgeon, lists the following important points about back pain:

- Human beings have had back pain throughout recorded history
- Back pain has not changed: it is no different, no more severe and no more common than it has always been
- What has changed is how we think about back pain and what we do about it
- We have turned a benign bodily symptom into one of the most common causes of chronic disability in Western society today
- But if we can create that epidemic, we can also reverse it.

Waddell's writing is pithy, smart, and makes intuitive sense. The messages are sound, evidence based, clear, and easy to follow. Like many others, he argues that the biomedical approach to back pain has not solved the problem and may even be adding to it via inappropriate intervention. He advocates passionately that we should all adopt a biopsychosocial framework. The following two messages taken from his book are pertinent here:

> The biopsychosocial model is not a new philosophy. Rather, it is a method, or a set of tools, to apply that ancient philosophy (of caring for sick people) to our daily practice. It allows us to combine the role of healer with the more ancient role of counsellor, helping patients to cope with their problem. The patients' role must also change from passive recipient of treatment to more active sharing of responsibility for their own progress.
>
> ...It is no longer enough to know about anatomy and pathology. The biopsychosocial approach opens a whole new perspective on how people behave and cope with illness. It reveals the limitations of our treatment and of our professional skills. It exposes us to the difficulties and stress of dealing with emotions. We must accept that patients are not neat packages of mechanics or pathology, but suffering human beings. Professional life may be much simpler if we stick to physical treatment of mechanical problems, but health care demands that we treat human beings.' (p.442)

Waddell goes out of his way to acknowledge the physical nature of back pain, that it is usually initiated by a physical problem, and that over the last 10 years the balance of back pain research has 'perhaps swung too far towards the psychosocial issues, to the neglect of the physical'. He argues that we need more research into the physical basis of non specific low back pain with the focus primarily on physical dysfunction rather than on anatomic and structural lesions. This stance is praiseworthy; however, 10 years of research may need as many years of integration into clinical reality. Perhaps in ten years' time books like this one, and the work of all the authors who have contributed to it, will receive a dash of recognition for initiating a practice change at a timely moment in our professional history?

Shifting therapist and patient thinking, from a largely unidimensional biomedical model based approach, to *incorporating* a multifaceted and multidimensional model, is the great philosophical and practical challenge confronting clinicians. Along with the first in the series, this volume rises to the challenge by providing the background information and practical pathways necessary for implementing changes in thinking and working practice.

Editing this volume of Topical Issues in Pain has been a pleasure; I am proud of what the authors have presented and I have been enlightened. I will be very surprised if you, the reader, do not get a great deal out of it too. Read, think, reflect and above all, integrate!

Louis Gifford, Falmouth
January 2000

Contributors

Julie Barber MSc
Research Fellow in Medical Statistics
Department of Medical Statistics and Evaluation
Imperial College School of Medicine
University of London
London UK

Suzanne Brook MCSP SRP
Clinical Specialist in Pain Management
Pain Management Centre
The National Hospital for Neurology and Neurosurgery
Queen Square
London UK

Amanda Farrin MSc
Trial Statistician
Department of Health Sciences and Clinical Evaluation
University of York
York UK

Louis Gifford MCSP BSc MAppSci
Chartered Physiotherapist
Kestrel, Swanpool
Falmouth UK

Vicki Harding MCSP SRP
Research and Superintendent Physiotherapist
INPUT Pain Management Unit
St. Thomas' Hospital
London UK

David Jackson MCSP
Research Physiotherapist
Institute of Rehabilitation
University of Hull
Hull UK

Nicholas Kendall PhD
Senior Lecturer
Department of Orthopaedic Surgery and Musculoskeletal Medicine
Christchurch School of Medicine
University of Otago
Christchurch New Zealand

Jennifer Klaber Moffett PhD MSc MCSP
Senior Lecturer in Rehabilitation
Deputy Director, Institute of Rehabilitation
School of Medicine
University of Hull
Hull UK

Hugh Llewelyn-Phillips MCSP
Senior Physiotherapist
Marmaduke Street Health Centre
Hull
Hull UK

Heather Muncey BA MCSP RMN
Physiotherapy Manager
Frenchay Hospital
Bristol UK

Toby Newton-John BA (Hons) M.Psychol, C.Psychol
Principal Clinical Psychologist
Department of Pain Management
National Hospital for Neurology and Neurosurgery
London UK

Hazel O'Dowd MSc C.Psychol
Chartered Clinical Psychologist
Pain Management
Frenchay Hospital
Bristol UK

Christina Papadopoulos MSc MCSP
Chartered Physiotherapist
Academia Centre
Larnaca Cyprus

George Peat PhD BSc MSc MCSP
Research Fellow
Primary Care Sciences Research Centre

Keele University
Staffordshire UK

Lisa Roberts MCSP SRP
Superintendent Physiotherapist and Lecturer in Physiotherapy
School of Occupational Therapy and Physiotherapy
University of Southampton
Southampton UK

Sally Bell-Syer BSc
Research Fellow
Department of Health Studies
University of York
York UK

David Torgerson PhD
Senior Research Fellow
Centre for Health Economics
University of York
York UK

Paul J. Watson MSc BSc MCSP
Research Fellow
Rheumatic Diseases Centre
Hope Hospital
Salford UK

Contents

Introductory essays

The patient in front of us: from genes to environment

LOUIS GIFFORD

In the current climate of professional insecurity and threatening market-place forces, it helps if physiotherapy can demonstrate to those who purchase its services that it is moving forward, keeping up to date, being cost effective and providing the public with a desirable service. The pressure is on. For example, in 1998 Cherkin and colleagues published the results of work that compared the outcomes for low back pain from chiropractic, McKenzie physical therapy, and an educational booklet. The outcomes need to be scrutinised in detail to be fair, but the publicised result of the research goes like this:

> Chiropractic and McKenzie treatments, which in this study cost about $235 more than the booklet, did not lead to decreased recurrences of back pain or to reductions in visits or costs of back care during the two years following treatment.

Conclusions:

> ...given the limited benefits and substantial costs of chiropractic manipulation and McKenzie physical therapy, treatments of this type should be used sparingly.

It is possible that the results will be generalised to all forms of therapy for back pain and sceptical referring practitioners will then take comfort in performing their usual speedy examination, giving a few words of reassurance and advice followed by handing out the latest back pain booklet, secure in the belief they are acting on 'the latest and most cost effective evidence'. They may have a point, but the complexity of factors that play a role in precipitating chronic pain and chronic disability are such that some at risk patients require thoughtful and time consuming assessment and management in the *early days* of their problem. This is the key time. Linton's (1998, 1999) work, has shown that identifying and addressing the known risk factors in early management of back pain can reduce chronic disability by 8 fold over 'treatment as usual'.

1

The interventions Linton (1998) used involved understanding and dealing with the anxieties and fears patients have about causing pain and causing structural damage with movement and activity, plus other psychosocial issues discussed at length in this book. What is evident from this work, is that alongside cognitive behavioural strategies that improve the patients' ability to cope, lies the fundamental issue of restoration of the patients' trust and confidence in their physical structure during activity. Hence the emphasis on incorporation into rehabilitation strategies of physical programmes aimed at providing a progressive restoration of confident physical function. Restoration of 'confidence', is about *proficient* examination, *helpful* education and *practical* experience. *This is a highly skilled area and one which is unique to the physiotherapy profession.* Guiding the patient into gradually more normal function, using practical tasks and exercises in ways where the patient always feel in control, feels safe, is a part of the decision making process, and can see where a particular exercise or movement is leading, are a few of the important issues.

The patient in front of us

Integrating psychological and social issues into practice is not an easy matter for professions that are linked historically to tissue/injury/pathology-based explanations and treatments for all pains. Overcoming a natural antipathy to integrate 'other' issues, concepts and explanations is a major step towards effective practice change.

The patient in front of us can have many problems, even one with such an apparently simple thing as a recently twisted ankle or a modestly sprained back. The more you enquire, the more information you seek, the more you tend to find. There may be loss of physical function and disability; there may be physical impairments—like losses of range of movement, tender areas, painful movements, or muscle imbalances; there may be anxieties and distress; there may be anger and unhelpful beliefs about the nature of the problem and about the effects of treatment; patients may have a significant fear of movement and harm; they may be under pressure from work and work colleagues, or may have financial problems and pressures; their standing in their social or work community may be under threat, and so forth. The term 'barriers to recovery' that Paul Watson uses, is so useful to think about when with a patient (see Chs 2 & 3). But perhaps a word of caution is needed: skilled therapists delve only to the depth of enquiry required for optimum outcome, and do so in a way that is quite comfortable for the patient. This skill is a product of high levels of knowledge, correct interpretation, and practised communication and handling.

Figure I.1 represents the traditional hierarchy of the sciences (see Rose 1997). This conventional perspective proceeds from the hard, reductionist and mechanistic lower levels that are most easily measured, controlled and analysed, to the upper softer, vaguer and more nebulous psychological and sociological levels. The disciplines at these upper levels have struggled to be accepted as scientific disciplines in their own right and still evoke general scepticism. Change in culture produces a change in attitude, and hypotheses

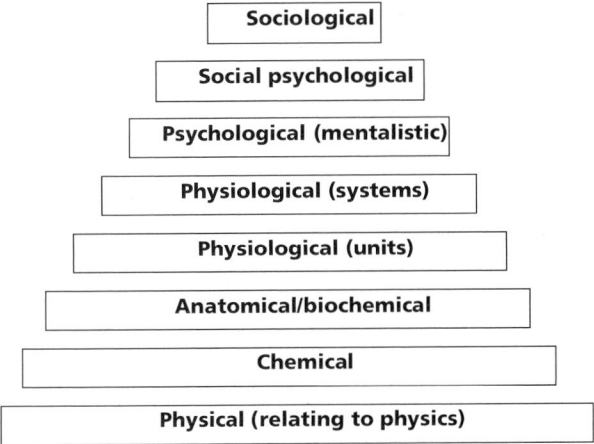

Fig. I.1 The traditional hierarchy of the sciences (adapted from Rose 1997)

and paradigms that were unacceptable and derided a few years ago may well offer pathways for the future. In this book we are dealing with the medical and physiotherapy culture related to patients in pain and their management and understanding. The plea is for integration of thinking and input from all levels of the scientific hierarchy.

From genes to environment

Scientists tend to operate within their own tightly knit communities. Until recently it has been quite rare to find a scientific thinker and writer who seeks explanations and understanding from specialities beyond a specific discipline. Each level of the scientific 'hierarchy' may well have its own explanations and answers for a given phenomenon, and adherents often defend their position by openly and unproductively criticising those offered from competing disciplines. This is especially so in the field of pain science and pain therapy, where a plethora of explanations and treatments for pain and disability derive from the many different disciplines and clinicians involved. These include a spectrum reaching from the social scientists right down to the biochemists and geneticists, with treatment inputs coming via sociologists, clinical psychologists, rehabilitationists, manual therapists, alternative therapists right down to the pharmacologists and, now, gene manipulators. In general the overall tendency is to fund and seek explanations for pain from ever more reductionist and economy driven paradigms. Hence the current wave of enthusiasm for genetic understanding and eventual genetic manipulation by drug interventions in the world of pain science (for example, Iadarola et al 1997, Julius 1999, Woolf et al 1999), rather than for the increasingly evidenced-based practices more strongly linked to the upper tiers of the heirarchy— where industry driven profit motives are least likely to feature and which are far more difficult and time consuming to practise than the simple act of prescribing and taking a pill.

Figure I.2 represents a hierarchy of levels that may be used for explanations of pain and disability. It also indicates the type of therapists available at each level.

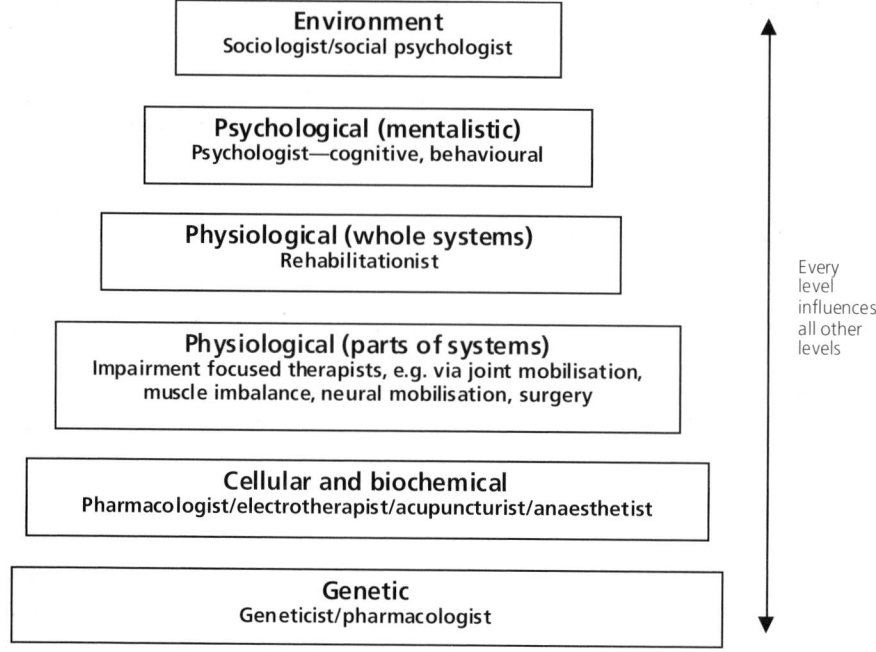

Fig. I.2 Hierarchy of explanations for pain and disability and related therapists

- At the top level is *environment*. Here, for example, chronic pain and disability may be linked to the patients' distress at work, to the way their family reacts to them or perhaps to some losses in their social life. Manipulate these and the patient may get better. Sociologists and social psychologists have a claim to pain treatments and management.

- At the *psychological* level, patients may have powerful beliefs that any physical movement is threatening to their weakened painful state and that rest is the best option for healing; or they may have such emotional turmoil that their interest in any form of healthy activity or life style is non-existent. Educate more healthy beliefs and demonstrate that their fears are unfounded, help them overcome their emotional turmoil, improve their coping strategies and reinforce more appropriate behaviour and patients may get better. Psychologists clearly have a role in pain.

- The *physiological: whole system* level relates to systems that may be considered to be faulty in some way, hence, temporarily or permanently altered function of the nervous, endocrine, musculoskeletal, locomotor, or visceral systems, and so forth. From a physical therapist's viewpoint this level may more easily relate to faulty or altered gross movement patterns and loss of function—it is here that research and therapy focus on ***disability.*** (In the clinical reasoning literature the term *general physical dysfunction* has been used synonymously, see Gifford 1997, Gifford & Butler 1997, Butler 1998). Thus, the patient with back pain may be unable to bend and this affects ability to dress, to sit comfortably, to drive the car, and to sit at the desk for work. Treatment may focus on exercises to gradually improve flexion, to pace up sitting and bending tolerance. For the sprained ankle, treatment may focus on normal gait or on starting a gradual and progressive weight bearing programme. Rehabilitationists are central to this level of management.

- The *physiological: parts of systems* level can relate to more specific findings. For example, a joint under question might have modest restriction of accessory movement, ligaments, tendons, muscles, muscle groups, or a specific nerve may demonstrate increased mechanical sensitivity. Other issues might include loss of range, muscle imbalance, even loss of structural integrity or instability. This level relates to an ***impairment*** focus by the researcher or clinician. (In the clinical reasoning literature the term *specific physical dysfunction* has been used synonymously, see Gifford 1997, Gifford & Butler 1997, Butler 1998.) Altered function at this level might be addressed by manual therapists or surgeons.

- The *cellular and biochemical* level looks at pain from the perspective of changes in the tissue environment and changes in cells and pathways in the nervous system. Thus pain and disability may relate to changes in inflammatory chemicals in freshly injured muscle or ligament, to alterations in neuropeptides or receptor populations in nociceptors and nociceptor pathways subserving the injury, or to altered immune functions and altered neuroendocrine reactivity and so on. This paradigm for pain offers help via chemical manipulation of the tissue and pathways as well as the cellular environment—hence the pharmacological claims to the management and treatment of pain. Involvement at this level might be via pharmacology, electrotherapy, acupuncture or perhaps manual therapy.

- Currently, the lowest, most 'reductionist' level is the *genetic* level of research, thinking and intervention. This is worth discussing as it serves as a useful platform to relate to effects and interactions from other levels.

There are presently two schools of thinking with regard to genes and pain. The first view accepts that states like pain sensitivity, response to analgesics and susceptibility to painful pathologies are subject to great inter-individual variability (like all bio-physiological and bio-psychological phenomena), and that genetic factors have a role to play here (Mogil 1999). The bottom line is that some of us may be genetically 'programmed' or 'susceptible' to more lasting pain states, following the same injury or pathology, than are others. Environmental influences on gene 'expression' are of course acknowledged. Gene therapy, as it was originally conceived would be used to correct genetic defects by replacing or substituting the defective gene with a new, more appropriately functional copy (Iadarola et al 1997). In essence the idea for pain treatment using this approach to gene therapy is to implant functional copies of new genes into appropriate sensory processing neurones (e.g. into nociceptors or nociceptor pathways) in order to confer new properties on them. Thus, the activity of the 'defective' gene is overridden and with the new gene's activity the cell changes its characteristics to become less sensitive. In genetic terms, the altered genotype changes the phenotype—the very structure and characteristics of the cell. A current research focus is targeting the spinal cord and dorsal root ganglion as potential sites of gene transfer (Iadarola et al 1997).

A second view seeks to alter gene 'expression' rather than actually change the gene for another one. At least this sounds more feasible! Appreciate that a specific gene is a unique series of amino acids on a molecule of DNA and that genes act as templates to build and produce relevant RNA molecules that go on to act as further templates for the construction of cellular proteins. When a gene 'expresses' it has to be switched on. A given gene produces or 'expresses' a protein specific to that gene. During the life of any given cell genes are continuously being switched on and off in order to manufacture, or stop the manufacture of, proteins needed/not needed by the cell to help it function and survive. The process of switching genes on and off is a fundamental part of cell homeostasis and very much a part of the normal day to day physiological processing for all active cells in all cellular organisms. For considerations with regard to pain and alterations in sensitivity we need to appreciate that the same mechanisms are operative. Genes are being switched on and off in response to injury and genes are being switched on and off in response to therapy. This needs closer scrutiny.

Electrical sensitivity and the ability to pass impulses via saltatory conduction is a characteristic of neurones that relies on the very rapid passage of Na^+, K^+ and Ca^{++} ions in and out of the cell through pores in the axoplasmic cell membrane (Shepherd 1994). These membrane pores are called 'ion channels' (Figs I.3 & I.4) and are capable of opening and closing in response to conditions locally (Kandel et al 1995, Tanner et al 1997). For example, some ion channels may be opened by nearby electrical activity—and are called 'voltage gated' channels; others may be opened by chemicals like adrenaline, noradrenaline, bradykinin, prostaglandins or hydrogen ions. Some open in response to mechanical stresses. Ion channels that are opened (or closed) by chemicals contain receptors and are termed 'ligand gated' ion channels. Ion channels, and their receptors if they have them, are protein molecules that are produced as a result of specific gene activity in the cell body of the neurone concerned. The more active ion channels and receptors that a given neurone has, the more sensitive it becomes. Further, the type of sensitivity characteristic of the cell is dependent on the type of receptor population present. Thus large populations of active mechanoreceptors signify a cell that is highly sensitive to touch and pressure—hence the clinical finding of mechanical allodynia/primary hyperalgesia (discussed in Gifford 1997, Gifford 1998a). Large numbers of adrenoreceptors signify a cell that is highly responsive to adrenaline and noradrenaline, and so forth.

6

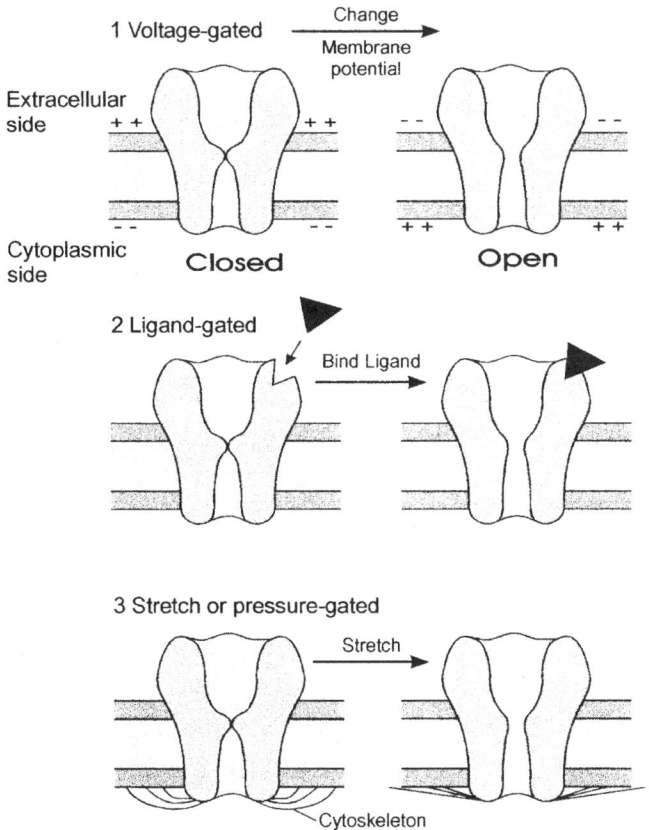

Fig. I.3 Ion channels in the cell membrane of sensory neurones:
1. Voltage gated. 2. Ligand gated. 3. Stretch or pressure gated channels.

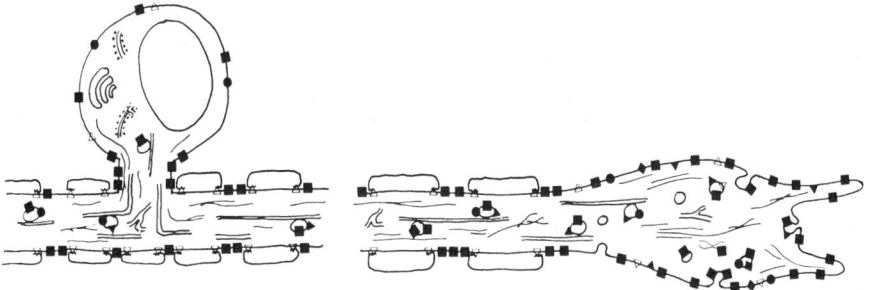

Fig. I.4 Schematic representation of a single sensory neurone highlighting ion channels and receptor proteins in the cell wall. Adapted from: Devor et al 1994
∇ K+ channel ● Ca++ channel
■ Na+ channel ▲ Adrenoreceptor = ligand gated ion channel sensitive to adrenaline.
♦ Mechanoreceptor or Stretch activated receptor

When tissues are injured the nociceptive cells innervating that tissue begin to increase their sensitivity and start to fire more easily, some may even fire spontaneously. Increased sensitivity and spontaneous firing is a product of the availability of *active* ion channels and receptors and their relative numbers (Tanner et al 1997). Immediately after an injury many inactive or 'refractory' receptors in the membranes of the local nociceptors become activated. Hence the relatively rapid increase in sensitivity of the injury area. At the same time, chemicals which are produced by the injured tissues or immune cells in the injury area pass into the nociceptors and, via axoplasmic transport, eventually reach the cell body of the neurone. Once there they are known to stimulate specific gene activity and hence protein synthesis (McMahon et al 1997). This is a wonderful example of a cellular level '*sample, scrutinise* and *act*' process discussed in Chapter 2 of Volume 1 of Topical Issues in Pain (Gifford 1998). The nervous system chemically *samples* its target tissues; if they are damaged it detects the presence of injury related chemicals, *scrutinises* them and then mounts an appropriate *response*. Part of this response is to produce more ion channels and receptors so that the neurone can increase its sensitivity. The neurone may also 'upregulate' its production of inflammatory neuropeptides— needed in the tissues to produce inflammation and hence initiate the healing process (McMahon et al 1997).

New receptors that are produced and transported back to the peripheral terminals of the neurone become implanted in the cell membrane with the result that the cell further increases its sensitivity. This is clearly a process that takes a while. The message of importance behind these events, is that gene activity influences the sensitivity of the cell by ultimately altering its membrane structure. The inclusion of more ion channels and receptors changes the cell physically and changes its dynamic properties. This demonstrates the plasticity of the system that enables its adaptive response to the threat posed by tissue injury. At its core is the activation and expression of appropriate genes that act as templates in the process of protein synthesis. Importantly, what has just been described occurs not just in the periphery where it is most easily appreciated, researched and described, but also throughout the whole sensory, processing and response systems involved. Change in response means altered gene expression and altered morphology anatomy and responsiveness, all along the involved pathways.

At the heart of the geneticists' approach to pain is the 'regulation' of this expression. At the 1999 World Congress on Pain in Vienna there were a total of 16 poster presentations relating to the scientific manipulation of genes and gene expression for the treatment of pain. The manipulation on offer was wholly at the same reductionist level, in other words, by understanding the chemistry of sensitisation another chemical may be applied that can intervene and prevent or reverse it.

Thinkers might step back from this and reason that if this type of process is fundamental to pain and sensitivity it must also be influenced by all types of therapies that are successful. I would agree and it makes for quite thought provoking therapeutic philosophising.

A biological rationale for unity

No matter what you do to a patient, from whatever level you focus, changes in gene expression will occur if the patient makes some changes. That every practitioner is ultimately a gene therapist is a nice idea, is unifying, and is, as far as I can see, quite rational. Also, if you are a patient you can be your own gene manipulator if you get involved in self help. Every therapist *could* argue (and perhaps one day soon *should* argue) that fundamental to their 'technique' or 'input' is the modulation of gene expression. I might be no different in my influence as a physiotherapy practitioner from a healer, a medicine man, a magnetic or copper arm band with healing properties, a session of Reiki, a cranial manipulation, a grade II p-a on a zygapophyseal joint, a muscle rebalance session, a McKenzie extension exercise, an education session that changes the patient's perspective on their pain to a less fearful one, a successful rehabilitation session where a formerly feared movement is conquered, or a positively negotiated arrangement with a patient's employer that results in a comfortable stress free return to work (Fig. 2). Based on this type of logic it seems unwise to criticise therapies that you find unusual/different/unorthodox. If patients have improved in some way from a therapy, there must be a mechanism underlying that improvement. The suggestions here reduce therapeutic effects down to a common mechanism involving alterations in gene expression, changes in receptor populations and neural reactivity. In many ways this is a far more responsible explanation than the classic insult of labelling another's successes as mere placebo. The view here is that the placebo is a biological phenomenon that often takes quite remarkable therapist skills to access to its full potential.

The problems practitioners have in standing up for their particular brand of therapy is that they tend to isolate themselves at a particular mechanistic level. For example, some manual therapists might explain their success with a patient in terms of improved local joint function. This is the model of explanation that I was trained in and used for many years. For a psychologist the explanation might be in terms of altered thinking, coping and behaviour; for an acupuncturist in terms of altered yin and yang, or altered central nervous system endorphins, depending on the training. A pharmacologist might view the world of therapy in terms of targeted physiological changes; a Reiki therapist in terms of energy fields and so forth. Explanations for effect like these are naturally reductionist and unidimensional, confined to the theory underlying the discipline concerned, often inadequate, and may be part truths or even totally wrong because they are ignoring the *multidimensional nature of biological processing*. Once we learn to appreciate that a fundamental biological truth is that all levels in Figures I.1 and I.2 interact (see the arrow on Fig. I.2), we can begin to see a much more profound multilevel and multidimensional picture. Single level management and thinking is constrained, is unlikely to be as productive as it could be, and often leads to arguments and tension. Think of each level in Figure I.2 as a cave with many smaller caves within representing a particular method or therapy. Then consider that it might be well worth the practitioners within coming out of their particular caves and looking around and into some of the others. For most practitioners it is relatively easy to take on the perspectives of those who are on adjacent levels. A herbalist can work in conjunction with an iridologist or a reflexologist but is unlikely to make much headway with an orthopaedic surgeon. Think about it in the terms suggested here and you realise that, philosophically, the entrance of the orthopaedic surgeon's cave lies quite close to the entrance to the caves where the alternative practitioners live; their philosophies are really all based on the identification of some form of impairment and its passive correction. Little is likely to be done by the majority of these practitioners in relation to promoting function or activities related to life and work, or active coping strategies, or decreasing fear about structural weakness or the nature of pain.

The argument here is for the emergence and appropriate integration of all levels because they all interact and interrelate biologically. For instance, change the way a patient thinks about a problem or a feared movement and you have the potential to change gene expression, sensitivity, pain response, muscle co-ordination and muscle strength, emotions and relationships. Add further potency by using a practical session whereby the patient is helped to find a way of actually starting to do the feared movement in a safe and controlled way. In some situations it may be appropriate to find a movement or even perform a passive technique on the patient that they find helpful in improving movement or reducing pain. Suggesting or asking for appropriate medication for pain control may be required, and so forth. The well established style of only doing 'one-technique-at-a-time', while occasionally necessary, may actually be missing a huge potential in terms of efficiency and cost effectiveness.

Treatments from professionals inputting at the bottom of the hierarchy can influence the top and vice versa. A particular message of this volume is that *some levels are more powerful than others* in influencing decline or wellbeing and recovery; these relate to the *environment, and the thoughts, feelings, beliefs, behaviours and functioning* of the patient—**the top three levels** in Figure I.2. If clinicians are to work efficiently to rehabilitate and prevent chronic incapacity then issues pertinent to these levels need their attention, understanding and integration into patient management. Those operating with models at lower levels need urgently to look upwards just as those above need to take an open minded look at those operating below. One day the well equipped therapist might be equally at ease using and integrating management skills derived from all levels. Let us hope, for the sake of the patient in front of us, that we are nearing a satisfying denouement underpinned by biological rationality. Perhaps we are about to witness the break-up of defensive boundaries with rigid enclosed thinking going quietly out of fashion?

REFERENCES

Butler DS 1998 Integrating pain awareness into physiotherapy—wise action for the future. In: Gifford LS (Ed) Topical issues in pain. Whiplash science and management. Fear-avoidance behaviour and beliefs. Physiotherapy Pain Association Yearbook 1998-1999 CNS Press, Falmouth pp:1-23

Cherkin DC, Deyo RA, Battie M et al 1998 A comparison of physical therapy, chiropractic manipulation and provision of an educational booklet for the treatment of patients with low back pain. New England Journal of Medicine 339(15): 1021-1029

Devor M et al 1994 Sodium ion channel accumulation in injured axons as a substrate for neuropathic pain. In: Boivie P, Hansson P, Lindblom U (Eds) Touch temperature, and pain in health and disease: mechanisms and assessments. Progress in Pain research and Management. Vol 3. IASP Press, Seattle

Dworkin RH 1997 Which individuals with acute pain are most likely to develop a chronic pain syndrome? Pain Forum 6(2): 127-136

Gifford LS 1997 Pain. In: Pitt-Brooke (Ed) Rehabilitation of Movement: Theoretical bases of clinical practice Saunders, London 196-232

Gifford LS 1998 The mature organism model. In: Gifford LS (Ed) Physiotherapy Pain Association Yearbook 1998-1999. Topical issues in pain. Whiplash - science and management. Fear-avoidance beliefs and behaviour. CNS Press, Falmouth pp. 45-56

Gifford LS 1998a Central mechanisms. In: Gifford LS (Ed) Physiotherapy Pain Association Yearbook 1998-1999. Topical issues in pain. Whiplash—science and management. Fear-avoidance beliefs and behaviour. CNS Press, Falmouth pp. 67-80

Gifford LS, Butler DS 1997 The integration of pain sciences into clinical practice. Hand Therapy 10(2): 86-95

Iadarola MJ, Lee S, Mannes AJ 1997 Gene transfer approaches to pain control. In: Borsook D (Ed) Molecular neurobiology of pain. Progress in Pain Research and Management, Vol. 9 IASP Press, Seattle pp. 337-359

Julius D 1999 Expression cloning of sensory receptors. In: Max M (Ed) Pain 1999 An updated review. Refresher course syllabus IASP Press, Seattle pp. 515-522

Kandel ER, Schwartz JH, Jessell TM (Eds) 1995 Essentials of neural science and behavior. Prentice Hall, London

Linton SJ 1996 Early interventions for the secondary prevention of chronic musculoskeletal pain. In: Campbell J N (Ed) Pain 1996 An updated review. Refresher course syllabus IASP Press, Seattle pp. 305-311

Linton SJ 1997 Overlooked and underrated? The role of acute pain intensity in the development of chronic back pain problems. Pain Forum 6(2): 145-147

Linton SJ 1998 The socioeconomic impact of chronic back pain: is anyone benefiting? Pain 75: 163-168

Linton SJ 1999 Cognitive-behavioral interventions for the secondary prevention of chronic musculoskeletal pain. In: Max M (Ed) Pain 1999 An updated review. Refresher course syllabus IASP Press, Seattle pp. 535-544

Linton SJ, Bradley LA 1996 Strategies for the prevention of chronic pain. In: Gatchel RJ, Turk DC (Eds) Psychological approaches to pain management Guilford Press, New York pp. 438-457

Linton SJ, Bradley LA, Jensen I et al 1989 The secondary prevention of low back pain: a controlled study with follow-up. Pain 36: 197-207

McMahon SB, Bennett DLH, Koltzenburg M 1997 The biological effects of nerve growth factor on primary sensory neurons. In: Borsook D (Ed) Molecular neurobiology of pain. Progress in pain research and managemnt, Vol 9. IASP Press, Seattle pp. 59-78

Mogil J S 1999 The genetics of pain. Abstracts: 9th World Congress on Pain, Vienna, Austria. IASP Press, Seattle p. 259

Rose S 1997 Lifelines. Biology, freedom, determinism. Penguin Books, London

Shepherd G M 1994 Neurobiology 3rd Edition. Oxford University Press, New York

Tanner KD, Gold MS, Reichling DB et al 1997 Transduction and excitability in nociceptors: dynamic phenomena. In: Borsook D (Ed) Molecular neurobiology of pain. Progress in pain research and management Vol 9. IASP Press, Seattle pp. 79-105

Woolf CJ, Mannion RJ, Costigan M 1999 Molecular approaches for the study of pain-differential gene expression. In: Max M (Ed) Pain 1999 An updated review. Refresher course syllabus IASP Press, Seattle pp. 509-514

Interpreting the results of treatment

(See Appendices 1 and 2 for explanations of research terms and abbreviations used in the text)

GEORGE PEAT

'Evidence-based medicine is the conscientious, explicit and judicious use of current best evidence in making decisions about the care of individual patients' (Sackett et al 1996). Best evidence for the efficacy and effectiveness of treatment is provided by randomised controlled clinical trials. Indeed, it has been asserted that large, high quality randomised controlled clinical trials (RCT) and systematic reviews of RCTs are our best chance of getting close to the truth about the effectiveness of treatments (McQuay & Moore 1998).

At the same time as efforts have increased to design, conduct, report and combine RCTs, clinicians involved in the treatment of patients have been encouraged to adopt similar outcome measurement in routine practice. In the field of pain management, providing treatment without collecting data has been described as a 'high risk strategy' (Report of a Working Group of The Pain Society 1997). The pressure to 'prove' that the treatment you are carrying out is effective is familiar to most clinicians. Evaluating outcome in routine practice, however, differs in many important respects from evaluation in clinical trials, most notably in the lack of adequate comparison or control groups.

The criteria for selecting outcome measures in clinical trials (Box 1) have been well-reviewed (Fitzgerald et al 1998) and will not be the primary concern here.

Box 1 Eight criteria for evaluating outcome measures

> **A**ppropriateness
> **R**eliability
> **V**alidity
> **R**esponsiveness
> **P**recision
> **I**nterpretability
> **A**cceptability
> **F**easibility

The question instead is this: once you summarise the results, how do you judge if there has been real change? The following discussion will centre on two specific points:

1   Can observed changes following treatment be attributed specifically to the intervention?

2   Can important change be distinguished from unimportant change, and if so, how?

Clinicians and researchers are urged to consider these matters *before* selecting, administering, and summarising outcome measures. The discussion and suggestions are aimed at quantitative evaluation of groups of patients measured before and after treatment without comparison groups. Qualitative or single case studies are not covered but can be reviewed elsewhere (see Kazdin 1982, Murphy et al 1998). Chronic pain will feature in much of the discussion reflecting the area of my clinical and research experience.

Throughout this chapter, I will attempt to illustrate some of the discussion points with practical examples drawn from data collected as part of the Manchester & Salford Pain Centre Back Pain Management Programme.

Table II.1 summarises outcome measurement from chronic low-back pain patients completing the three-week multidisciplinary Back Pain Management Programme (BPMP). Measures were administered immediately prior to the start of the BPMP and immediately after the three weeks. The results are expressed in the traditional format of group means for complete paired observations (i.e. excluding drop-outs and those with missing data).

Table II.1   Summary of results from a back pain management programme (adapted from Peat 1998). See Appendix 2 for Glossary of outcome measures.

Measure	Pre-BPMP Mean (sd)	Post-BPMP Mean (sd)	n
RMDQ (0-24)	14.3 (4.5)	9.4 (5.1)	188
MSPQ (0-39)	10.8 (6.4	8.7 (5.9)	178
MZ (0-69)	30.7 (10.4)	25.2 (8.8)	178
SFMPQ-VAS (0-100mm)	53.4 (20.7)	43.2 (21.4)	189
SFMPQ-SENS (0-33)	14.0 (6.7)	10.4 (6.2)	188
SFMPQ-AFF (0-12)	4.6 (3.2)	2.7 (3.0)	189
PRSS-CAT (0-45)	24.0 (8.5)	16.6 (9.5)	187
PRSS-COP (0-45)	27.3 (8.1)	32.5 (7.3)	188
PSEQ (0-60)	26.6 (11.2)	39.9 (12.9)	185
FABQ-PHYS (0-24)	15.3 (5.2)	8.3 (6.2)	173
Timed 20-metre speed walk (sec)	16.7 (6.6)	9.6 (3.6)	185
Step-ups in 30 seconds	10.5 (3.8)	15.0 (4.1)	191
Sit-stands in 30 seconds	7.7 (3.0)	11.4 (3.4)	191

The results demonstrate improvement in all measures. Even more impressive, the likelihood of observing such changes purely due to chance is less than 1 in 1000 for all measures.

Can we conclude that treatment is an unqualified success? We will return to this question after considering the alternatives.

Can observed changes be attributed to treatment?

Before attributing observed changes specifically to the treatment delivered it is helpful to consider possible alternative explanations. These can be grouped under natural history and non-specific treatment-related effects.

Natural history

It is tempting to regard interventions as the only potential source of change in patient status, particularly in chronic conditions. This ignores 'experiments of nature' (Feinstein, 1977) which allow a healthy person to change as they grow, make a healthy person ill, or take a person through the clinical course of a condition. To understand whether the changes we observe in outcome measures are due to our treatment we must accept that any change due to treatment takes place over and above the natural history of that condition. The refrain that 'it doesn't matter what you do, it'll get better/worse regardless' may simply be an expression of powerlessness to alter the condition's natural course. Different conditions have different typical courses. One need only contrast the different expected courses of cauda equina syndrome and 'simple low back pain'. An understanding of the natural history of the conditions that we treat can make clearer the contribution that treatment makes to observed changes in patient status.

Emerging epidemiological research emphasises the episodic nature of musculoskeletal pain (Deyo 1993, Von Korff 1994, Von Korff & Saunders 1996). Even in persistent pain, there is likely to be some degree of natural variability in severity. In these circumstances, the phenomenon of *regression to the mean* becomes important. Patients with higher than usual pain are more likely to register a return to normal levels on subsequent measurement. If patients seek help when their condition is at uncharacteristically high pain levels they are bound to return to normal levels irrespective of the treatment administered.

The effects of natural improvement and regression to the mean have traditionally been a source of glee for those working in chronic pain regarding the claims of those treating acute pain. Epidemiological evidence is now accumulating which refutes the belief that recent-onset pain recovers completely in most people. Natural history and regression to the mean are important in chronic pain (Whitney & Von Korff 1992, MacFarlane et al 1996). Now the glee is shared more equitably, perhaps it is time for all of us to take a sober look at these issues. Natural history effects may lead health care professionals and patients alike to reach false conclusions about the efficacy of worthless treatments administered during a flare-up (Von Korff 1992, Deyo 1993; see also Fig. II.1). It raises the ugly possibility that interventions may even *hamper* the natural course and recovery. There have been several reports on so-called 'iatrogenic' disability and it remains a contentious subject (Pither & Nicholas 1991, Loeser & Sullivan 1995, Peat & Sweet 1997, Kouyanou et al 1998).

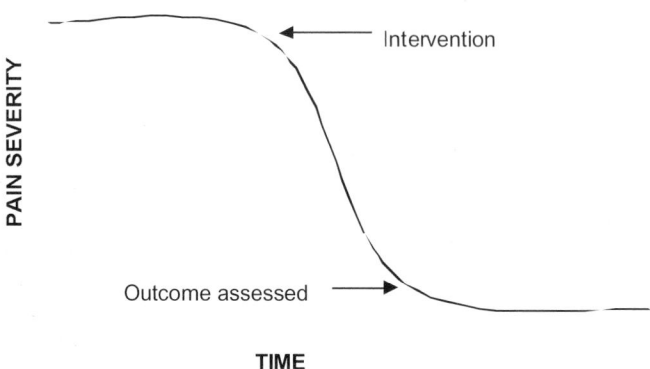

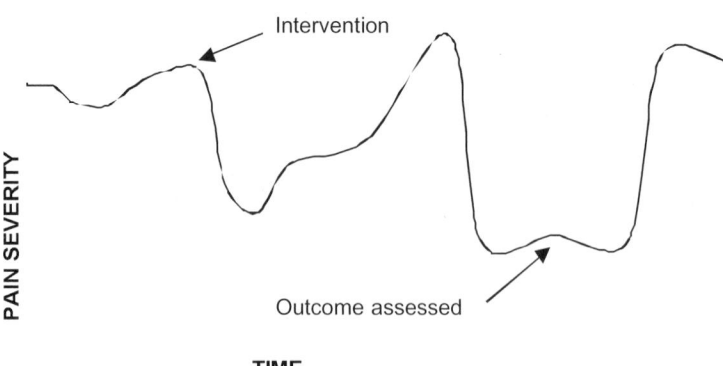

Fig. II.1   Hypothetical and actual course of chronic low back pain, (Adapted from: Deyo RA 1993 Practice variations, treatment fads, rising disability. Do we need a new clinical research paradigm? Spine 18(15): 2153-2162)

Non-specific effects of treatment

The Hawthorne effect

Between 1927 and 1933, as part of some of the most detailed investigation ever undertaken in social science, a group of investigators led by George Elton Mayo conducted an experiment at the Hawthorne plant of the Western Electric Company to examine whether variations in rest breaks could improve worker productivity. Six female workers were selected and placed in a separate parts assembly room where they could be monitored closely. During this time a total of 13 different arrangements for rest breaks and early finishes were studied. The results were surprising. Productivity began to rise shortly after the study began and showed continuous improvement thereafter *irrespective of which experimental condition was in place*. The improvements persisted even when the subjects returned to their usual 48-hour week.

Although several explanations were proposed, one has gained lasting recognition (despite being challenged later)—that there is a tendency of people being observed as part of a research effort to behave differently than they would otherwise. This is known as the **Hawthorne Effect**.

Does the Hawthorne Effect have any relevance to health care and the outcome of health care interventions? Does the feeling that someone is interested in or concerned with their health alter patients' behaviour? Support for the influence of the Hawthorne effect has been noted in some trials (e.g. Bouchet et al 1996). In an RCT of exercise for patients with knee osteoarthritis, reported compliance and selected outcomes were better in those who were informed that they would be reviewed than in those who were assessed unexpectedly (Chamberlain et al 1982). In practice, evidence remains largely anecdotal. Patients with chronic pain do remark that being believed and feeling that someone is taking them seriously are important steps in their rehabilitation. Does it matter exactly what specific treatment follows? Is the *process* of gathering a group of individuals together, scrutinising their behaviour, and monitoring and inquiring after their progress the main cause of important changes in patient distress and disability, rather than the treatment techniques that accompany it?

The placebo effect

In an editorial in *Pain*, Patrick Wall (1992) identified several myths surrounding this 'unpopular topic':

1 Placebo responders have nothing wrong with them
2 A third of people will respond to placebo
3 Placebo responders suffer from some kind of personality defect
4 Placebo is the same as doing nothing.

Each of these myths has been refuted and can no longer be upheld seriously. People respond to placebos inconsistently, the proportion across trials is highly variable (McQuay et al 1995), and no placebo-personality has been found. In medication trials at least, placebo responses appear to exhibit similar time-effect curves, peak, cumulative, and carryover effects as do active medications (Turner et al 1994).

Non-specific, treatment-related effects pose a real challenge to our clinical reasoning and the basis of clinical models that explain why patients change after treatment. Their importance was underlined in the National Institute of Health Consensus Statement on acupuncture:

> It should be noted that for any therapeutic intervention…the so-called 'non-specific' effects account for a substantial proportion of its effectiveness and thus should not be casually discounted. Many factors may profoundly determine therapeutic outcome, including the quality of the relationship between the clinician and the patient, the degree of trust, the expectations of the patient, the compatibility of the backgrounds and beliefs systems of the clinician and the patient, as well as a myriad of factors that together define the therapeutic milieu.
>
> NIH Consensus Statement Online (1997)

At this stage, readers may be wondering if there is any point in evaluating outcome at all. Before we discard it, we should consider the question that we initially posed; can changes in patients, observed by measuring outcome in routine practice, be attributed specifically to our treatment? The answer is probably not. However, even if we cannot disentangle specific from non-specific treatment effects and natural history, there are good reasons to monitor patient changes in routine practice. When the expected natural course of a condition is known, monitoring patient changes as we treat them may help identify delayed recovery or unexpected deterioration leading us to reappraise either the diagnostic triage or our treatment approach. Monitoring patient changes may enable us to identify subgroups of patients whose response to treatment is consistently different, causing us to adopt a different approach. These important functions, and many more, underline the value of measuring patient changes in routine practice. If we accept that such routine measurement is reasonable the problem that faces the clinician is how to discern 'real' or important changes from those that are unimportant.

Can important change be distinguished from unimportant change?

Surrogate outcomes

Surrogate outcomes are measures that are used to evaluate outcome but are in fact substitute end-points, used either because they are simpler, cheaper, and more convenient than measuring the true outcome of interest, or sometimes as a 'harder' alternative to 'soft data'. Their use is justified by claiming that they are strongly correlated with the real outcome of interest. Table II.2 gives some examples from medical trials of surrogate outcomes.

Table II.2 Surrogate outcomes in medical trials

Condition	True point of interest	Surrogate outcome
Osteoporosis	Osteoporotic fracture	Loss of bone mineral density
Ocular glaucoma	Visual field damage	Intraocular pressure
Chronic hepatitis	Hepatic failure and death	Markers for viral replication or liver enzymes
AIDS	Survival	Lymphocyte helper count
Hypertension	Incidence of stroke	Blood pressure readings

In practice, the surrogate may give a good indication of the true outcome. Then again it may not! The weakness of surrogate outcome measures can be understood by watching a football game on TV. Coverage of the game is now supported by an impressive array of statistics. At the end of a game you can be told the amount of possession, the number of corners, the number of shots on goal ad nauseum. But how many feel consoled by the fact that their team won more corners than the other side, had 90% of the possession, and had twice as many shots on goal, after being beaten 1-0.

In a recent trial of exercise for osteoarthritic knee pain, improvements in self-reported pain and disability were greater than gains in muscle strength (O'Reilly et al 1999). Had the researchers confined themselves to judging the effectiveness of treatment by muscle strength alone, they would have under-estimated its impact on important outcomes.

Audit and standard-setting have introduced process variables that have been regarded by some as treatment outcomes in themselves. In fact they are surrogates. As Feinstein (1989) elegantly phrased it,

> When the process is successfully carried out, we may congratulate ourselves on reaching the goal, while overlooking the appropriate target that should have been hit, but was not.

What you can do about surrogate outcomes

- Be clear about what the true end-point of interest to both yourself and the patient is—try to measure it as directly as possible
- Be aware of the limitations of measuring 'surrogate' outcomes—try to avoid over-extrapolating
- Set primary and secondary outcomes to distinguish between the main aims of treatment and subsidiary outcomes
- Don't assume that process equals outcome.

Determine the primary outcomes

Reducing disability and distress are the principle aims of pain management programmes and so are reasonable primary outcomes. There has been some concern over relying solely on patient self-report for outcome evaluation. A measure of observed functional performance was therefore also included as a primary outcome.

Outcome domain	Outcome measure
Self-rated interference	RMDQ
Distress	MSPQ + MZ
Behaviour	Step-ups in 30 seconds

Measurement artefact

If the facts used as a basis for reasoning are ill-established or erroneous, everything will crumble or be falsified.'

Claude Bernard, 1865 (in Bernard 1957)

The above quote continues to be a central tenet of scientific methodology and is relevant to outcome measurement. If our measures are inaccurate or erroneous, our judgement on treatment outcome will be flawed. This is not a chapter on specific measurement attributes but at a basic level it is clear that the reproducibility, responsiveness, and validity of measures contribute to the accuracy of determining whether important change has taken place. Measures which contain a high degree of random error, fail to register true change, or end up not measuring what we thought they were will mislead us when we try to work out whether there has been a change in patient status. For example, single measures of current pain intensity taken before and after treatment are unlikely to give a good estimate of changes in patients' usual pain (Jensen & McFarland 1993). Measuring functional improvement by return to work may fail to detect true change. Functional improvements are possible without return to work and return to work is influenced by many other factors besides functional ability (Deyo et al 1994).

If measurement of outcome is performed in such a way that compromises the ability or willingness of the patient to provide an accurate account of their status, or our ability to faithfully record it, the following judgement of treatment outcome is flawed. Bias in outcome measurement comes in many forms. A handful of simple examples are provided below.

Lack of independent assessor

In routine clinical practice, patients are often evaluated by the professional who has treated them. Even if we discount cases where results are deliberately manipulated, is the evaluation that comes from this arrangement accurate? Maybe, but ask yourself if you've ever modified your views when someone close to you has asked for 'an honest and frank opinion' about a subject that is obviously close to their heart. Blinded assessment is taken for granted in clinical trials but is not a feature of outcome evaluation in routine practice (Peat et al 1999 submitted manuscript). We may encourage or instruct patients differently if they are known to us from treatment—two factors that are known to influence performance in physical tests (Ikai & Steinhaus 1961, Guyatt et al 1984, Matheson et al 1992).

Reactive measures

After several months of running a pain management programme, a small change in the programme resulted in improvements on outcome measures. The small change was to invite patients to engage in a daily walking test. The outcome measure? A timed 20 metre speed walk. Measures that bear a very close relation to the treatment will often result in biased appraisal. They are unfortunately common in pain treatment outcome studies. Flor et al (1992) classed measures according to how likely they were to be influenced by patient and/or therapist bias. The least reactive were physiological measures, laboratory data, blind rating, and behavioural assessment. The most reactive were patient self-reported improvement, therapist improvement ratings, and instruments with an obvious relationship to treatment outcome.

Confirmation bias

This describes the process of biased recording where contradictory information is more likely to be ignored than that which confirms our existing opinions (Plant et al 1998).

What you can do about measurement artefact

- Where possible, use outcome measures that have been extensively tried and tested in the patient group that you plan to administer them to
- Don't rely on measures that are transparently related to your treatment
- Be consistent in the way in which you administer the measures to patients— use standard protocols if necessary.

Verifying measurement validity and reliability

The RMDQ is a LBP-specific questionnaire developed initially in primary care (Roland & Morris 1983). It has been extensively used in other studies and its test-retest reliability found to be acceptably high in LBP patients (r=0.88; Beurskens et al 1995, Kopec & Esdaile 1995).

The MSPQ and MZ were developed specifically for chronic low-back pain (Main 1984). They have been shown to have adequate test-retest reliability (Main 1983, Main 1984).

A 1-minute stair test developed by Harding et al (1994) in chronic pain patients demonstrated good test-retest reliability. The test was shortened to 30 seconds because of practical time restrictions on assessment. Because the test had been modified, its retest reliability over three weeks (the duration of the pain management programme) was examined and confirmed in the current population by a small-scale three-week test-retest study on waiting list patients (Peat 1998).

Reducing observer bias by standard protocols

It was not possible to use truly independent observers for all assessments although most of the functional tests were carried out by physiotherapists with minimal input into the running of the programme. A clear protocol for the functional tests was developed and all assessing physiotherapists were instructed in this. Questionnaires were administered at the Centre with instructions not to seek the help of others for completion. Most questionnaires were handed out by and returned to administrative staff at the Centre.

Unmasking the response of clinically important subgroups

Not all patients benefit equally from a treatment. Unfortunately, the common expression of outcome results by group averages masks potentially important differences in response between subgroups of patients (Feinstein 1996a, Guyatt et al 1998). Feinstein (1996a) has termed this 'statistical reductionism'. Does it matter if we lump the results of those who have made large improvements with those who have made no change or even worsened? It does if we wish to address *clinically* significant change as opposed to *statistically* significant change. If the average change following treatment is small but this contains a mixture of patients who made very large improvements and some who actually deteriorated, we would want to know something about these different groups.

Box 2 The importance of subgroups

Example

Summary of pain outcomes for 50 patients with chronic neck pain receiving 4 weeks of treatment in a physiotherapy department.

Average pain score (0-100mm VAS):   Pre-treatment   = 60
                                     Post-treatment = 35

When the results were looked at in detail, 12 patients had made no change at all. They were all reporting extremely high levels of pain at the point of starting treatment.

In the above example we have identified a subgroup who have responded differently to treatment and appear to have something in common that distinguishes them from the rest of the sample. Instead of accepting that average scores are generally improved we might want to enquire more closely into this group of 12 who did not benefit from treatment. Why was there no change? Was it something to do with the severity of their pain before treatment? Was something missed? Should alternative treatment options be considered for such patients in future?

Identifying subgroups has implications for selecting treatment options, and for translating results from clinical trials into practice (Deyo et al 1988). A necessary first step is to move from average results to defining changes on an individual basis.

Before starting treatment, how often can we articulate, in a way that can be measured, what a successful outcome will be for the patient in front of us? Determining successful outcome in pain treatment outcome studies is a 'neglected topic' (Turk et al 1993). The interpretability of some measures, such as quality of life measures, is difficult. How much change is important? In what area? This is a complex issue depending in part on who is asked and what the treatment is. Several approaches to defining changes on an individual basis have been used. Their development has been assisted as clinical trials have sought to communicate their results in a more directly understandable way (Sackett et al 1991, Moore et al 1996, Sackett & Haynes 1997, Williams 1997, Guyatt et al 1998). Some of the approaches are briefly outlined below.

Minimum detectable change

At the very best, we must be able to distinguish changes in measures that exceed the variability caused by random measurement error. Stratford et al (1996a) have described the application of this technique to RMDQ scores for patients with acute and subacute low-back pain in an outpatient setting. They found that clinicians could be fairly confident that a change of 4 or 5 points was unlikely to reflect measurement error.

Reliable change index

Jacobsen and Truax (1991) adopted a statistical approach to defining clinically significant change in which the aim of treatment is assumed to be to shift the patient from a dysfunctional population to within the limits of a normal or functional population. The amount of change between pre- and post-test scores is expressed as a reliable change index, that controls for the effects of measurement error. The concept has been refined (Speer 1992) and is now beginning to be used to summarise the outcome of pain treatments. Rather than report average results the proportion of patients making clinically significant improvements is specified (Rudy et al 1995, Slater et al 1997).

Minimal clinically important change

Jaeschke et al (1989) outlined an approach for defining individual change in which the minimal clinically important change was 'the smallest difference in score in the domain of interest which patients perceive as beneficial.' In practice this was calculated by comparing change scores with global ratings of improvement or deterioration.

Attainment of an absolute standard

Rather than analysing change scores, a different approach is to specify an absolute standard to be attained. In an RCT of a pain management programme for chronic pain by Williams et al (1996), two absolute criteria were used to evaluate outcome—using no analgesic or psychotropic drugs, and receiving no further treatment for pain (McQuay et al 1997). This method has the advantage of being clearly understandable. A disadvantage is that it takes no account of the amount of change. Baseline characteristics are therefore important.

Patient-specific measures

Each of the above methods helps outline how to distinguish the magnitude of change. In some settings there may be a number of legitimate targets for treatment. In chronic pain, reducing disability and distress are primary goals

(Report of a Working Group of the Pain Society 1997) but what about reducing maladaptive pain behaviours, cognitive coping techniques, sleep, fear, unnecessary health care use, medication reduction, work skills? Formally, patient-specific or patient-preference measures can be used to enable the individual to prioritise areas of change. Less formally the practice of goal-setting addresses the same issue: measuring treatment benefit by changes deemed important by the individual.

Further information on the relationship between methodology and assessing change scores can be found in Stratford et al (1996b) and in a recent overview of methods of defining clinically significant change (Jacobson et al 1999).

What you can do about unmasking the response of clinically important subgroups

- Be aware that average (mean) results can disguise the response of important subgroups of patients
- Make the distinction between statistically significant change and clinically
- Try to define individual important change—consider referring to existing studies for possible definitions, setting absolute standards, and patient-specific goals.

Defining individual change

Patient preference was not taken into account when calculating individual change. The calculations were therefore limited to the statistical concepts of minimum detectable change, reliable change or an absolute standard. The following choices were made with the support of evidence from previous studies.

RMDQ   improvement was defined as a reduction of 5 or more points (Stratford et al 1996a).

DRAM   improvement was defined as a reduction from initial classification of distressed (DS/DD) to normal (N) or at-risk (AR) categories. The change in Mod. Zung scores had to be greater than 1 s.d. of pre-PMP scores (Williams 1997). This worked out at a change of 11 points or more.

Step-ups   >50% improvement (Williams 1997).

Other considerations

What do the changes mean?

Changes in patient-based outcome measures, most notably self-report instruments, are not immediately easy to understand. What does a 5-point change in a measure mean? Fitzgerald et al (1998) suggest that part of the problem with the interpretability of these measures is that we are unfamiliar with them. Studies have sought answers to this by relating changes in these measures to more familiar or objective tests that are easier to interpret. An interesting approach for interpreting changes in quality of life measures was reported by Testa and Simonson (1996). They correlated changes in quality of life measures with changes associated with life events. A minor deterioration in quality of life measures corresponded to the stressful effects of a minor violation of the law; moderate deterioration with being fired from work; large deterioration with divorce or death of spouse or family member. Knowing that a patient has rated your treatment as about as helpful as getting sacked from work may be an effective way of translating measurement scores into more direct language, but the meaning may still be illusory and further work is needed. It is worth remembering that simple, clinical indexes serve as useful outcome measures as well as more complex psychometric questionnaires (Wright & Feinstein 1992).

Duration of effect

True, clinically important, changes that fail to last lose some of their value, particularly in chronic or recurrent conditions. In Feine and Lund's (1997) review of physical therapy and physiotherapy treatment modalities for chronic musculoskeletal pain, they concluded that patients did show improvement 'during the period that they are treated' but evidence on long-term efficacy was lacking. Again, more research is needed. The fact that patients are seldom followed up for clinically relevant periods of time after physiotherapy treatment means that we miss the chance to observe relapse and recurrence. This is probably more pronounced in hospital-based services than for those working in the community or in primary care who may have contact with individuals over years rather than weeks.

Attrition

Those designing clinical trials to evaluate treatment efficacy or effectiveness are sensitive to the problems that attrition causes. Those who drop out of treatment or fail to complete follow-ups are often simply excluded from calculations of treatment outcome. In clinical practice it is a case of 'out of sight, out of mind'. We base our judgements on treatment outcome on those patients who come back. However, if a significant number of patients drop out of treatment or do not attend follow-up there is a risk of bias when appraising outcome (Hennekens & Buring 1987). Often they differ from those who complete treatment in subtle ways. They need not necessarily represent treatment failure. For example, some patients will fail to attend simply because of the distance involved or being unable to take time off work (Coughlan et al 1995). More often than not, though, they cannot be regarded as treatment successes. Unless there is information to the contrary, they should be included in our evaluation of treatment amongst those not making clinically significant change. Participant flow diagrams that clearly describe what happened to all patients entering the treatment have been recommended for clinical trials (Begg et al 1996) and successfully applied to cohort studies in pain centres (Weir et al 1994).

Extending the length of evaluation

As the aims of the programme were to teach self-management skills the results at 6 month follow-up were felt to be important. The evaluation of outcome would need to be repeated at this stage as well as for immediate post-PMP changes.

Accounting for attrition

The results in Table II.1 (page 14) are slightly misleading. We do not know how many entered treatment and whose data was missing or who dropped out. If we are to extend the evaluation to 6 months we also need to account for people who were lost to follow-up or whose data at this assessment was missing. Figure II.2 below shows a simple participant flow chart.

There were no strong reasons to presume that drop-outs, missing data, or losses to follow-up contained substantial numbers of patients with a successful outcome. They were therefore counted in the analysis along with those who failed to make clinically detectable change.

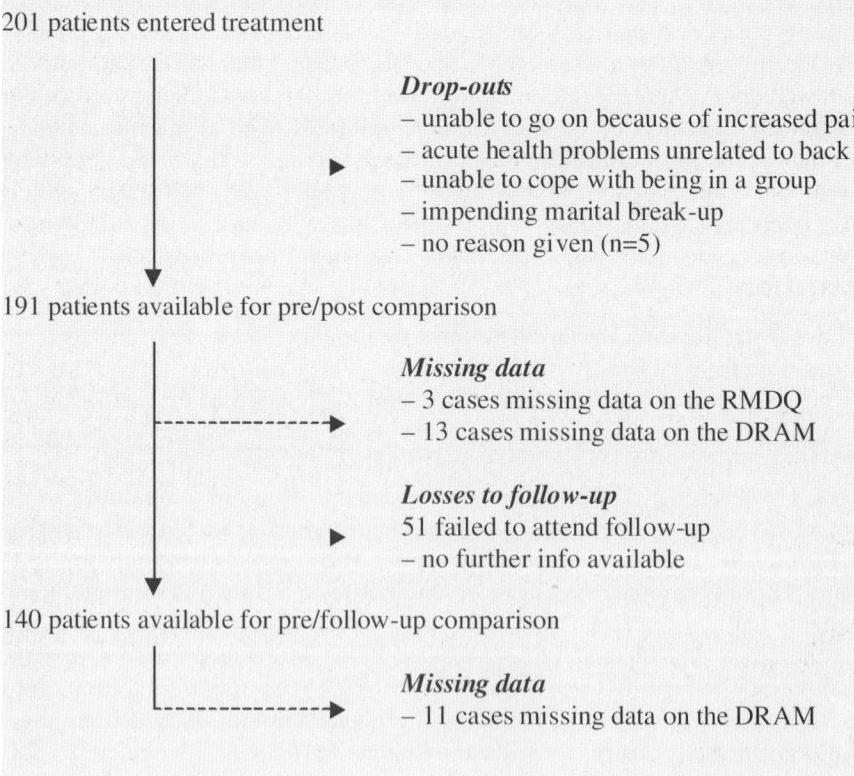

201 patients entered treatment

Drop-outs
– unable to go on because of increased pain
– acute health problems unrelated to back
– unable to cope with being in a group
– impending marital break-up
– no reason given (n=5)

191 patients available for pre/post comparison

Missing data
– 3 cases missing data on the RMDQ
– 13 cases missing data on the DRAM

Losses to follow-up
51 failed to attend follow-up
– no further info available

140 patients available for pre/follow-up comparison

Missing data
– 11 cases missing data on the DRAM

Fig. II.2 Participant flow chart showing sample attrition

Re-stating the results

Table II.3 summarises the results after incorporating some of the points discussed on distinguishing important change.

Table II.3 Re-statment of results from Table II.1.

Measure	Proportion of patients making clinically significant improvements	
	Pre- to post-	Pre- to Follow up
Self-rated interference (RMDQ)	92/201 (46%)	63/201 (31%)
Distress (MSPQ + MZ – i.e. DRAM)	33/101 (33%)	22/101 (22%)
Behaviour (step-ups in 30 seconds)	120/201 (60%)	83/201 (41%)

For pre-post results, all drop-outs and cases with missing data are included in the calculations as treatment 'failures'.

For pre-follow up results, all drop-outs, losses to follow-up and cases with missing data are included in the calculations as treatment 'failures'.

For calculating the proportion making clinically significant changes on the DRAM only those who were distressed at pre-PMP assessment were included in the calculation.

Interpreting the results

Almost a half of patients entering treatment reported reductions immediately after the PMP in self-reported interference. These were unlikely to be due to random measurement error. The figure dropped to just under a third by 6-month follow-up. Half of patients entering treatment were not classed as distressed. Of those who were, a third had made clinically significant improvements by the end of the three weeks. At 6 months, a fifth had maintained this. Three in every 5 patients starting the PMP improved by more than 50% on the step-up test. At 6 months, 2 in every 5 could be expected to have maintained this.

This leaves a large number of patients who appeared to make modest or negligible improvements as measured by self-rated interference, distress or observed functional performance. This does not preclude benefits in other areas that the patient may have deemed important. A more detailed review of those who failed to make improvements may reveal common features that distinguish them from the rest.

Action was taken to limit the effects of measurement artefact and bias. A conservative approach to dealing with attrition and missing data was adopted. There was no comparison group and we therefore cannot exclude or quantify natural history effects, Hawthorne effect or placebo response as being responsible for the observed changes.

Summary

This chapter has attempted to provide an introduction to issues surrounding the evaluation of treatment outcome in response to the beguilingly simple question, has there been real change? The view that evaluating treatment is simply a matter of taking measurement instruments off the shelf, administering them to patients, scoring them up, summarising them (preferably as group averages), performing a quick statistical test and concluding that the results prove that your treatment works, is sadly mistaken. Gaining an accurate impression of treatment effectiveness is often complex and laborious. Although statistics are involved, it is not primarily a statistical task. Clinical knowledge of the condition in question, the characteristics of the patients and the treatment under scrutiny are vital. Many of the issues described in this paper are best considered before embarking on measurement. Melzack and Wall (1988) suggested criteria for studies of psychological approaches to chronic pain management:

1 Treatment must demonstrate superiority over placebo.
2 Changes, both in magnitude and duration, must be clinically significant.
3 Changes must be transferable to the patients' normal day-to-day environment.
4 Skills acquired by patients must have long-term effectiveness.

The treatment and management of pain by physiotherapists faces similar challenges. Routine evaluation in clinical practice cannot answer all these questions but much can be done to improve the accuracy of our judgements about treatment outcome.

REFERENCES

Begg C, Cho M, Eastwood S, Horton R, Moher D, Olkin I, Pitkin R, Rennie D, Schulz KF, Simel D, Stroup DF 1996 Improving the quality of reporting of randomized controlled trials. The CONSORT statement. Journal of the American Medical Association 276:637–639

Bernard C 1957 An introduction to the study of experimental medicine. Dover Publications, New York. p 13

Beurskens AJ, de Vet HC, KokeAJ, van der Heijden GJ, Knipschild PG 1995 Measuring the functional status of patients with low back pain. Assessment of the quality of four disease-specific questionnaires. Spine 20:1017–1028

Bouchet C, Guillemin F, Briancon S 1996 Nonspecific effects in longitudinal studies: impact on quality of life measures. Journal of Clinical Epidemiology 49:15–20

Carmines EG, Zeller RA 1979 Reliability and validity assessment. In: Sullivan JL. (Ed.) Quantitative applications in the social sciences. Sage, London

Chamberlain MA, Care G, Harfield B 1982 Physiotherapy in osteoarthrosis of the knees. A controlled trial of hospital versus home exercises. International Journal of Rehabilitation Medicine 4:101–106

Coughlan GM, Ridout KL, Williams AC, Richardson PH 1995 Attrition from a pain management programme. British Journal of Clinical Psychology 34:471–479

Deyo RA 1993 Practice variations, treatment fads, rising disability. Do we need a new clinical research paradigm? Spine18:2153–2162

Deyo RA, Bass JE, Walsh NE, Schoenfeld LS, Ramamurthy S 1988 Prognostic variability among chronic pain patients: implications for study design, interpretation, and reporting. Archives of Physical Medicine and Rehabilitation 69:174–178

Deyo RA, Andersson G, Bombardier C, Cherkin D, Keller RB, Lee CK, Liang MH, Lipscomb B, Shekelle P, Spratt KF, Weinstein JN 1994 Outcome measures for studying patients with low back pain. Spine 19:2032S–2036S

Feine JS, Lund JP 1997 An assessment of the efficacy of physical therapy and physical modalities for the control of chronic musculoskeletal pain. Pain 71:5–23

Feinstein AR 1977 Clinical biostatistics. C.V. Mosby, St Louis

Feinstein AR 1989 Models, methods, and goals. Journal of Clinical Epidemiology 42:301–308

Feinstein AR 1996a Two centuries of conflict-collaboration between medicine and mathematics. Journal of Clinical Epidemiology 49:1339–1343

Feinstein AR 1996b Twentieth century paradigms that threaten both scientific and humane medicine in the twenty-first century. Journal of Clinical Epidemiology 49:615–617

Fitzgerald R, Davey C, Buxton MJ, Jones DR 1998 Evaluating patient-based outcome measures for use in clinical trials. Health Technology Assessment 2(14):19–45

Flor H, Turk DC 1988 Chronic back pain and rheumatoid arthritis: predicting pain and disability from cognitive variables. Journal of Behavioural Medicine 11:251–265

Flor H, Fydrich T, Turk DC 1992 Efficacy of multidisciplinary pain treatment centers: a meta–analytic review. Pain 49:221–230

Guyatt GH, Pugsley SO, Sullivan MJ, Thompson PJ, Berman LB, Jones NL, Fallen NL, Taylor DW 1984 Effect of encouragement on walking test performance. Thorax 39:818–822

Guyatt GH, Kirshner B, Jaeschke R 1992 Measuring health status: what are the necessary measurement properties? Journal of Clinical Epidemiology 45:1341–1345

Guyatt GH, Juniper EF, Walter SD, Griffith LE, Goldstein RS 1998 Interpreting treatment effects in randomised trials. British Medical Journal 316:690–693

Harding VR, Williams AC, Richardson PH, et al 1994 The development of a battery of measures for assessing physical functioning of chronic pain patients. Pain 58:367–375

Hennekens CH, Buring JE 1987 Epidemiology in medicine. Little, Brown, Boston. 272–286

Ikai M, Steinhaus AH 1961 Some factors modifying the expression of human strength. Journal of Applied Physiology 16:157–163

Jacobsen NS, Truax P 1991 Clinical significance: a statistical approach to defining meaningful change in psychotherapy research. Journal of Consulting Clinical Psychology 59:12–19

Jacobson NS, Roberts LJ, Berns SB, McGlinchey JB 1999 Methods of defining and determining the clinical significance of treatment effects: description, application, and alternatives. Journal of Consulting Clinical Psychology 67:300–307

Jaeschke R, Singer J, Guyatt GH 1989 Measurement of health status. Ascertaining the minimally clinically important difference. Controlled Clinical Trials 10:407–415

Jensen MP, McFarland CA 1993 Increasing the reliability and validity of pain intensity measurement in chronic pain patients. Pain 55:195–203

Kazdin AE 1982 Single-case research designs. Methods for clinical applied settings. Oxford University Press, Oxford

Kopec JA, Esdaile JM 1949 Functional disability scales for back pain. Spine 1995 20:1943–1949

Kouyanou K, Pither CE, Rabe-Hesketh S, Wessely S 1998 A comparative study of iatrogenesis, medication abuse, and psychiatric morbidity in chronic pain patients with and without medically explained symptoms. Pain 76:417–426

Loeser JD, Sullivan M 1995 Disability in the chronic low back pain patient may be iatrogenic. Pain Forum 4:114–121

McQuay HJ, Moore RA 1998 An evidence-based resource for pain relief. Oxford University Press, Oxford

McQuay HJ, Moore RA, Eccleston C, Morley S, de C Williams AC 1997 Systematic review of outpatient services for chronic pain control. Health Technology Assessment 1(6):97–110

McQuay H, Carroll D, Moore A 1995 Variation in the placebo effect in randomised controlled trials of analgesics: all is as blind as it seems. Pain 64:331–335

29

Macfarlane GJ, Thomas E, Papageorgiou AC, Schollum J, Croft PR, Silman AJ 1996 The natural history of chronic pain in the community: a better prognosis than in the clinic? Journal of Rheumatology 23:1617–1620

Main CJ 1984 Psychological factors in chronic low back pain. Thesis submitted for the degree of Doctor of Philosophy, University of Glasgow

Main CJ 1983 The Modified Somatic Perception Questionnaire (MSPQ). Journal of Psychosomatic Research 27:503–514

Main CJ, Waddell G 1984 The detection of psychological abnormality in chronic low back pain using four simple scales. Current Concepts in Pain 2:10–15

Main CJ, Wood PD, Hollis S, Spanswick CC, Waddell G 1992 The Distress and Risk Assessment Method. A simple patient classification to identify distress and evaluate the risk of poor outcome. Spine 17:42–51

Matheson LN, Mooney V, Caiozzo V, Jarvis G, Pottinger J, DeBerry C, Backlund K, Klein K, Antoni J 1992 Effect of instructions on isokinetic trunk strength testing variability, reliability, absolute value, and predictive value. Spine 17:914–921

Melzack R 1987 The short–form McGill Pain Questionnaire. Pain 30:191–197

Melzack R, Wall PD 1988 The challenge of pain (2nd edn). Penguin, London

Moore A, McQuay H, Gavaghan D 1996 Deriving dichotomous outcome measures from continuous data in randomised controlled trials of analgesics. Pain 66:229–237

Murphy E, Dingwall R, Greatbatch D, Parker S, Watson P 1998 Qualitative research methods in health technology assessment: a review of the literature. Health Technology Assessment 2(16):1–276

NIH Consensus Statement Online 1997 Acupuncture. Nov 3–5 [24 June 1999] 15(5) 1–34

Nicholas MK 1989 Self-efficacy and chronic pain. Paper presented at the annual conference of the British Psychological Society, St Andrews

O'Reilly SC, Muir KR, Doherty M 1999 Effectiveness of home exercise on pain and disability from osteoarthritis of the knee: a randomised controlled trial. Annals of Rheumatic Disease 58:15–19

Peat GM 1998 Functional limitation in chronic low-back pain. Doctoral thesis, University of Manchester

Peat GM, Sweet CA 1997 Does previous physical therapy contribute to self-reported disability in chronic low-back pain? Journal of Back and Musculoskeletal Rehabilitation 9:29–33

Peat GM, Moores L, Goldingay S, Hunter M 1999 Pain management programme follow-ups. An audit of current practice in the United Kingdom, submitted manuscript

Pither C E, Nicholas M K 1991 The identification of iatrogenic factors in the development of chronic pain syndromes: abnormal treatment behaviour? In: Bond M R, Charlton J E, Woolf C J (Eds) Proceedings of the VIth World Congress on Pain. Elsevier, Amsterdam 429–433

Plant MA, Richards JS, Hansen NK 1998 Potential bias of data from functional status measures. Archives of Physical Medicine and Rehabilitation 79:104–106

Report of a Working Party of the Pain Society of Great Britain and Ireland. 1997 Desirable criteria for pain management programmes. The Pain Society

Roland M, Morris R 1983 A study in the natural history of back pain. Part I: Development of a reliable and sensitive measure of disability in low-back pain. Spine 8:141–144

Rudy TE, Turk DC, Kubinski JA, Zaki HS 1995 Differential treatment responses of TMD patients as a function of psychological characteristics. Pain 61:103–112

Sackett DL, Haynes RB 1997 Summarising the effects of therapy: a new table and some more terms. Evidence Based Medicine 103–104

Sackett DL, Haynes RB, Guyatt GH, Tugwell P 1991 Clinical epidemiology. A basic science for clinical medicine (2nd edn). Little Brown, Boston

Sackett DL, Rosenberg WMC, Gray JAM, Haynes RB, Richardson WS 1996 Evidence-based medicine: what it is and what it isn't. British Medical Journal 312:71–72

Slater MA, Doctor JN, Pruitt SD, Atkinson JH 1997 The clinical significance of behavioral treatment for chronic low back pain: an evaluation of effectiveness. Pain 71:257–263

Speer DC 1992 Clinically significant change: Jacobson & Truax (1991) revisited. Journal of Consulting Clinical Psychology 60:402–408

Stratford PW, Binkley J, Solomon P, Finch E, Gill C, Moreland J 1996a Defining the minimum level of detectable change for the Roland-Morris Questionnaire. Physical Therapy 76:359–365

Stratford PW, Binkley J, Riddle DL 1996b Health status measures: strategies and analytic methods for assessing change scores. Physical Therapy 76:1109–1123

Testa MA, Simonson DC 1996 Assessment of quality-of-life outcomes. New England Journal of Medicine 334:835–840

Turk DC, Rudy TE, Sorkin BA 1993 Neglected topics in chronic pain treatment outcome studies: determination of success. Pain 53:3–16

Turner JA, Deyo RA, Loeser JD, Von Korff M, Fordyce WE 1994 The importance of placebo effects in pain treatment and research. Journal of the American Medical Association 271:1609–1614

Von Korff M 1992 Epidemiological and survey methods: chronic pain assessment. In Turk DC, Melzack R. (Eds) Handbook of pain assessment. Guildford Press, New York 391–408

Von Korff M 1994 Studying the natural history of back pain. Spine 19:2041S–2046S

Von Korff M, Saunders K 1996 The course of back pain in primary care. Spine 21:2833–2839

Waddell G, Newton M, Henderson I, Somerville D, Main CJ 1993 A Fear-Avoidance Beliefs Questionnaire (FABQ) and the role of fear–avoidance beliefs in chronic low back pain and disability. Pain 52:157–168

Wall PD 1992 The placebo effect: an unpopular topic. Pain 51:1–3

Weir R, Browne G, Roberts J, Tunks E, Gafni A 1994 The Meaning of Illness Questionnaire: further evidence for its reliability and validity. Pain 58:377–386

Whitney CW, Von Korff M 1992 Regression to the mean in treated versus untreated chronic pain. Pain 50:281–285

Williams AC. 1997 NNTs used in decision-making in chronic pain management. Bandolier Evidence Based Health Care 22:3

Williams AC, Richardson PH, Nicholas MK, Pither CE, Harding VR, Ridout KL, Ralphs JA, Richardson IH, Justins DM, Chamberlain JH 1996 Inpatient vs. outpatient pain management: results of a randomised controlled trial. Pain 66:13–22

Wright JG, Feinstein AR 1992 A comparative contrast of clinimetric and psychometric methods for constructing indexes and scales. Journal of Clinical Epidemiology 45:1201–1218

Appendix 1

Research terms and abbreviations

Attrition Patients whose outcome cannot be evaluated because of drop-out during treatment, discharge by staff or failure to contact or be contacted during the follow-up period.

Concurrent validity A type of criterion-related validity in which the measure and the criterion are compared at the same point in time.

Construct validity The extent to which a measure relates to other measures consistent with theoretically derived hypotheses concerning the concepts being measured.

Content validity The extent to which a measure reflects a specific domain of content, e.g. a self-reported questionnaire measuring fear-related beliefs ideally should not contain items related to beliefs and attitudes which are not fear-related.

Criterion-related validity The extent to which a measure is related to the criterion (in some cases a gold standard) that it purports to represent. It consists of concurrent validity and predictive validity, e.g. the criterion validity of a driving test might be evaluated by correlating it with how well people drive in everyday life.

Hawthorne effect The tendency for people being observed as part of a research effort to behave differently than they would otherwise.

Internal consistency A way of estimating the reliability of a measure (usually self-report questionnaire) from a single test administration. Usually summarised by Cronbach's alpha which indicates how strongly the inter-item correlations are.

Inter-rater reliability The assessment of reliability between two or more raters. Denotes the extent of clinical agreement.

Intra-rater reliability The assessment of reliability by one rater on more than one occasion.

Predictive validity A type of criterion-related validity in which the measure is compared with a future criterion, e.g. comparing subacute LBP patients' scores on the

	Yellow Flags screening tool with future occurrence of chronic disability.
Reactive measurement	Refers to the possibility that the very process of measuring a phenomenon can induce a change in the phenomenon itself (Carmines & Zeller, 1979).
Regression to the mean	A phenomenon that occurs when a second measurement is made only on those individuals with extreme initial levels. As a result, the second measurement tends on average to be less extreme than the initial one. This is particularly likely where there is a high degree of variability in a condition or measure.
Reliability	Concerns the reproducibility and internal consistency of a measure.
Reproducibility	The extent to which an experiment, test, or any measuring procedure yields the same results on repeated trials (Carmines & Zeller 1979). It deals with random error.
Responsiveness	The ability of a measure to detect small but important changes over time (Guyatt et al 1992).
s.d. (Standard deviation)	A measure of the spread of data.
Sensitivity to change	The term 'responsiveness' is to be preferred because of possible confusion with the use of the term 'sensitivity' in connection with prediction.
Surrogate outcome measure	A substitute for direct measurement of the true outcome we wish to know about.
Validity	The extent to which a measure does what it is intended to do.

Appendix 2

Outcome measures

DRAM   Distress Risk Assessment Method (Main et al. 1992). A classification of psychological distress based on patients' responses to the Modified Somatic Perceptions Questionnaire (MSPQ, see below) and Modified Zung (MZ, see below). Patients' levels of distress are classed as Normal, At Risk, Distressed-Somatic, Distressed-Depressed.

FABQ   Fear-Avoidance Beliefs Questionnaire (Waddell et al. 1993). A self-report, self-complete measure developed for use in low-back pain groups, particularly those with less severe distress and disability. Contains two scales relating to fear of physical activity (FABQ-PHYS—4 items) and work-related activity (FABQ-WORK—10 items)

MSPQ   Modified Somatic Perceptions Questionnaire (Main 1983). A 22-item self-report, self-complete questionnaire (13 scored, 9 dummies) developed in chronic low-back pain patients to quantify the degree of heightened somatic awareness.

MZ   Modified Zung (Main & Waddell 1984). A 23-item self-report, self-complete questionnaire developed in low-back pain patients to quantify depression/low mood.

PRSS   Pain-Related Self-Statements (Flor & Turk 1988). An eighteen item self-report, self-complete questionnaire consisting of two scales—catastrophising (PRSS-CAT—9 items) and active coping (PRSS-COP—9 items). Developed and tested in low-back pain and rheumatoid arthritis patients to measure the use of cognitive coping statements.

PSEQ   Pain Self-Efficacy Questionnaire (Nicholas 1989). A 10-item self-report, self-complete questionnaire designed to measure chronic pain patients' self-efficacy beliefs regarding pain control and functioning in spite of pain.

RMDQ   Roland & Morris Disability Questionnaire (Roland & Morris 1983) is a simple self-report, self-complete questionnaire designed to measure functional limitation. It was developed for low-back pain in primary care. Consists of 24 statements to which the patients can answer 'describes me today' or 'does not describe me today' (therefore measures functional limitation on the day of completion).

SFMPQ

Short-Form McGill Pain Questionnaire (Melzack 1987). A shortened version of the McGill Pain Questionnaire designed for research purposes or settings where time was limited. Self-report, self-complete. Consists of 4 scales designed to measure different aspects of pain experience—a visual analogue scale for current pain intensity (SFMPQ-VAS), descriptors for sensory (SFMPQ-SENS) and affective (SFMPQ-AFF) dimensions of pain quality, and an anchor scale for present pain intensity (SFMPQ-PPI)

VAS

Visual Analogue Scale.

The challenge of change in practice

HEATHER MUNCEY

This chapter looks at change as it affects physiotherapy practice within health care at the beginning of the 21st century. Change is all around us and many health care practitioners feel its pressure within their working environment. It is not, however, always easy to see the overall direction or to identify what is valid change. Least of all is it easy to know how to change and what constitutes responsible practice.

This book focuses on physiotherapy practice in the realm of musculoskeletal medicine and advocates the use of the biopsychosocial model for the assessment and management of musculoskeletal pain (see Chs 1 & 2). There is considerable evidence to support this approach. Many therapists use elements of it in their everyday practice but as an overall framework it represents a significant shift from use of a model within which they have been trained and have worked for most of their professional lives.

The traditional medical model attempts to link cause with effect and sets out a framework of clinical examination and investigation leading to a diagnosis on the basis of which a cure aimed at the cause is effected. In the physical therapies the diagnoses and treatments have tended to be predominantly tissue orientated. In addition, during the last part of the 20th century physiotherapy has been dominated by a 'guru' culture propagating frameworks of practice largely unsupported by any evidence. This may be viewed as an attempt to gain credibility in the medically dominated culture and to fit the square peg of a rehabilitation profession into the round hole of a biomedical model. Physiotherapists in musculoskeletal medicine have focused on the pain as the primary problem and have directed efforts towards alleviating or at least reducing this. Regaining or improving function has been an integral part of the treatment programme. However, on the whole, this has remained secondary.

Patient and practitioner expectations of the outcome of treatment have not matched the actuality. The model does not take into account other dimensions involved in the development and maintenance of the problems, such as psychosocial factors. The result may be a tendency to blame the patient when the cure is not forthcoming (Harding 1998a). Therapists also feel a sense of failure in that they do not know enough or are not good at their jobs. In fact, this reductionist model has proved inadequate to explain and support the role of the physiotherapist which in general has been considered to be that of a rehabilitationist.

Rehabilitation is one of the activity groupings assigned to physiotherapy by the National Casemix Office (1997) along with assessment/consultancy, enablement, maintenance, palliative care and health education. These are further categorised within types of cases amongst which are 'musculoskeletal' and 'pain.' There are many definitions of rehabilitation but one of the most commonly used is that of the World Health Organisation 1980:

The aim of care is the amelioration of a pathological condition and/or the restoration of function where a potential for improvement exists but the final level of improvement is uncertain.

Enablement is defined as:

Care given to empower an individual's potential for increased function when due to disabilities the ultimate level of function is unknown.

Perhaps a more enlightening and useful definition of rehabilitation as it applies to musculoskeletal medicine may be:

A problem solving and educational process aimed at restoring a state of health or wellbeing and independence. (Watson 1996)

In any event, rehabilitation models of impairment and disability recognise that disability is not synonymous with illness and acknowledge social factors as well as the role of iatrogenesis in the maintenance and development of disability (Harding 1998a).

In the light of the above some therapists are looking towards models of care other than the medical model in an attempt to optimise their practice. This chapter, therefore, looks at issues around introducing a new model of practice to a profession or a group of staff within that profession. It considers some current issues within health care, some theories and models which may help to inform the change process, and discusses some key concerns for those embarking upon this adventure!

Setting the scene

Throughout the 20th century, health care sciences have proliferated and flourished in an unprecedented way. Along with this, and within the context of a society shaped by the rise and development of capitalism and the journey into a global economy, the majority of health care in the Western World is now delivered within large organisations. The philosophy of health care has been pulled and pushed on one hand by the political masters and on the other by the rise of technology. At the same time the position of the 'organisation' within society has altered so that where it was once seen as solid and dependable this is now less so.

In the United Kingdom, as in other western countries, political changes reflecting an individualist rather than a pluralist perspective have resulted in the call for different approaches to the delivery of health care. The move has been from a nurturing towards an enabling culture but the passage has not been smooth! The 1980s saw the market applied to healthcare delivery but with the mediation of Thatcherism. With the 'New Labour' movement in the late 1990s, this has shifted towards a culture of the patient as a partner with a set of responsibilities accompanying previously defined rights. The purchaser/ provider split has become less overt and with the lack of the market as a regulator, other ways have had to be found to spread the finite resource creaking under the ballooning and potentially uncontainable demand.

The call for evidence-based practice is one of these ways. The trend is clear—purchase on the basis of evidence. This simple message is misted by the lack of evidence of any kind, for or against, for many traditionally accepted practices. In addition, how to access and assimilate the existing evidence is a complex task for already busy clinicians to contemplate. The government in the United Kingdom has assisted to some extent with Research and Development initiatives and with the setting up of institutions to assist clinicians in the review of evidence and, for example, in the preparation of clinical practice guidelines. However, a further (and probably the most key and challenging) step has been more or less ignored. This is the intricate and ongoing process of translation of evidence into practice. The result is that many practices shown to be ineffective are continued and many demonstrated to be effective are not implemented.

Evidence-based practice

Sackett (1997) defined evidence-based practice as 'Integrating individual clinical expertise with a critical appraisal of the best available external clinical evidence.' So previous experience and individual expertise still have a role. The dilemma appears to sit at the interface between this and the integration of 'best available external evidence.'

Why do therapists persist with clinically ineffective approaches?

'Physiotherapists rely heavily on initial training when selecting treatment techniques' (Turner & Winfield 1997). Recalled experiences of clinicians are reported to overestimate efficacy and lag behind available evidence reflecting individual enthusiasm rather than knowledge base (Grimeshaw et al 1995). Likewise, nurses are found to support practices and developments without sound research bases, some of which have even been shown to be detrimental to patients (Boore 1995).

Hunt in 1981 set out some reasons why nurses do not put research into practice. These were that they did not know about the research, did not understand the findings, did not believe the findings, did not know how to use them, or were not allowed to use them. Hunt (1996) points out though that 'just presenting the evidence to practitioners in an attempt to develop evidence based practice is unlikely to achieve the desired results.'

So how much does the body of evidence available to physiotherapists encourage change? There are still areas where physiotherapy practice is unsupported by evidence. On the other hand, biomedical research has provided some relevant evidence although this perspective has some limitations when applied to physiotherapy.

Biomedical research favours experimental design for research. This perspective ignores a significant defining characteristic of human beings—the capacity for self reflection and consequent ability to change our future (Parry 1997). The perspective considers cause and effect but does not fit well with physiotherapy practice which encompasses other aspects of health and disease such as human behaviour and its relationship to adjustment to disability, enablement and self management. So physiotherapy practice needs to look to perspectives other than the biomedical in order to move forward to support its practice with evidence. More appropriate support for the role may be of more interest to the profession so that it draws its attention in a more engaging way. Qualitative research from the social sciences, for example, may complement quantitative research from the biomedical perspective to broaden our understanding, help gain acceptance by the profession, and guide our practice.

The availability and type of evidence discussed above are two considerations but, in addition, another pressing question is how much evidence is required to form a strong basis for change in practice?

If one piece of good quality evidence demonstrates harm this is generally considered to be enough to warrant making change immediately. Otherwise, when evidence demonstrates benefit, there is no clearly accepted formula considered definitely to indicate change. It is generally accepted that at the least a study should be replicated and in most cases a good quality review of the literature should be done. Clinical experience and expert opinion are useful when evidence is not available (Partridge 1996). Although the value of experience and opinion is accepted, in this case it is important to recognise that it is a frail basis for practice and that more robust support should be sought continually. In reality, new evidence may be forthcoming at any time and keeping practice up to date is an ongoing process. Other texts detail levels of evidence in order of strength (Phillips 1986, White 1997). However, when referring to this literature it is important to remember that these 'tables' and 'schedules' mostly appertain to biomedical research and to keep in mind the limitations discussed above.

Strategies for integrating evidence into practice

One strategy for the integration of evidence based practice is the use of a Research Utilisation Model. There are many such models applicable to the health sciences (e.g. Brownman et al 1995, Stetier 1994). These vary in how they approach the change process. In general they encompass a definition of the problem, a statement of current practice and variations, a definition of the purpose and expected outcomes of the change. A good quality review of the literature and ranking of its value is always recommended. Finally, there is an implementation plan and subsequent evaluation and ongoing review so that change does not remain static.

Another strategy for implementation of research findings into practice is the use of Clinical Practice Guidelines. Grimeshaw et al (1995) define these as 'systematically developed statements to assist practitioner-patient decisions about appropriate health care in specific clinical circumstances.' The use of good quality and cost effective clinical practice guidelines is one way in which purchasers of health care services may gain some assurance about the standards of practice in terms both of its process, to which attention is often not paid, as well as the outcome of care. Grimeshaw et al's 1995 review of the implementation of clinical guidelines showed that these effected a change in practitioner behaviour resulting in a significant change in process and outcome of care.

Nevertheless, even with the help of these methods, in developing evidence-based practice the most challenging stage remains that of the translation of evidence into practice (Walsh 1995) and the successful management of the change process itself.

Physiotherapy education is changing so that therapists are now more able to appraise published evidence critically. However, even when this is clear in its support for change it is often still not applied to practice (Brownman et al 1995). Why is this? Grimeshaw et al (1995) observed the phenomenon that 'providing information to practitioners by itself is rarely sufficient to stimulate corresponding change in practice'. Could this lack of response to information alone be a feature of human behaviour applicable to therapists as well as patients? Do other strategies need to be enlisted before behaviour change occurs? Other chapters in Volume 1 of this series have discussed therapeutic approaches to change in the behaviour of patients (Harding 1998b & c, Shorland 1998). But what of therapists? There is certainly some argument for education to be, in general, participative rather than didactic. Implementation strategies should be related to clinical decision making, involve the user, and be integrated into the health care process, although evidence for specific strategies in defined circumstances is not yet available (Grimeshaw et al 1995).

Amongst other things, when planning change there is a need to take into account the culture of the profession as well as the environment within which the change is to occur. Although some research utilisation models include consideration of the environment, it will be helpful to move into the occupational psychology literature to explore further some ideas around change in the work environment.

Cultural and organisational change

In the United Kingdom, and in many other countries, physiotherapists work within large or relatively large organisations in the public or private sector. Organisational theorists have pointed to the accelerating rate of change in society (Kirkbridge 1993). All organisations are set within an environmental context and are subject to a variety of pressures exerted by that environment. These pressures may be political, economic, social, cultural or technological, are constantly changing, and require the organisation to adapt in order to survive. Individuals within those organisations and, in particular, managers need to develop skills and competencies to cope with this (Morgan 1989). Professional managers, senior clinicians and those responsible for planning, developing, and delivering services in health care organisations are no less subject to this multiplicity of pressure. The United Kingdom National Health Service (NHS) is an example of an organisation where such pressure occurs. Those working within it may feel they are subject to an ever shifting set of demands. Ground does not remain firm beneath the feet! Philosophies, structure and processes, goalposts and expectations within the culture are on the march! As a result, it may sometimes be less than clear how to create a service in which objectives, the means of achieving them, and even a way to recognise when they are reached are clear. No wonder it is difficult for individual practitioners in the physical therapies to have a clear sense of what they are trying to achieve and to take on an appropriate model of care to assist them in their task.

This discussion is not intended as a primer for service management! However, it may be helpful at this stage for practitioners wishing to move staff, however large or small the groups, to a biopsychosocial model of care to be aware of the debates around organisational theory and how these may relate to managing such a change within a local therapy service.

The majority of organisational theories lie within the modernist perspective. They view change as incremental so that the organisation may maintain a fit with its environment. Time is seen as linear and change as always for the best. That is, change is viewed as progress. The implication is that change may be managed.

Alternatively, some other theories, broadly within the postmodernist perspective (e.g. Peters 1987) point to the increasingly chaotic environment. They question whether change is always for the best, and whilst allowing that change can be directed are not confident that this ensures that the outcome will be as planned.

So both perspectives view change as an always present dynamic which does not need to be introduced. However, modernist theories consider that change may be managed and postmodernist theories argue that it cannot. Keeping these two perspectives in mind, some of the theories within them will now be considered.

From the end of the World War II until the 1970s the **process change model** of Lewin (1951) was prevalent in organisational theory. Change was seen as occasional within a usually stable situation. In this model Lewin described dynamic forces driving and restraining in different directions, resulting in a state of equilibrium. Change was said to occur in three stages: unfreezing of the equilibrium, change, and then refreezing into a new state of equilibrium. Since the 1970s with massive economic, political, technological and cultural shifts this view has reversed so that stability is now seen as relatively rare with long periods of turbulent change as the norm.

Models of organisation-environment linkage, on the other hand, allow that organisations are driven by external environment demands. Internal triggers such as new management or altering staff ideas may also affect change. In a complex organisation like the NHS many external and internal triggers will constantly be in operation. Change has to be planned, developed and executed and the individual and group complexities surrounding this process recognised, acknowledged and dealt with in order to achieve the aim.

Allaire and Firsiotu (1985) argued that a problem in either case may be that staff do not recognise the need for change and may even deny the validity of evidence and data produced to support it. In order for change to occur the misfit with the current environment needs to reach the organisational consciousness. So threats and opportunities such as redundant technology or methods, and changing political or social demands need to be recognised and assessed. In other words, there needs to be 'acceptance and ownership' of the need for change. Resistance to change is discussed later but first let us look at some models of change.

Models of the change process

Most of these are variations on Lewin's model and may be categorised as top-down/bottom-up or hard-soft/soft-hard approaches. A brief description of a cross section of models will set out some choices of style in approach to change.

Phillips (1983) described a top-down model where leading managers recognise the need for change. They then raise concerns amongst staff and direct actions with which to address the changes. During this process service philosophies and core values may be redefined but a frequent problem in this model is that staff do not truly take the redefinitions on board or recognise what they need to do to effect the required change. With this in mind managers may target areas other than people in which to make change. These may be structure and processes, technology, or tasks.

'Leavitt's diamond' (1964) describes that change in one of these four areas will affect the other areas (see Fig. III.1).

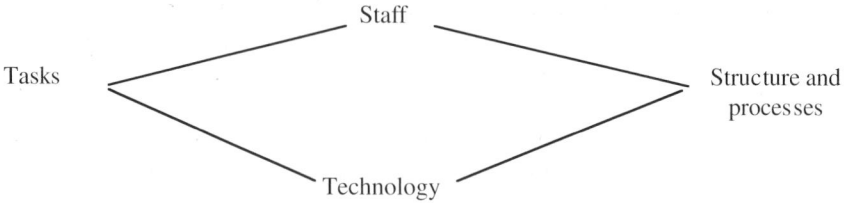

Fig. III.1 Leavitt's Diamond

Examples of this might be:

Structure and process	New procedures or the implementation of guidelines.
Technology	Evidence of the effective way to manage a problem.
Tasks	Individuals' job designs or explicit performance goals.
Staff	Each of the three areas above will affect the way that staff behave.

Once behaviour change begins it is vital to reinforce it by recognising achievements and providing rewards. In doing this, by optimising the learning which occurs through the process and by planning for future continuing change, an opportunity is created to ensure that future change is less traumatic. Change must then be consolidated and evaluated (Killmann 1989). Despite the fact that top-down models are used frequently there is little evidence that they actually work.

Bottom-up models, on the other hand, start by targeting individual beliefs and attitudes in order to change behaviour.

The so called **task alignment model** (Beer et al 1990) does this by considering the context within which individuals function. It starts by changing the person's organisational roles and relationships. Within this, each individual then has some flexibility to find methods of achieving the stated standards and goals.

Style of approach

Another dimension of the change process is the style of approach. This may be, for example, whether it is 'hard' or 'soft.' Bate (1990) describes four approaches along this spectrum:

The **conciliatory approach** is derived from the theory of small group dynamics. It attempts to avoid confrontation and employees are consulted. The best of the old way is included in the new and 'throwing the baby out with the bath water' is avoided. Individuals' skills are acknowledged and valued, change takes place gradually and is flexible. It may be too slow for some situations.

The **aggressive approach** on the other hand is very directive and is more suited to a crisis situation. It attacks traditional values and there is a danger of strong resistance and of the changes not being maintained when the initiator is no longer around.

The **indoctrinative approach** tries to teach core values by systematic socialisation (e.g. via education and training) in the hope that this will change behaviour. There is, however, little evidence that this works. In staff, as we observe with patients, 'information alone' rarely achieves the desired result. The majority of staff need to accept and own the need for change before progress can be made.

The **corrosive approach** believes that behaviour influences beliefs and attitudes. For example, leaders of a service within a large organisation may feel they cannot wait for direction from above so may go ahead with change themselves. This is empowering and flexible but results in erratic change when the organisation is viewed as a whole. In addition, if things go wrong, the responsible leaders may be allocated the blame.

Changing the culture of a profession

In reality, any change in culture occurs along a continuum and different approaches are required at different times. How might this apply to changing the culture of a profession such as physiotherapy?

Maybe we need to be shocked out of our current state by use of the aggressive approach. This might explain the cries for change over recent years in the way we consider the management of pain both from within and from outside our own profession. Once the message is recognised it needs to be accepted and this is more readily effected by a switch to the conciliatory style where consultation and discussion facilitate acceptance. Education and training to spread the word works within the indoctrinative approach helping to incorporate the new model into the individual therapist's personal frame of reference. This teaching then needs to be directed into learning and action for change. The corrosive approach will assist in the adoption of new attitudes by networking services already making the changes so that the new culture is adopted. The conciliatory approach comes into its own again here where participation facilitates behavioural change and the consolidation and maintenance of a new culture.

How to approach making the change

This information may be applied to the more global notion of changing a profession's practice or, more specifically, to changing that of a local service. It can be considered in steps:

1 **Establish a sense of urgency**. Identify the need for change, the present reality or a major opportunity to make change, and a clear purpose.

2 **Identify the leaders**. To take forward the change the key members of staff will need to work together as a team with the same aim in mind and develop supportive processes to achieve this.

3 **Create a vision**. To direct the change effort a clear vision is required along with the strategies which will achieve this.

4 **Communicate the vision and strategies**. Teach by the example of the leaders in order to achieve the desired behaviour change and the sharing of the vision.

5 **Empower others**. They can then act upon the vision.

6 **Remove obstacles to change**. For instance, undermining systems such as policies, procedures or routines.

7 **Encourage risk taking**. Create a supportive and fulfilling environment where new ideas, activities and actions may be discussed.

8 **Plan and create short term goals**. This will help performance improvement to become visible. Those involved in these improvements should be recognised and rewarded.

9 **Consolidate improvements and produce more change**. Foster a continuing learning environment. The increased credibility and enthusiasm generated by the achievement of short term goals can be harnessed to further change structures, processes, policies, etc. which do not fit the vision. It will be helpful at this stage to re-invigorate the process with new projects, etc.

10 **Institutionalise the new approach**. Make clear the link between the new behaviour and the achievements of the service. Ensure that the leaders develop and that there is a means of succession if they leave.

(Bath Consultancy 1998)

Making change within an organisation whether it be a large corporation, a service or department within a larger concern or a small group of specialist staff is a complex process. Recognising this is essential for success. A key element is identifying attitudes to change and unblocking resistance either in oneself or in staff members.

Resistance to organisational change

'It is usual to feel fainthearted at the prospect of change.'

George Eliot *Middlemarch* 1873

Change may be viewed as a threat to the *status quo* and it is not uncommon to encounter resistance by individuals to a proposed change. Why does this occur? Other chapters in this book discuss some barriers to change in those we encounter in the pain population (Chs 4, 6 & 7). How do colleagues at work respond to the idea of change in their behaviour in terms of implementing a different model of care?

Individuals at work may not be able to see the need for change particularly if their role does not require them to consider the more global effects of the environment on their organisation or service. They may also feel that the service is currently operating successfully. Even when leaders point out the changing environment it may be easier to deny that these changes will affect them than to act. Even if they are persuaded of the need to act they may be unable to decide on how to do so. Fear of the unknown or of the consequences of action may make them reluctant to move forward.

So fear is an issue in the organisational change process as well as in the individual behaviour change with which therapists attempt to engage pain sufferers (see fear avoidance chapters in Gifford 1998). But what does the employee fear? Surely not increased pain or potential harm as a result of the behaviour change? Perhaps it is pain of a different kind! A change in working conditions, new standards of practice or new skills required, decreased job satisfaction or rewards, or simply fear of the unknown. Fear is a potent force and needs to be recognised, acknowledged, and dealt with in order to effect significant change.

However, locating the blame for resistance to change in the individual alone may be inappropriate and, in some of the models described above, will be viewed as reductionist. Arguments based on the individual employee may be insufficient to explain the level of resistance and certainly fail to take into account the individuals' interaction with their environment. Neither does they allow for potential organisational, political, economic, technological or environmental barriers to change.

So how do we recognise and overcome barriers to change? As a first step in exploring these questions let us consider the definition of organisational development. Organisational development is 'a systematic effort applying behavioural science knowledge to the planned creation and reinforcement of organisational strategies, structures and processes for improving an organisation's effectiveness' (Huse & Cummings 1985). So again our knowledge and skills in the behavioural approach come into their own.

An important first step in dealing with this phenomenon is to identify the reasons for resistance so that it can be avoided or converted to commitment to the change. It is, of course, important to identify attitudes and beliefs which may underpin resistance behaviour in order to move towards altering this. Some common reasons for resistance in individuals follow.

Common reasons for resistance to change

- **Loss of control**. When change is imposed from above without participation in the process the feeling of loss of control may provoke fear, anxiety and resistance.
- **Excess uncertainty**. Too many things shifting at once create uncertainty and resistance.

- **The surprise factor**. Sudden change without warning does not allow time to absorb and acclimatise to the change.
- **The difference effect**. The introduction of new approaches requires questioning of the old approach which may be uncomfortable.
- **Loss of face**. Adoption of a new approach may imply that the old one was wrong and result in a feeling of being undervalued.
- **Concerns about future competence**. If new skills will be required there may be anxiety about whether these can be learned and how well they can be put into practice. Role, status and comfort at work may be at risk.
- **Ripple effect**. A change at work may impact upon other areas in the employee's life. For example, learning new skills requires time and energy and may affect home life.
- **More work**. The old job may have been automatic and comfortable, requiring little effort. A new approach will take more time, require more thought, and an investment and energy.
- **Past resentments**. Employees who have experienced problems within the organisation in the past may be less enthusiastic about committing to changes required by it.
- **Sometimes the threat is real**. Threat to role, status or even job may be perceived within the change. Sometimes this is in fact real. If this is so, it should be acknowledged early in the process to accommodate adaptation and problem solving with the individual.

Resistance to change may take different forms and is not always readily recognised as such. However, this does occur in patterns of more or less helpful behaviours. It is interesting to know what some of these might be in order to aid early recognition and problem solving. Figure III.2 shows some behaviours, sometimes known as the ladder of transition, with the most helpful behaviour at the top and least at the bottom.

Developing a commitment to change

It is not enough to have a plan for how to make change. It is clear that staff resistance to change may interfere with the process either at its initiation or at any point throughout. The previous discussion gives some suggestions as to how to tackle this issue. Having identified the sources of resistance and approached the solution, how do we move to building commitment to the new approach? Suggestions here may be seen as a corollary to the reasons why resistance occurs.

Involving staff in planning fosters a sense of control, participation and ownership. Room for some choice within the overall change framework will enhance this. Clear information about the nature of the change, why it is needed, and how it will be achieved is vital. A picture of what the service will look like after the change helps so that goal achievement is more easily recognised. Dividing the process into small, manageable steps with clearly defined goals at each stage will enhance the sense of purpose and direction.

	MOST PRODUCTIVE BEHAVIOUR
Making change happen and implementing the planned changes	
Planning for change and producing action plans for change	↑
Solving problems and dealing with the effects of change	
Confronting issues and putting change issues on the table	
Moaning and groaning and complaining about change	
Blaming and determining whose fault it is	
Avoidance and not being there to discuss change	
Denial and acting as if it will not happen	
Passive resistance – withholding support for change	
Overt resistance – openly working to resist change.	↓
Sabotage – destructive activity to stop change	LEAST PRODUCTIVE BEHAVIOUR

Fig. III.2 The 'transition ladder'

Providing information in plenty of time will give staff opportunity to discuss, reflect, and absorb the proposed changes. In this way they can become accustomed to the idea before they are required to make a commitment to it. Learning theory advises us that learning is cyclical and occurs through a process of planning, reviewing, thinking, and doing. This requires time. If you are the leader of the change it will help if you constantly repeat your commitment to the change and your reasons for this.

Requirements of staff should be made clear and explicit. It may help to have written standards, protocols, procedures, guidelines, etc. Check back with staff that they have understood what you think you have said! This is not meant to be patronising but to assist staff in knowing exactly what is expected of them at all stages.

When changes start to occur provide positive reinforcement for the desired behaviour. The meeting of standards or demonstration of a new competency, for example, should be rewarded with clear positive feedback. In this way early successes may provide role models to enhance the change.

Find a way of helping staff feel compensated for the extra effort they are putting into the change. Generating enthusiasm for clearly demonstrated improved results may be one way of doing this.

Some staff will feel the change benefits them less than others. If this is so, acknowledge it, allow time for people to express nostalgia for the old ways, and their regret at the movement away from those ways. It will then, however, be necessary to move on to create enthusiasm about the new ways and what this will mean in the future.

Why change initiatives may fail

There are many reasons why change initiatives may fail either completely or partially to achieve the stated objectives. Viewing change as a process the following ten common reasons may contribute at any stage to a greater or lesser extent to lack of success:

1 **Too ambitious.** Attempting to be too ambitious in the change project may be a result of failure to assess the current situation appropriately, or planning the change at the wrong time, in the wrong place or with the wrong staff and resources. Presenting staff with a project which is just too big to contemplate will, inevitably, not work.
2 **Importing someone else's solution.** Once the 'problem' or present situation has been identified correctly and the need for change accepted, the solution needs to be tailored to the specific set of circumstances. Adopting strategies used by another service, where circumstances will be different, may lead to failure. Considering someone else's overall framework and looking at their methods may help to identify potential pitfalls or to generate creative thinking locally, but taking into account specific local circumstances is vital for success.

3 **Too many initiatives.** It will be difficult to enlist the commitment of staff who have experienced many previous initiatives which have not been carried through to their endpoint. The perception of yet another idea destined to produce more inevitably unproductive work, which will be lost in the morass of future similar unfinished initiatives, will result in dislocation between staff and leaders and difficulty in generating enthusiasm.

4 **Ignoring the culture.** Changing the working model of a profession or staff group, such as moving from the biomedical to the biopsychosocial model as a basis for physiotherapy practice, is a major alteration in culture. Broadly speaking, it is likely that many staff groups at the present time will be working predominantly within the medical model. An assessment of the present thinking of individuals provides a picture of what work needs to be done in order to achieve the change. This may vary from an almost complete lack of recognition of the reductionist nature of the biomedical model and of issues within healthcare in the present environment; through an undefined lack of satisfaction with current practice style and outcomes; to an in depth understanding of other models of practice and ability to make a comparative analysis of these models, link this with and translate it into practice. Further, the style of approach to the change should be identified in order to 'fit' the presenting and underlying culture and needs to vary according to the specific stage of the change. This requires empathetic but clearly focused monitoring throughout.

5 **Emotions not acknowledged.** Failure to take account of the impact of emotional cycles of transition misses an important factor. Change initiatives not only require of individuals and groups a change in behaviour, but also represent in many cases a challenge to attitudes and beliefs and to status and rewards within the organisation. Attitudes and beliefs, behaviour and emotions, interact and affect each other and cannot be viewed in isolation. The emotional response throughout the change process needs to be recognised and acknowledged in a way which allows it to be worked through in order to produce positive results.

6 **Avoiding key issues.** This may occur if leaders are concerned about and unprepared for dealing with embarrassment or threat. An unresolved key issue will sabotage the change process and needs to be faced and dealt with.

7 **Delegation without authority.** Delegating tasks without delegating the appropriate responsibility and authority inevitably results in lack of clarity of role and frustration from the inability to action tasks. Expectations of all staff should be made clear and the authority to take action should be given.

8 **No feedback flow.** No feedback flow between policy and operation learning cycle can be a problem. Careful feedback needs to occur so that adjustments may be made on the basis of the state of progress. This needs to occur in both directions. If it is absent, leaders and staff may become out of step and the process dislocated and fragmented. Communication systems should be set up and monitored for effectiveness.

9 **Solutions without ownership of problems.** The acceptance and ownership of the 'problem' on the part of key staff must be ascertained before embarking on the search for a solution. Attempting to work out a solution to a problem which is not accepted will mean that staff fail to see the relevance of an initiative and are not engaged with the process. This will provoke resistant behaviour in some form and may result in a previously cohesive team being disrupted and ineffective in whatever model it is working.

10 **Insufficient skills development.** Insufficient personal skills development for pioneers of change means that the wherewithal to 'do the deed' is lacking. Skills development is important for the leaders of change and also for the workforce who are to implement it. Many physiotherapists will feel that their skills in musculoskeletal therapy are at a reasonable if not highly competent level. Changing models may produce a feeling of 'de-skilling' It is important to recognise that, although many physiotherapists already use aspects of the biopsychosocial model, the change process may require a more complete and systematic approach. Recognition of previously held skills, their incorporation into the new framework, and identification of the new skills required are important steps in the change process. Once learning needs are identified for the team, and for individuals within it, a programme for developing these skills must be planned. Learning needs to be evaluated in practice against progress in achieving overall objectives.

(Bath Consultancy 1998)

Conclusion

There are many things to consider when introducing change into the workplace and some of these have been discussed.

If we agree that, as health care professionals, it is our aim to provide the best care for our patients then it behoves us to examine what 'best care' may be and to continually evaluate our services set against this. Expectations of health care users and of health care professionals shift with changes in their environment and this also needs to be taken into account. Inevitably, therefore, if evaluation is ongoing then so will the change process be ongoing.

As an example, in considering the current health care environment, this book advocates the use of a biopsychosocial model in the management of musculoskeletal pain. This will represent some change for many practitioners and services.

Coping with these changes in a therapeutic setting is a major consideration for the individual practitioner and for those leading service provision. This chapter has attempted to discuss some of the relevant issues for both and to indicate some steps which may be taken in order to identify and agree the necessary changes and to implement them effectively.

The ongoing process of change is a challenge which we must meet in order to understand and continue to provide 'best care' for our patients.

REFERENCES

Allaire Y, Firsiotu M 1985 How to implement radical strategies in large organisations. Sloan Management Review 26, Spring 3

Bate SP 1990 A description and evaluation of four different approaches to the management of cultural change in organisations. Proceedings of the Fourth Annual Conference of the British Academy of Management, Glasgow

Bath Consultancy 1998 Personal ommunication. University of Bath, UK

Beer M, Eisenstat RA, Spector B 1990 Why change programs don't produce change, Harvard Business Review 68 (6):158–166

Boore J 1995 From research to practice and back again. Paper presented at the 1995 Royal College of Nursing Research Society annual conference, University of Ulster

Brownman P, Levine MN, Mohide A, Hayward RSA, Richard KI, Gafni A, Laupacis A 1995 The practice guidelines development cycle: a conceptual tool for practice guidelines development and implementation. Journal of Clinical Oncology 132 (5):502–512

Eliot, G 1873 Middlemarch: a study of provincial life. William Blackwood and Sons, Edinburgh

Gifford L S (Ed) 1998 Physiotherapy Pain Association Yearbook 1998–1999 topical issues in pain. Whiplash—science and management. Fear-avoidance beliefs and behaviour. CNS Press, Falmouth

Grimeshaw J, Freemantle N, Wallace S, Russell I, Hurvitz B, Wait I et al 1995 Developing and implementing clinical practice guidelines. Quality in Healthcare 4:55–64

Harding V 1998a Application of the cognitive behavioural approach. In: Rehabilitation of movement: theoretical basis of clinical practice. Pitt–Brooke J, Reid H, Lockwood J, Kerr J (Eds). W.B. Saunders, London pp539–583

Harding V 1998b Minimising chronicity after whiplash injury. In: Gifford L S (Ed) Physiotherapy Pain Association Yearbook 1998–1999. Topical issues in pain: Whiplash science and management; Fear avoidance behaviour and beliefs. CNS press, Falmouth pp105–114

Harding V 1998c Cognitive-behavioural approach to fear and avoidance. In: Gifford L S (Ed) Physiotherapy Pain Association Yearbook 1998–1999. Topical issues in pain: Whiplash science and management; Fear-avoidance beliefs and behaviour. CNS press, Falmouth pp173–191

Hunt J 1981 Indicators for nursing practice: the use of research findings. Journal of Advanced Nursing 6:189–194

Hunt JM 1996 Barriers to research utilisation. Journal of Advanced Nursing 23:423–425

Huse EF, Cummings DG 1985 Organization development and change 3rd Edn. St Paul West

Killmann R 1989 A completely integrated programme for creating and maintaining organizational success. Organizational Dynamics 18(1):5–19

Kirkbridge P 1993 Managing hange. In: Stacey R (Ed) Strategic thinking and the management of change: international perspective on organisational dynamics. Kogan Paige

Leavitt HJ 1964 Applied organizational change in industry. In: Cooper WW, Leavitt HJ, Shelly MW (Eds) New perspectives in organizational research. Wiley, New York

Lewin K 1951 Field theory in social science. Harper & Row, New York

Morgan K 1989 Riding the waves of change. Sage, London

National Casemix Office 1997 Physiotherapy groupings. Version 1.1 Community Healthcare Resource Group. April

Parry A 1997 New paradigms for old: musing on the shape of clouds. Physiotherapy 83(8):423–433

Partridge C 1996 Evidence based medicine: implications for physiotherapy, Physiotherapy Research International. 1:69–73

Peters T 1987 Thriving on chaos: handbook for a managerial revolution. Pan, London

Phillips JR 1983 Enhancing the effectiveness of organizational change management. Human Resource Management 22(12):18–39

Phillips LRF 1986 A clinicians guide to the critique and utilisation of nursing research. Appleton Century Crofts, Connecticut

Sackett DL 1997 Evidence based medicine. Seminars in Perinatology 21(1):3–5

Shorland S 1998 Management of chronic pain following whiplash injuries. In: Gifford L S (Ed) Physiotherapy Pain Association Yearbook 1998–1999: Topical Issues in pain. Whiplash science and management; Fear-avoidance beliefs and behaviour. CNS Press, Falmouth 115–134

Stetier CB 1994 Refinement of the Stetier Marram model for application of research findings to practice. Nursing Outlook 42: 15–25

Turner P, Winfield TWA 1997 Physiotherapists use of evidence based practice: a cross national study. Physiotherapy Research International 2(1):17–29

Walsh K 1995 Given in evidence. Health Service Journal 105 (5459):28–29

Watson G 1996 Neuromusculoskeletal physiotherapy: encouraging self management. Physiotherapy 82(6):352–357

White SJ 1997 Evidence based practice and nursing: the new panacea? British Journal of Nursing 63:175–178

World Health Organisation 1980 International classification of impairments, disabilities, and handicaps. World Health Organisation, Geneva, Switzerland

Exercise for low back pain: clinical outcomes, costs, and preferences

Reproduced with kind permission from British Medical Journal 1999 319:279-283

JENNIFER KLABER MOFFETT, DAVID TORGERSON, SALLY
BELL-SYER, DAVID JACKSON, HUGH LLEWELYN-PHILLIPS,
AMANDA FARRIN, JULIE BARBER

Low back pain is common and, although it may settle quickly, recurrence rates are about 50% in the following 12 months (Croft 1997). Recent management guidelines recommend that an early return to physical activities should be encouraged, (Clinical Standards Advisory Group 1994, Waddell et al 1996) but patients are often afraid of movement after an acute onset of back pain. Trials of specific exercise programmes for acute back pain have not shown them to be effective, (Malmivaara et al 1995, Faas et al 1993) but a specific exercise programme may have to be tailored to suit the individual patient and so is less likely to be effective for a heterogeneous group of patients.

However, there is some evidence that a general exercise programme, which aims to increase individuals' confidence in the use of their spine and overcome the fear of physical activity, can be effective for patients with chronic back pain (of more than six months' duration). A recent randomised trial of a supervised exercise programme in a hospital setting reported significantly better outcomes at six months and two years for the exercise group compared with the control group (Frost et al 1995, 1998). Whether this approach would be effective and cost effective for patients with low back pain of less than six months' duration in a primary care setting is unknown.

An important methodological problem occurs when it is not possible to blind subjects to the treatment they receive, since outcome is probably directly influenced by their preconceived ideas regarding the effectiveness of intervention (McPherson et al 1997). Thus, in trials where a double blind procedure is not feasible, participants who are not randomised to their treatment of choice may be disappointed and suffer from resentful demoralisation (Bradley 1993), whereas those randomised to their preferred treatment may have a better outcome irrespective of the physiological efficacy of the intervention. However, this problem may be partly ameliorated if patients' treatment preferences are elicited before randomisation, so that they can be used to inform the analysis of costs and outcomes (Clement et al 1998, Torgerson et al 1996).

In this paper, we report a fully randomised trial for the treatment of subacute low back pain in which the analysis was informed by patient preference.

Subjects and methods

Recruitment of subjects

Eighty-seven general practitioners agreed to participate in the study, and the principal investigator (JKM) visited each practice to discuss participation. Selection of general practitioners was based in the York area and restricted by the need to provide easy access for patients to the classes. Only one invited practice declined to participate. Single handed practices were not invited. The general practitioners referred patients directly to the research team or sent a monthly list of patients who had consulted with back pain. Inclusion criteria were patients with mechanical low back pain of at least four weeks' duration but less than six months, aged between 18 and 60, declared medically fit by their general practitioner to undertake the exercise, and who had consulted one of the general practitioners participating in the study. Patients with any potentially serious pathology were excluded, as were any who would have been unable to attend or participate in the classes. The exclusion criteria were the same as described by Frost et al (1998) except that concurrent physiotherapy rather than previous physiotherapy was an exclusion criterion in this trial.

Evaluation

Patients who seemed eligible were contacted by telephone and if they were interested in participating in the study were invited to an initial interview, at which the study and its implications for participants were explained. Patients who met all the eligibility criteria and consented to participate attended a first assessment a week later.

This included a physical examination (to exclude possible serious spinal pathology) and collection of baseline data by means of validated measures of health status. The main outcome measures were the Roland back pain disability questionnaire (Roland & Morris 1983), which measures functional limitations due to back pain, and the Aberdeen back pain scale (Ruta et al 1994), which is more a measure of clinical status. The Roland disability questionnaire consists of a 24 point scale: a patient scoring three points on the scale means that he or she reports, for example, 'Because of my back I am not doing any of the jobs that I usually do around the house, I use a handrail to get upstairs, and I lie down to rest more often.' We also administered the EuroQoL health index

(EQ-5D) (Brooks 1996) and the fear and avoidance beliefs questionnaire (FABQ) (Waddell et al 1993).

The second assessment was carried out at the patients' general practice six weeks after randomisation to treatment. The brief physical examination was repeated, and the patients were asked to complete the same outcome questionnaires.

In addition, patients were asked to complete pain diaries in the week before their first assessment and in the week before their second assessment. The diaries were used to assess subjective pain reports and asked 'How strong is the pain?' and 'How distressing is the pain?' (Frost et al 1995, Jensen & McFarland 1993).

We also evaluated patients at six and 12 months' follow up by sending them outcome questionnaires to complete and return.

Randomisation and treatments

A pre-prepared randomisation list was generated from a random numbers table and participants were stratified by practice in blocks of six. The trial co-ordinator ensured concealment of allocation from the clinical researchers by providing the research physiotherapist with a sealed envelope for a named patient before baseline assessment. A note inside the envelope invited the participant either to attend exercise classes or to continue with the current advice or treatment offered by his or her general practitioner. (One of the referring general practitioners used manipulation as usual treatment on most of his patients so that up to 37 patients in each arm of the study could also have received manipulation.) Each patient had an equal chance of being allocated to the intervention or the control group. Before patients were given their envelope they were asked whether they had any preference for the treatment assignment. The participants opened the envelope after leaving the surgery.

Intervention group

The exercise programme consisted of eight sessions, each lasting an hour, spread out over four weeks, with up to 10 participants in each class. The programme was similar to the Oxford fitness programme (Frost et al 1998) and included stretching exercises, low impact aerobic exercises, and strengthening exercises aimed at all the main muscle groups. The overall aim was to encourage normal movement of the spine. No special equipment was needed. Participants were discouraged from viewing themselves as invalids and from following the precept of 'Let pain be your guide.' They were encouraged to improve their individual record and were selectively rewarded with attention and praise. Although partly based on a traditional physiotherapy approach, the programme used cognitive-behavioural principles. One simple educational message encouraging self reliance was delivered at each class. Participants were told that they should regard the classes as a stepping stone to increasing their own levels of activity.

Controls

Patients allocated to the control group continued under the care of their doctor and in some cases were referred to physiotherapy as usual. No attempt was made to regulate the treatment they received, but it was recorded.

Economic analysis

We recorded patients' use of healthcare services using a combination of retrospective questionnaires and prospective diary cards, which they returned at 6 and 12 months' follow up. From this information we estimated the cost of each patient's treatment. We compared the mean costs of treatment for the two groups by using Student's t tests and standard confidence intervals. However, as cost data were highly positively skewed, these results were checked with a non-parametric 'bootstrap' (Efron & Tibshirani 1993). The economic evaluation addressed both costs to the NHS and the costs to society. Participants were not charged for the classes, in line with any treatment currently available on the NHS.

Statistical analysis

Our original intention was to recruit 300 patients, which, given a standard deviation of 4, would have provided 90% power at the 5% significance level to detect a 1.5 point difference between the two groups in the mean change on the Roland disability questionnaire. However, recruitment of patients to the study proved much slower than expected, and, because of the limitations of study resources, recruiting was stopped after 187 patients had been included into the study (see Fig. IV.1). This smaller sample reduced the power to detect such a difference to 72%, but there was still 90% power to detect a 2 point difference in outcome.

Our analysis was based on intention to treat. We estimated the effects of treatment on the outcome measures by means of analysis of covariance, with the change in scores as the dependent variable and adjustment being made for baseline score and patient preference. We used Student's t tests to analyse the data from the pain diaries as the baseline scores were quite similar.

Results

Study population

Of the 187 patients included in the trial, 89 were randomised to the intervention and 98 to the control group. Figure IV.1 shows their progress through the trial. In both groups those with the most severe back pain at randomisation were less likely to return follow up questionnaires: the mean Roland disability questionnaire score for responders at one year follow up was 5.80 (SD 3.48) compared with a mean score of 9.06 (4.58) for non responders respectively (P=0.002).

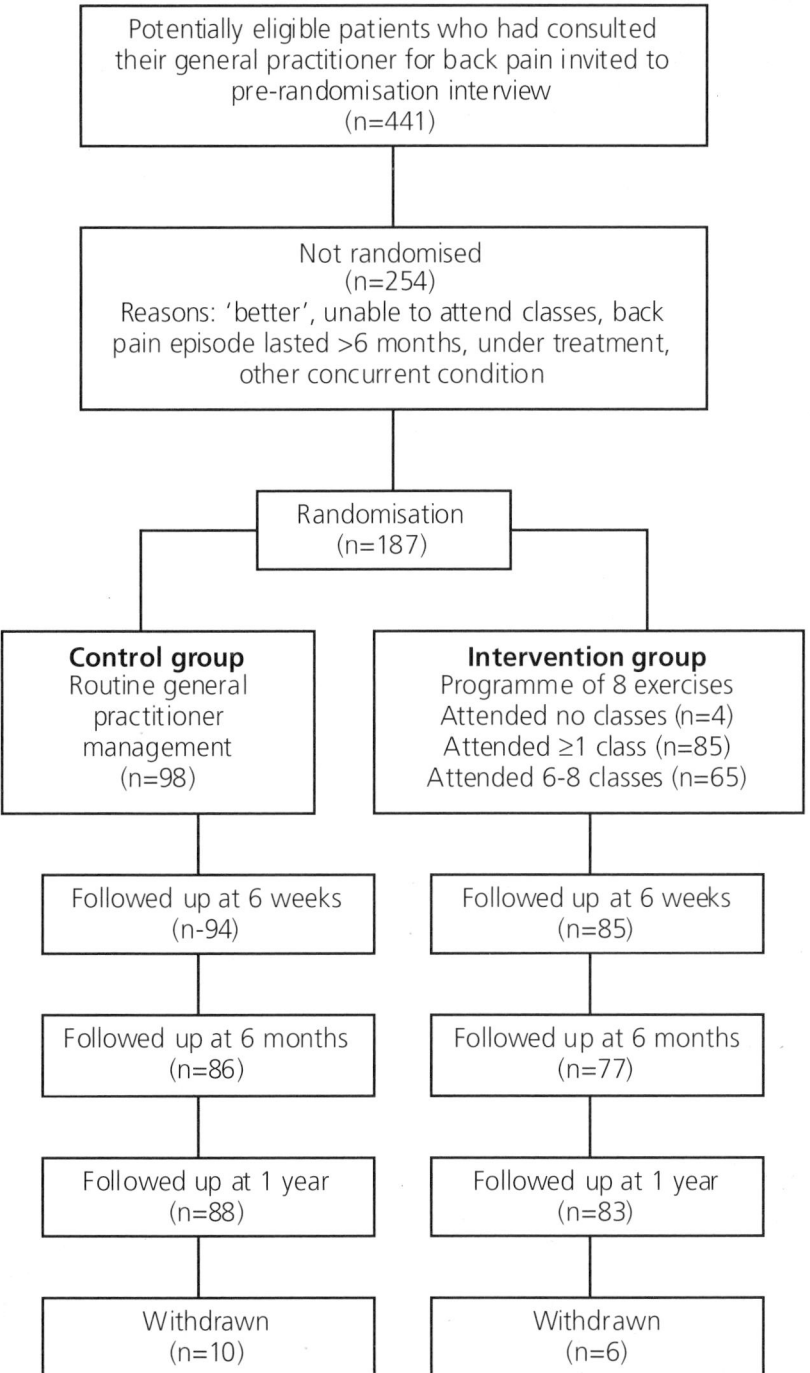

Fig. IV.1 Flow chart describing patients' progress through the trial

Baseline characteristics

The clinical and demographic characteristics of the patients in the two groups were fairly well balanced at randomisation (Table IV.1), although those allocated to the intervention group tended to report more disability on the Roland disability questionnaire than did the control group. Most patients (118, 63%), when asked, would have preferred to be allocated to the exercise programme. Attendance of the classes was considered quite good, with 73% of the intervention group attending between six and eight of the classes. Four people failed to attend any classes and were included in the intention to treat analysis. No patients allocated to the control group took part in the exercise programme.

Table IV.1 Baseline characteristics of patients with mechanical low back pain included in study. Values are means (standard deviations) unless stated otherwise

Variable	Control group (n=98)	Intervention group (n=89)
Age (years)	42.6 (8.62)	41.1 (9.21)
No (%) of women	55 (56)	51 (57)
No (%) of non-smokers	69 (70)	64 (72)
No (%) preferred allocation to exercise	65 (66)	53 (60)
No (%) had physiotherapy in past 6 months	23 (24)	18 (20)
Visits to GP in past 6 months	2.45 (2.36)	2.22 (3.32)
Roland disability questionnaire score		
(0-24 points)	5.56 (3.94)	6.65 (4.02)
Aberdeen back pain scale (0-100 points)	25.52 (10.85)	29.73 (11.07)
Fear-avoidance beliefs questionnaire		
Work (0-42 points)	13.7 (9.83)	14.7 (10.10)
Physical activities (0-24 points)	12.7 (5.47)	13.8 (5.26)
EuroQoL health index (0-1 point)	0.73 (0.15)	0.71 (0.16)

Clinical outcomes

Table IV.2 shows the mean changes in outcome measures over time, from randomisation to final follow up at one year. After adjustment for baseline scores, the intervention group showed greater decreases in all measures of back pain and disability compared with the controls. At six weeks after randomisation, patients in the intervention group reported less distressing pain than the control group (P=0.03) and a marginally significant difference on the Roland disability questionnaire scores. Other variables were not significantly different, but the differences in change were all in favour of the intervention group. At six months the difference of the mean change scores of the Roland disability questionnaire was significant, and at one year the differences in changes of both the Roland disability questionnaire and the Aberdeen back pain scale were significant (Table IV.2). Most of the intervention group improved by at least three points on the Roland disability questionnaire: 53% (95% confidence interval 42-64%) had done so at six weeks, 60% (49-71%) at six months, and 64% (54-74%) at one year. A smaller proportion of the control group achieved this clinically important improvement: 31% (22-40%) at six weeks, 40% (29-50%) at six months, and 35% (25-45%) at one year.

Table IV.2 Changes in back pain scores from baseline values in intervention and control groups at 6 weeks, 6 months, and 1 year follow up

| | Mean change in scores* | | | |
| | Control | Intervention | | P |
Outcome measure	group	group	Difference (95% CI)	value)
At 6 weeks	**(n=94)**	**(n=85)**		
Roland disability questionnaire	-1.94	-2.86	0.92 (-0.02 to 1.87)	0.06
Aberdeen back pain scale`	-8.99	-11.58	2.59 (-0.37 to 5.55)	0.09
Pain diary	(n=89)	n=82)		
Strength	-9.4	-12.2	2.8 (-1.67 to 7.30)	0.22
Distress	-5.0	-10.2	5.13 (0.41 to 9.85)	0.03
Fear and avoidance beliefs questionnaire				
Work	-1.26	-2.98	1.72 (-0.34 to 3.78)	0.10
Physical activities	-2.02	-3.26	1.24 (-0.27 to 2.74)	0.11
EuroQoL health index	0.022	0.030	-0.10 (-0.09 to 0.07)	0.84
Mean (range) number visits to GP	0.41 (0-6)	0.20 (0-3)	NA	0.09
At 6 months	**(n=86)**	**(n=77)**		
Roland disability questionnaire	-1.64	-2.99	1.35 (0.13 to 2.57)	0.03
Aberdeen back pain scale	-8.11	-10.26	2.15 (-1.63 to 5.93)	0.26
EuroQoL health index	0.067	0.080	-0.01 (0.06 to 0.04)	0.60
Mean (range) number visits to GP	0.89 (0-8)	0.49 (0-4)	NA	
At 1 year	**(n=88)**	**(n=83)**		
Roland disability questionnaire	-1.77	-3.19	1.42 (0.29 to 2.56)	0.02
Aberdeen back pain scale	-8.48	-12.92	4.44 (1.01 to 7.87)	0.01
EuroQoL health index	0.089	0.111	-0.02 (-0.08 to 0.04)	0.47

* Adjusted for baseline scores
NA = Not applicable

Patients' preference

We examined the effect of patients' baseline preference for treatment on outcome after adjusting for baseline scores and main effects. Preference did not significantly affect response to treatment. The intervention had similar effects on both costs and outcomes regardless of baseline preference. For example, the change in the Roland disability questionnaire score at 12 months in the control group was 1.93 for patients who preferred intervention and 1.18 for those who were indifferent (95% confidence interval of difference 1.05-2.55), and in the intervention group the change in score was 3.10 for those who preferred intervention and 3.15 for those who were indifferent ((95% confidence interval of difference 1.47-3.08). As the interaction term (preference by random allocation) was non-significant, the results shown in Table IV.2 exclude the preference term.

Economic evaluation

Patients in the intervention group tended to use fewer healthcare and other resources compared with those in the control group (Table IV.3). However, the mean difference, totalling £148 per patient, was not significant: the 95% confidence interval suggests there could have been a saving of as much as £442 per patient in the intervention group or an additional cost of up to £146. Patients in the control group took a total of 607 days off work during the 12 months after randomisation compared with 378 days taken off by the intervention group.

Discussion

Our results support the hypothesis that a simple exercise class can lead to long term improvements for back pain sufferers. Studies have shown that a similar programme for patients with chronic back pain can be effective in the hospital setting (Frost et al 1995, 1998). In this study we show the clinical effectiveness for patients with subacute or recurrent low back pain who were referred by their general practitioner to a community programme.

Current management guidelines for low back pain recommend a return to physical activity and taking exercise. In particular, they recommend that patients who are not improving at six weeks after onset of back pain, which may be a higher proportion than previously realised (Croft 1997), should be referred to a reactivation programme. The programme we evaluated fits that requirement well. It shows participants how they can safely start moving again and increase their levels of physical activity. It is simple and less costly than individual treatment.

It seemed to have beneficial effects even one year later, as measured by functional disability (Roland disability questionnaire) and clinical status (Aberdeen back pain scale). The mean changes in scores on these instruments were small, with many patients reporting mild symptoms on the day of entry to the trial. However, a substantially larger proportion of participants in the

Table IV.3 Use of services and their costs associated with back pain in the two study groups at 12 months follow up

Variable	Intervention group (n=70)*	Control group (n=74)*	Difference (95% CI) (Student's t test)
Health services			
No of exercise classes	70	0	
Total cost (£25.20/person /programme of 8 classes)	£1764	0	
No of vists to GP	139	266	
Total cost (£16/visit)	£2224	£4256	
No of visits to a physiotherapist	65	146	
Total cost (£18/visit)	£1170	£2628	
No of visits to a chiropractor or osteopath	27	25	
Total cost (£20/visit)	£540	£500	
No of visits to orthopaedic surgeon	0	1	
Total cost (£174/visit)	0	£174	
No of MRI investigations	1	1	
Total cost (£300/visit)	£300	£300	
No of x-ray investigations	4	3	
Total cost (£20/visit)	£80	£60	
No of nights in hospital	0	2	
Total cost (£150/night)	0	£300	
Total health service related costs	£6078	£8218	
Mean (SD) cost per patient	£86.83 (105.19)	£111.05 (205.11)	24.23 (-29.94 to 78.39) (P=0.38†)
Median (90% range) cost per patient	£41.20 (25.20-353.20)	0 (0-532.00)	
Equipment (beds, stove modification, car seat)			
No of pieces of equipment:	4	4	
Total cost (item cost £10-800)	£2123	£2091	
Days off work			
Total no of days off work:	378	607	
Total cost (£45/day)‡	£17 010	£27 315	
All costs (including equipment and days off work)			
Total costs	£25 211	£37 624	
Mean (SD) cost per patient	£360.15 (582.27)	£508.43 (1108.79)	148.28 (-145.92 to 442.48) (P=0.32§)
Median (90% range) cost per patient	£115.20 (25.20-1688.40)	£50.00 (0-2728.00)	

Notes

MRI = magnetic resonance imaging.

* Based on 144 subjects without missing data on resource use or costs.

† Bootstrap comparison of means P=0.38, accelerated 95% CI corrected for bias (-22.00 to 81.90).

‡ Based on gross domestic product per capita 1996.

§ Bootstrap comparison of means P=0.33, accelerated 95% CI corrected for bias (-89.78 to 506.14).

exercise classes gained increases of over three points on the Roland disability questionnaire at six weeks, six months, and one year, which might be clinically important. At six weeks, participants in the exercise classes reported significantly less distressing pain compared with the control group, although the intensity of pain was not significantly different. This is consistent with findings from a study of chronic back pain patients in Oxford, in which changes in distressing pain were much greater than were the changes in intensity of pain (Frost et al 1995).

People with back pain who use coping strategies that do not avoid movement and pain have less disability (Williams & Keefe 1991, Eŝtlander & Harkapaa 1989, Holmes & Stevenson 1990, Rosenstiel & Keefe 1983, Slade et al 1983). In our study the participants in the exercise classes were able to function better according to Roland disability questionnaire scores than the control group at six months and one year after randomisation to treatment, and at one year they also showed a significantly greater improvement in clinical status as measured by the Aberdeen back pain scale. This increase in differences in effect between the intervention and control groups over time is consistent with the results from long term follow up in comparable back pain trials (Meade et al 1995, Cherkin et al 1998).

Key messages

- Patients with back pain need to return to normal activities as soon as possible but are often afraid that movement or activity may be harmful.

- An exercise programme led by a physiotherapist in the community and based on cognitive-behavioural principles helped patients to cope better with their pain and function better even one year later.

- Patients' preferences for type of management did not affect outcome.

- Patients in the intervention group tended to use fewer healthcare resources and took fewer days off work.

- This type of exercise programme should be more widely available.

Study design

The design of this study was a conventional randomised controlled trial in that all eligible patients were randomised. However, the participants were asked to state their preferred treatment before they knew of their allocation. A study of antenatal services showed that preferences can be an important determinant of outcome (Clement et al 1998), but we did not find any strong effect of preference on the outcome, although a much larger sample size would be needed to confidently exclude any modest interaction between preference and outcome (McPherson et al 1997). This information may be useful to clinicians in that it suggests that exercise classes are effective even in patients who are not highly motivated. Our trial design, of asking patients for their preferences at the outset, has substantial advantages over the usual patient preference design, in which costs and outcomes cannot be reliably controlled for confounding by preference.

Conclusions

Our exercise programme did not seem to influence the intensity of pain but did affect the participants' ability to cope with the pain in the short term and even more so in the longer term. It used a cognitive-behavioural model, shifting the emphasis away from a disease model to a model of normal human behaviour, and with minimal extra training a physiotherapist can run it. Patients' preferences did not seem to influence the outcome.

REFERENCES

Bradley C 1993 Designing medical and educational studies. Diabetes Care 16: 509–518

Brooks R with EuroQoL Group 1996 EuroQoL: the current state of play. Health Policy 37: 53–72

Cherkin D, Deyo R, Battie M, Street J, Barlow W 1998 A comparison of physical therapy, chiropractic manipulation, and provision of an educational booklet for the treatment of patients with low back pain. New England Journal of Medicine 339: 1021–1029

Clement S, Sikorski J, Wilson J, Candy B 1998 Merits of alternative strategies for incorporating patient preferences into clinical trials must be considered carefully [letter]. BMJ 317:78

Clinical Standards Advisory Group 1994 Back pain. London: HMSO

Croft P (Ed) 1997 Low back pain. Radcliffe Medical Press, Oxford

Efron B, Tibshirani R 1993 An introduction to bootstrap. Chapman & Hall, New York

Estlander A, Harkapaa K 1989 Relationships between coping strategies, disability and pain levels in patients with chronic low back pain. Scandinavian Journal of Behaviour Therapy 18:56–69

Faas A, Chavannes A, van Eijk JTM, Gubbels J 1993 A randomized, placebo-controlled trial of exercise therapy in patients with acute low back pain. Spine 18:1388–1395

Frost H, Klaber Moffett J, Moser J, Fairbank J 1995 Evaluation of a fitness programme for patients with chronic low back pain. British Medical Journal 310:151–154

Frost H, Lamb S, Klaber Moffett J, Fairbank J, Moser J 1998 A fitness programme for patients with chronic low back pain: 2 year follow–up of a randomised controlled trial. Pain 75:273–279

Holmes J, Stevenson C 1990 Differential effects of avoidant and attentional coping strategies on adaption to chronic and recent–onset pain. Health Psychology 9:577–584

Jensen M, McFarland C 1993 Increasing the reliability and validity of pain intensity measurement in chronic pain patients. Pain 55:195–203

Malmivaara A, Hakkinen U, Aro T, Heinrichs M, Koskenniemi L, Kuosma E et al. 1995 The treatment of acute low back pain—bed rest, exercises or ordinary activity? New England Journal of Medicine 332: 351–355

McPherson K, Britton A, Wennberg J 1997 Are randomised controlled trials controlled? Patient preferences and unblind trials. Journal of the Royal Society of Medicine 90:652–656

Meade T, Dyer S, Browne W, Frank A 1995 Randomised comparison of chiropractic and hospital outpatient management for low back pain: results from extended follow up. British Medical Journal 311:349–351

Roland M, Morris R 1983 A study of the natural causes of back pain. Part 1: Development of a reliable and sensitive measure of disability in low–back pain. Spine 8:141–144

Rosenstiel A, Keefe F 1983 The use of coping strategies in chronic low back pain patients: relationship to patient characteristics and current adjustments. Pain 17:33–44

Ruta D, Garratt A, Wardlaw D, Russell I 1994 Developing a valid and reliable measure of health outcome for patients with low back pain. Spine 19:1887–1896

Slade P, Troup J, Lethem J, Bentley G 1983 The fear avoidance model of exaggerated pain perception II Preliminary studies of coping strategies for pain. Behaviour Research and Therapy 21:409–416

Torgerson D, Klaber Moffett J, Russell I 1996 Patient preferences in randomised trials: threat or opportunity? Journal of Health Services Research and Policy 1(4):194–197

Waddell G, Feder G, McIntosh A, Lewis M, Hutchinson A 1996 Low back pain evidence review. Royal College of General Practitioners, London

Waddell G, Newton M, Henderson I, Somerville D, Main C 1993 A fear–avoidance beliefs questionnaire (FABQ) and the role of fear–avoidance beliefs in chronic low back pain and disability. Pain 52:157–168

Williams D, Keefe F 1991 Pain beliefs and use of cognitive–behavioral coping strategies. Pain 46:185–190

1

Biopsychosocial assessment and management

1

Flagging the danger signs of low back pain

LISA ROBERTS

Low back pain is not a disease, but a symptom (Walsh 1992) which affects most people at some point in their lives, and costs the NHS almost £500 million per year (CSAG 1994). As chartered physiotherapists, much of our clinical practice involves treating people with low back pain, and therefore having a clear understanding of how to assess patients with this symptom is vital. But how adept is our assessment? What do we learn from asking 'special questions' in a patient interview? Can we really determine whether serious spinal pathology might be present from our clinical examination?

This chapter investigates these issues and reports on a study outlining what general practitioners (GPs) consider to be 'danger signs' for serious spinal pathology, i.e. the signs and symptoms justifying immediate hospital advice (not necessarily an admission). These results are discussed, together with the controversial evidence base for some of these signs, derived from literature reviews. The chapter aims to 'flag up' and heighten awareness of these danger signs, and perhaps, challenge some of our assumptions about spinal assessments.

The biopsychosocial model

It is important that our spinal assessments consider the holistic nature of low back pain. We are not considering an anatomical structure such as a disc or zygapophyseal joint, nor a pathological process such as a fracture or a degenerate spine, but a *person* experiencing low back pain.

In an attempt to conceptualise this holistic perspective, Waddell (1987) outlined the biopsychosocial model, a theoretical framework, which may explain many clinical observations. This model is a useful alternative to the traditional medical model and suggests that there is far more to consider than just the pain itself as Figure 1.1, often used to depict the model, shows.

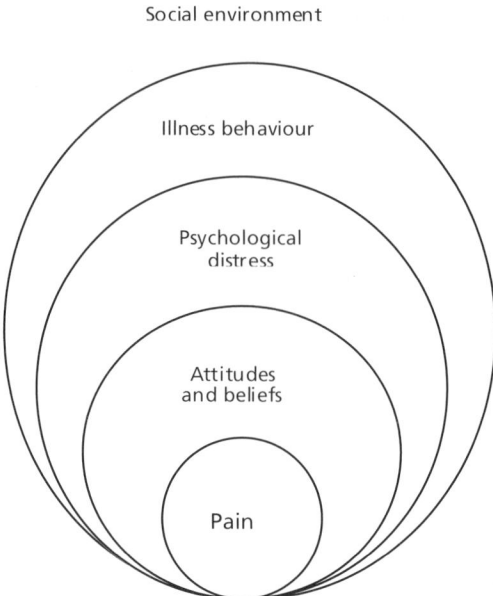

Fig. 1.1 Biopsychosocial model of low back disability (Waddell 1987)

When considering a biopsychosocial context, addressing danger signs may appear to focus on the 'bio' aspect, however it must be remembered that our whole clinical assessment of a person experiencing back pain should still be within a holistic psychosocial context.

The *Back Home* study

In an attempt to understand more about acute low back pain, funding was obtained in 1993 from the Research and Development Directorate to develop and test the effectiveness of a leaflet for patients and produce a diagnostic guide for GPs to assist them in their clinical assessment. The hypothesis of the study was that 'an optional GP diagnostic guide supplemented by a patient information leaflet (called *Back Home*) improves the ability of people with acute low back pain to manage the episode of pain at home'. (Acute low back pain was defined as a new episode of 'pain' [as described by a patient] in an area bounded by T12 and the lowest ribs superiorly, the gluteal folds inferiorly, and the contours of the trunk laterally).

This randomised controlled trial was undertaken in Southampton and the New Forest between June 1994 and December 1996. However, before any developmental work could be done on designing the leaflet or diagnostic guide, it was first necessary to see how GPs were currently managing people with acute low back pain. (This was before the Clinical Standards Advisory Group (CSAG) report was available.) Therefore the 'Back Home' team (consisting of a consultant rheumatologist, GP, research physiotherapist, physiotherapy manager, lecturer in physiotherapy, and statistician), developed a questionnaire for GPs, covering many aspects of back pain management. Included in the questionnaire was an open question: 'What signs and symptoms do you consider are 'danger signs' for a patient with acute low back pain *i.e.* those which would necessitate immediate hospital attention?'

The questionnaire was pilot tested with 31 GPs in Salisbury and re-mailed two weeks later to establish test-retest reliability. The results are reported from a 71% response rate (n = 22). In response to the question about danger signs, GPs listed responses (mean 2.2 per GP), that were assigned to 21 categories. The top 8 responses (*i.e.* signs or symptoms selected by more than one GP) can be seen in Table 1.1.

Table 1.1　General practitioner's top 8 perceptions of danger signs. Results from the pilot questionnaire asking GPs to identify what they considered to be danger signs for a patient with acute low back pain

Response	*Number*
Signs/symptoms of bladder/bowel disturbances	10
Problems with sphincter control	8
Severe/disabling pain	6
Gross neurological complications	3
Obvious root signs	3
Objective signs	2
Paralysis	2
Progressive weakness/loss of reflexes	2

One difficulty in categorising data in this way is that it could be argued that 'problems with sphincter control' may also be deemed 'bladder / bowel disturbances'. If the sphincter under consideration is either the anal or bladder sphincters, then this will be true; however, this cannot automatically be assumed, and so the categories are treated separately.

Having sought opinions from the GPs, we were particularly interested in the reported evidence base for danger signs, and so turned to the literature.

What evidence is there for danger signs (or red flags?)

Reviewing the literature revealed a surprisingly poor evidence base for danger signs. The reported studies were primarily either individual case histories, or studies with few subjects, and often lacked clinical details.

Evidence exists in the CSAG report (1994), which describes a diagnostic triage for back pain and categorises patients' back pain as:

a) simple backache (defined as 'common "mechanical" back pain which is musculoskeletal in origin and in which symptoms vary with different physical activities');
b) nerve root pain; and
c) possible serious spinal pathology.

In classifying patients with possible serious spinal pathology, the report identified danger signs, which the authors termed 'red flags'. These 'red flags' are further subdivided into two groups:

a) signs and symptoms requiring emergency referral to a spinal surgeon; and
b) signs and symptoms suggesting possible serious spinal pathology:

Box 1 'Red flags' identified in the Clinical Standards Advisory Group report (1994)

---

1. Signs/symptoms requiring emergency referral to a spinal surgeon

- difficulty with micturition
- loss of anal sphincter tone/faecal incontinence
- saddle anaesthesia about anus, perineum or genitals
- widespread (>1 nerve root) or progressive motor weakness in legs
- gait disturbance

2. Signs/symptoms suggesting possible serious spinal pathology

- age of onset <20 or >55 years
- violent trauma e.g. fall from a height, RTA
- constant, progressive, non-mechanical pain
- thoracic pain
- previous medical history — carcinoma
- systemic steroid use
- drug abuse, HIV
- systemically unwell
- weight loss
- persisting severe restriction of lumbar flexion
- widespread neurology
- structural deformity

Prior to publication of the CSAG report, we had independently established a hierarchy of danger signs in preparation for the GP questionnaire. This was based upon the literature, the clinical experience of the interdisciplinary research team (rheumatology, general practice, and physiotherapy), and opinions sought from medical colleagues in neurosurgery, orthopaedics, and casualty departments at Southampton University Hospitals Trust.

From this evidence, when signs were usually reported to be indicative of serious spinal pathology, they were termed 'probable danger signs'. When evidence was more controversial, they were considered 'possible danger signs', and when little or no evidence could be found, they were deemed 'probably not danger signs'.

Box 2 Research group classification of signs

---

1 **Probable danger signs**

- extensor plantar response
- neurological signs at multiple levels
- saddle anaesthesia

2 **Possible danger signs**

- [constant] night pain
- bilateral leg signs

3 **Probably not danger signs**

- severe local back pain
- loss of reflex at one level
- unilateral sciatic symptoms below the knee.

The list was not intended to be definitive, but aimed to address the less obvious histories than trauma, previous history of carcinoma, systemic steroid use, etc. Having identified these signs, the next stage was to establish what evidence exists for these three 'probable' and two 'possible' danger signs.

Probable danger signs

Extensor plantar response

The plantar response has been described as the most important reflex in the body and yet the one most frequently misinterpreted (Bickerstaff 1973). The phenomenon was first described in 1896 by Joseph Babinski, a Polish neurologist, working in a syphilitic ward at the Pitie Hospital in Paris (O'Reilly 1992) and he coined the term 'phénomène des orteils' (phenomenon of the toes) for this sign (Youl 1989). Babinski (in O'Reilly 1992), observed that stroking the lateral aspect of the foot facilitated 'dorsiflexion of the big toe in patients with meningovascular syphilis affecting the corticospinal tract'. He went on to describe a sign, evoked by nociceptive stimulus, that consisted of dorsiflexion of the toes and ankle, with flexion at the knee and hip (Walshe 1956). In 1903 Babinski added abduction or fanning of the toes, which he called 'le signe de l'éventail' (sign of the fan), to his original description, but noted that this was not a constant component (Youl 1989, Walshe 1956). It has been reported that Babinski found fanning of the toes occasionally occurred in healthy people, but was often found in patients with early pyramidal tract lesions before the plantar response became extensor (Grant 1987). Later, in 1912, Babinski expressed his view that the plantar response was part of a general flexion reflex (Walshe 1956), however, the speed of the extensor response was slower than that of the normal flexor response (Grant 1987).

The presence of an extensor response in clinical practise indicates a disturbance in function of the pyramidal system and this notion is supported by clinical and experimental agreement (Bickerstaff 1973). It is interesting that Babinski is reported to say (in MacGregor 1987) 'This sign, although it indicates the presence of a pyramidal system disturbance, does not denote its severity', and MacGregor (1987) comments on his use of the term *pyramidal system* as oppose to pyramidal tract. However, MacGregor does not discuss whether this is a translation, (since Babinski's papers were originally written in French).

The presence of the sign does not necessarily indicate a lesion of the pyramidal tract, and indeed there is some debate over whether the pyramidal tract is responsible for the response or whether other descending fibre systems may be involved (O'Reilly 1992). It is important to remember that the sign does not give any indication of the degree of damage (Grant 1987), and an extensor plantar response may be found in some groups of people who are not experiencing dysfunction of the pyramidal tract including: people in a coma (Bickerstaff 1973); infants—due to immaturity of the pyramidal tracts (Grant 1987); elderly patients with psychiatric disease (Maher et al 1992); hypo-glycaemia (O'Reilly 1992, Mayo Clinic 1971); post-ictally (after cardiovascular accident) (O'Reilly 1992); and even in people who are in a very deep sleep (O'Reilly 1992). If no response is elicited on testing, this may be due to either the patient not being relaxed or being cold (Bickerstaff 1973). It can also be difficult to interpret the sign if the soles of the feet are particularly tender or sensitive (Grant 1987).

Little evidence is reported on the reliability of clinically testing the plantar response. Indeed Maher et al (1992) reported that the specificity and sensitivity of the sign had never been studied. They examine the reproducibility of the sign by assessing intraobserver and interobserver variation in 24 physicians 'with some years of clinical experience, all of whom were members or fellows of a Royal College'. The physicians were divided into six groups of four, and the extent of their agreement within each group of two patients was assessed. The result of this interobserver variation was that in only 50% of the examinations was there total agreement between the four doctors. When considering intraobserver variation, only 14 physicians agreed completely with their assessments on two separate occasions. These findings are both surprising and disturbing, since greater reliability might be expected from experienced physicians. It would be both interesting and challenging to investigate the reliability of the plantar response test performed by chartered physiotherapists working in neurological and musculoskeletal fields, since testing this sign also forms part of our neurological examination.

Neurological signs at multiple levels

The evidence for neurological signs at multiple levels being indicative of likely serious spinal pathology, is based on knowledge of anatomy and pathology. Herniated discs are sometimes cited as mimicking extraosseous spinal tumours (Guyer et al 1988), and Epstein (1970) determined that approximately 1% of patients presenting with symptoms consistent with disc herniation have intraspinal tumours—a sobering statistic. In addition the clinician needs to be able to differentiate between symptoms resulting from multiple level degenerative disease and possible serious spinal pathology.

Unfortunately many studies reported in the literature are not specific in describing the details of the clinical signs present in their patients. For example Levy et al (1986) report that 30% of their series of 66 patients with neurofibromas had 'motor dysfunction with weakness', and 40% of the patients had increased lower extremity reflexes with extensor plantar responses, but it is unclear as to the extent of these signs and how they were measured. Grubb et al (1994) report that 21 out of 36 patients with primary Ewing's sarcoma of the spine presented with 'neurologic deficit', but again, no precise details were described, and so it is impossible to establish whether the deficit was from multiple levels. Likewise, Delamarter et al (1990) report a series of 29 patients with 'primary osseous thoracic and lumbar vertebral neoplasms' over a 17 year period, and state that 'sixteen patients had demonstrable neurologic deficits, including motor weakness in eight, sensory changes in six, lower extremity spasticity in six, abnormal deep tendon reflexes in six, and bowel and bladder incontinence in three'. Such descriptions still omit detail of the levels involved, however it is clear that for bowel and bladder incontinence, multiple levels will be affected, as the nerves supplying the bladder form the vesical plexus (Williams & Warwick 1986).

Case studies, although often less generalisable than clinical studies or reported series, may contain more detail. For example, Guyer et al (1988) report details of a 13 year old girl who presented with low back pain and occasional right leg pain, numbness and tingling, and an unsteady gait. The CT scan showed an 'erosive lesion S1 vertebrae and intermedullary mass', subsequently found to be a neurilemmoma. The authors warn clinicians to be suspicious of a 'teenager presenting with symptoms of disc herniation', presumably because from epidemiological studies, disc herniation and degenerative disease in this age group are rare.

Despite the non-specific reports cited, some evidence of neurological signs at multiple levels being indicative of possible serious spinal pathology does exist. Nayernouri (1985) describes a series of 20 patients with neurilemmomas, where 9 patients had 'back pain and bilateral sciatica with signs implicating two or more roots of the cauda equina'. Donaldson et al (1993) reviewed a group of 15 patients with 'symptomatic metastatic melanoma to the spine' where 7 patients presented with neurological findings: 'Most patients had multiple spinal level involvement with an average of 3.1 levels per patient (range 1 to 9 levels)'.

Saddle anaesthesia

In texts describing clinical examination of the spine, a positive finding of saddle anaesthesia 'makes immediate surgical referral imperative' (Paterson & Burn 1986), as an 'urgent decompression may be indicated' (Grieve 1991). Dinning and Schaeffer (1993) state that permanent bladder and rectal dysfunction will result if the compression of the cauda equina is not relieved speedily and effectively. In such texts, saddle anaesthesia is described as a feature of 'cauda equina syndrome' (according to Deyo 1986, along with rectal sphincter tone, bilateral leg weakness or reflex loss). However in many case histories of patients with spinal tumours resulting in symptoms of cauda equina compression, saddle anaesthesia is reported surprisingly rarely. Three possible reasons for this may be:

1 Incomplete records (as many are reported in retrospective series of case histories);
2 Because the focus of reporting has been on clinical signs rather than the patients' symptoms; or
3 When details are included, they are nebulous *e.g.* Levy et al (1986) describe 'bowel or bladder difficulties', giving no indication of the nature of these difficulties.

It is not just urinary retention that we need to be vigilant for; Grieve (1991) defines 'sphincter problems' as 'loss of control, retention, hesitancy, urgency or a sense of incomplete evacuation'.

Despite these issues, some evidence that saddle anaesthesia is indicative of serious spinal pathology has been reported. For example, Matthew and Todd (1993) state that 'sensory disturbance in the saddle (perineum and buttocks) region occurs in both intramedullary and extramedullary tumours and invariably accompanies a disturbance in sphincter function'.

Even though saddle anaesthesia should raise the suspicion of serious spinal pathology, there is much that we still do not understand. For example, Frierson-Stroud (1990) reports in an autopsy series, that 30-70% of oncology patients have spinal epidural metastases but only 5% have spinal cord compression. He freely admits that the reason 'why no more patients exhibit this sequela is not known', and concludes that 'it is conceivable that as patients live longer, the incidence will rise'.

Possible danger signs

(Constant) night pain

For many clinicians, alarm bells ring if patients describe their pain as 'constant'. It is then important to ascertain what happens to the pain at night because surely, for pain to be described as truly 'constant', this must also include night pain? A number of studies report case histories of patients with spinal tumours, who sometimes describe their pain as being worse at night (Delamarter et al 1990, Nayernouri 1985). However night pain may not always be present when serious pathology exists. For example, Boriani et al (1992) report the findings from a series of 30 patients with osteoblastomas of the spine. All 30 patients complained of 'continuous local pain, with only four noting an increase in pain at night'. Likewise in nine patients with non-malignant intraspinal tumours at the Texas Back Institute, only three complained of night pain and/or pain that increased in the supine position (Guyer et al 1988). Perhaps the most alarming findings are reported in a series of 55 patients with severe pain from spinal instability secondary to metastatic cancer, where 'all 55 patients presented with a history of malignancy and severe pain in the dorsal or lumbar spine which was mechanical in nature and relieved by lying absolutely still' (Galasko 1991). Such patients might easily be referred for physiotherapy.

It is important to establish whether night pain is reported by the patient, and if so, in conjunction with what other signs and symptoms? Having a clear understanding of patients' aggravating and easing factors will help determine if the pain reported is due to a 'mechanical' cause, or whether serious spinal pathology should be suspected. It is vital to exclude environmental factors such as the patient's bed, and pathological processes such as inflammation, or arthritis. Having eliminated these issues, it is highly probable that night pain or truly constant pain constitutes possible serious spinal pathology, and Nayernouri (1985) particularly describes 'night pain relieved by walking' as an important sign to watch for, as do Matthew and Todd (1993). Delamarter et al (1990) conclude that 'constant pain unresponsive to conservative therapy, night pain, and pain enhanced by laying supine, are suggestive of a neoplastic process'. The physiotherapist must therefore be vigilant, particularly as patients with acute and severe nerve root pain frequently report significant night pain.

Bilateral leg signs

When considering bilateral leg signs, many studies do not specify whether reported signs are indeed bilateral. In the Levy et al (1986) series of 66 patients with spinal cord neurofibromas, 40% of the patients presented with 'increased lower extremity reflexes, with extensor plantar responses', however again detail was omitted as to whether these signs were bilateral. Once again, case reports may yield more detailed information. Guyer et al (1988) describe a case report in which a 33 year old patient reported recurrent low back pain and unilateral leg pain but after a long automobile drive, she reported low back pain and bilateral leg pain, then three days later noted 'weakness in her lower legs and urinary hesitancy'. Emergency myelogram revealed a complete block from T11 to L3, and at surgery this was found to be due to an ependymoma. The authors also report a second case, this time in a 37 year old patient, where one of the features mentioned was progressive weakness of both legs, which was due to a neurilemmoma.

In the light of such evidence, this might suggest that serious spinal pathology could be present in a patient presenting with bilateral leg signs, hence its classification as a 'possible danger sign'.

Probably not danger signs

Throughout the literature reviews evidence for loss of reflex at one level or unilateral sciatic symptoms below the knee were not reported in any of the case histories or studies reviewed. Hence they were classified as 'probably not danger signs' in our hierarchy, and used to intersperse with the other 'probable' and 'possible' danger signs. Likewise, severe local back pain was also placed in this category, because although it was sometimes described as a feature of the cases presented, as Delamarter et al (1990) state, it 'is not diagnostic and can be associated with other spinal disorders'. It is also a personal and emotional experience, which is difficult to measure. Thus, it is the *details about the pain*, such as its aggravating and easing factors, diurnal patterns etc, which are essential to record in a patient interview.

The final GP questionnaire

From the findings of the GP pilot questionnaire in Salisbury and the literature reviews, the main GP questionnaire was developed. Questions included details of the assessment, advice given about everyday activities, treatment strategies, referrals for x-rays and consultations, demographic information about the GPs themselves, and a visual analogue scale rating GP satisfaction with their current approach to the management of acute low back pain.

The danger signs question which formed part of the final questionnaire was revised so that GPs were asked to tick 'yes' or 'no' for each of the eight items in answer to the question (see Box 3).

Box 3 Final GP signs/symptoms questionnaire

What signs and symptoms do you feel justify immediate hospital advice for a patient with acute low back pain?	Yes	No
a) Severe local back pain	❏	❏
b) Bilateral leg signs	❏	❏
c) Loss of reflex at one level	❏	❏
d) Extensor plantar response	❏	❏
e) Constant night pain	❏	❏
f) Unilateral sciatic symptoms below the knee	❏	❏
g) Saddle anaesthesia	❏	❏
h) Neurological signs at multiple levels	❏	❏

The final questionnaire was sent to 97 GPs in the New Forest area and 139 in Southampton i.e. all GP practices in the area (except two, deemed atypical, which were linked to the University of Southampton).

The response rate was 70% (n=166) and the results were very interesting! For example, generally GPs reported themselves as being not very satisfied with their current approach to managing back pain, with one third of them (n=55) rating their satisfaction with their back pain management as 4 out of 10 or less on a visual analogue scale (where 0=totally unsatisfied, and 10=totally satisfied). The median satisfaction score=5.1 (Little et al 1996).

Regarding the danger signs question specifically, the results are shown in Table 1.2, where it can be seen that the GPs in our survey considered 'saddle anaesthesia' to be the danger sign of most concern and 'unilateral sciatic symptoms below the knee' to be of least concern.

Table 1.2 Results from final questionnaire asking GPs to identify whether they considered 8 selected items to be danger signs for a patient with acute low back pain. Results show numbers and percentages of GPs who responded 'yes' to each item. When the total response is less than 166, this signifies some GPs omitted to respond to the item.

Hierarchy of importance	Specific signs	Yes (n)	Yes (%)
Probable danger signs	Extensor plantar response	$83/150$	55
	Neurological signs at multiple levels	$135/159$	85
	Saddle anaesthesia	$147/157$	94
Possible danger signs	[Constant] night pain	$47/150$	31
	Bilateral leg signs	$84/157$	54
Probably not danger signs	Severe local back pain	$12/156$	8
	Loss of reflex at one level	$16/152$	11
	Unilateral sciatic symptoms below the knee	$4/152$	3

It is encouraging that our three 'probable danger signs' coincided with the three signs GPs considered most likely to be worthy of seeking immediate hospital advice for a patient with acute low back pain. However, the proportion of GPs who did not consider these as danger signs was surprisingly high.

One possible explanation for this could be that GPs feel confident in their management of patients with acute low back pain, but results from the visual analogue scale, rating their satisfaction with their management of this symptom, appear to suggest otherwise (although measuring satisfaction is not a direct measure of confidence). Other possible explanations for these results could be that GPs underestimate the significance of these clinical signs, or that they are aware of the controversies surrounding the literature and favour not seeking *immediate* hospital advice. Since the introduction of clinical guidelines by the Royal College of General Practitioners (Waddell et al 1996) and the Clinical Standards Advisory Group (1994), it would be interesting to re-examine this issue to see whether there is now greater awareness of danger signs among practising GPs.

When comparing our hierarchy of danger signs with the CSAG report (1994), the latter does not specifically mention extensor plantar response or night pain, both of which featured strongly with the Southampton GPs, (however constant, progressive and non-mechanical pain was identified as a symptom which suggests possible serious spinal pathology). Evidence from the literature suggests that it would be prudent to add these two signs and symptoms to the list outlined in the CSAG report.

Having discussed evidence for danger signs, it is worth considering the questions that we ask in our patient interviews which might help to identify possible serious spinal pathology. Perhaps the key is identifying very clear information about aggravating and easing factors, the nature of the pain, and diurnal patterns (over a 24-hour period). In addition, accurate questioning about past medical history, medication, sensation and weakness is vital, together with details about bladder and bowel function and general health. This list is not definitive, and it is worth challenging our assumptions: What might the answers be to these questions if the patient had underlying serious spinal pathology, and would our level of questioning be sufficiently sensitive to detect it? An initial, careful, patient interview can yield vital information, which is a solid foundation on which to build the clinical examination.

Nerve root pain

Once it is established that 'danger signs' or 'red flags' are not present in a patient, the next stage is to decipher whether their signs and symptoms are due to nerve root involvement. Nerve root pain is sometimes described as 'radicular pain', and may be caused by disc prolapse, chemical irritation via inflammatory metabolites, spinal stenosis or surgical scarring.

In their diagnostic triage, the CSAG identified the signs and symptoms of nerve root pain as:

a) unilateral leg pain more intense than back pain
b) pain generally radiates to foot or toes
c) numbness and paraesthesia in the same distribution
d) nerve irritation signs (i.e. decreased straight leg raise test which reproduces leg pain)
e) motor, sensory or reflex change limited to one nerve root
f) reasonable prognosis, where 50% recover from an attack within six weeks

(CSAG 1994).

Such signs and symptoms are often confused with somatic referred pain, and Bogduk (1994) gives one of the clearest accounts of radicular pain and includes a description of the pain as shooting or lancinating, of characteristic quality and distribution, which travels down the lower limb in a band-like distribution, less than 5 cm wide. He attributes the cause to be nerve root irritation or compression e.g. sciatica and cites it as relatively rare. For true radicular pain, the pain must be accompanied by other features of nerve root compression i.e. numbness, weakness or paraesthesia. Bogduk (1994) goes further in saying 'In the absence of such accompanying features, it is very difficult to maintain that root compression is the cause of any pain'. Thus, nerve root pain cannot be diagnosed clinically without accurate questioning and neurological examination.

Application to physiotherapy

Box 4 summarises implications for the profession. Having identified the importance of a detailed, accurate, spinal assessment, we need to understand the implications of every question that we ask and every clinical test that we do. The skill comes in knowing not only what questions to ask and what tests to perform, but also in knowing how to interpret the findings.

Box 4 Physiotherapy and the danger signs of low back pain

> • As chartered physiotherapists, we need to be clear why we are asking every question in our patient interviews and understand what to assess in our patient examinations.
> • Performing the tests is not enough: We need to know the relevance of the findings.
> • There is a consensus that some signs and symptoms exist which if present, may indicate serious spinal pathology.
> • A few signs and symptoms exist which if present, require emergency referral to a spinal surgeon.
> • Having excluded 'danger signs' or 'red flags', it is necessary to establish whether nerve root pain is present.
> • As Grieve (1991) states: 'The recognition of neoplastic disease, earlier rather than later, depends more on awareness, vigilance and suspicion rather than a set of rules. One must *always* be thinking of it, all the time and every time.'

REFERENCES

Bickerstaff E 1973 Neurological examination in clinical practice. Blackwell Scientific Publications, Oxford 199–200

Bogduk N 1994 Innervation, pain patterns and mechanisms of pain production. In: Twomey L, Taylor J (eds). Clinics in physical therapy. Physical therapy of the low back 2nd edn. Churchill Livingstone, New York 93–109

Boriani S, Capanna R, Donati D, Levine A, Picci P, Savini R 1992 Osteoblastoma of the spine. Clinical Orthopaedics and Related Research 278:37–45

Clinical Standards Advisory Group 1994 Back pain. Report of a CSAG committee on back pain. HMSO, London

Delamarter RB, Sachs BL, Thompson GH, Bohlman HH, Makley JT, Carter JR 1990 Primary neoplasms of the thoracic and lumbar spine. An analysis of 29 consecutive cases. Clinical Orthopaedics and Related Research 256:87–100

Deyo RA 1986 Early diagnostic evaluation of low back pain. Journal of General Internal Medicine 1:328–338

Dinning TAR, Schaeffer HR 1993 Discogenic compression of the cauda equina: a surgical emergency. Australian and New Zealand Journal of Surgery 63:927–934

Donaldson WF, Peppelman WC, Yaw KM 1993 Symptomatic metastatic malignant melanoma to the spine. Journal of Spinal Disorders 6(4):360–363

Epstein JA 1970 Common errors in the diagnosis of herniation of the intervertebral disk. Industrial Medicine 39(11):47–54

81

Frierson-Stroud L 1990 Malignant spinal cord compression: when a backache signals danger. Texas Medicine 86(1):48–52

Galasko CSB 1991 Spinal instability secondary to metastatic cancer. Journal of bone and joint surgery 73B:104–108

Grant R 1987 The neurological assault on the great toe (1893–1911). Scottish Medical Journal 32:57–59

Grieve G 1991 Mobilisation of the spine. Churchill Livingstone, Edinburgh:53, 171

Grubb MR, Bradford LC, Pritchard DJ, Ebersold MJ 1994 Primary Ewing's sarcoma of the spine. Spine 19(3):309–313

Guyer R, Collier R, Ohnmeiss D, Stith W, Hochschuler S, Rashbaum R, Vanharanta H, Loguidice V 1988 Extraosseous spinal disease mimicking disc disease. Spine 13(3):328–331

Levy WJ, Latchaw J, Hahn JF, Sawhny B, Bay J, Dohn DF 1986 Spinal neurofibromas: a report of 66 cases and a comparison with meningiomas. Neurosurgery 18(3):331–334

Little P, Smith L, Cantrell T, Chapman J, Langridge J, Pickering R 1996 General practitioners' management of acute back pain: a survey of reported practice compared with clinical guidelines. British Medical Journal 312:485–488

MacGregor JM 1987 That up–going toe. South African Medical Journal 71(9):592–594

Maher J, Reilly M, Daly L, Hutchinson M 1992 Plantar power: reproducibility of the plantar response. British Medical Journal 304:482

Matthew P, Todd N 1993 Diagnosis of intradural conus and cauda equina tumours. British Journal of Hospital Medicine 50(4):169–174

Mayo Clinic and Mayo Foundation 1971 Clinical examinations in neurology. W.B. Saunders Co., Philadelphia, 175

Nayernouri T 1985 Neurilemmomas of the cauda equina presenting as prolapsed lumbar intervertebral disks. Surgical Neurology 23:187–188

O'Reilly S 1992 The extensor plantar response. Irish Medical Journal 85(2):49

Paterson J, Burn L 1986 Examination of the back. MTP Press Limited, Lancaster: 62, 91

Waddell G 1987 A new clinical model for the treatment of low–back pain. Spine 12(7):632–44

Waddell G, Feder G, McIntosh A, Lewis M, Hutchinson A 1996 Low back pain evidence review. Royal College of General Practitioners, London 1–34

Walsh K 1992 An epidemiological study of low back pain. Doctoral Thesis, University of Southampton Faculty of Medicine

Walshe F 1956 The Babinski plantar response, its forms and its physiological and pathological significance. Brain 79:529–556

Williams P, Warwick R (eds) 1986 Gray's anatomy 36th edn. Churchill Livingstone, Edinburgh: 1407

Youl BD 1989 A neurological double entente [letter]. Archives of Neurology 46(11):1167

ACKNOWLEDGEMENTS

I would like to thank my colleagues in the 'Back Home' team who worked jointly on this project:

Judith Chapman, Lecturer in Physiotherapy, School of Occupational Therapy and Physiotherapy, University of Southampton; Paul Little, GP and Wellcome Training Fellow, Primary Care, Faculty of Medicine, University of Southampton; Ted Cantrell, Consultant in Rheumatology and Rehabilitation, Department of Rheumatology and Rehabilitation, Southampton University Hospitals Trust; Ruth Pickering, Lecturer in Medical Statistics, Department of Medical Statistics and Computing, University of

Southampton; John Langridge, Manager of Physio-therapy Services, Department of Physiotherapy, Southampton University Hospitals Trust.

In addition I would like to thank all the GPs in Salisbury, Southampton and the New Forest who participated in this study, the Research and Development Directorate for their financial support, and Debbie Prince MCSP and Dr Paul Roberts for their helpful comments on the manuscript.

2

Psychosocial predictors of outcome from low back pain

PAUL WATSON

Physical therapy rehabilitation, which has tended to concentrate on a biomedically orientated approach to the assessment and management of acute and sub-acute problems, may now be entering a new era of drawing on a wider repertoire of skills to help patients. The wealth of research into the predictors of outcome from physical therapy and manual therapy interventions has demonstrated that psychosocial factors are much more important in the prediction of outcome than physical factors. Research into the outcome of specific physical therapy practices such as exercise and manual therapy in the management of low back pain, for example, has sometimes been equivocal. Authors working in this field have provided evidence both for and against the efficacy of exercise or manual therapy (Koes et al 1991, Koes et al 1994, Koes et al 1996, Faas 1996). The general consensus of opinion on passive modalities such as ultrasound, traction, or heat/cold therapies appears to be that they are generally ineffective (van der Heijden et al 1995). The sceptic's view may be that physiotherapy is not effective in managing acute or sub-acute pain, when these modalities are subjected to randomised controlled trials in isolation.

Is physiotherapy solely biomedically orientated?

The term 'biomedical model' refers to a solely tissue or pathology based interpretation of the patient's problem where there is an assumed linear relationship between tissue dysfunction and loss of function. Hence, biomedically orientated treatment focuses on the resolution of that dysfunction with the expectation that function will be restored and disability resolved.

The physiotherapy profession is often viewed by outsiders with reference to the material taught in its schools and on post graduate courses, the focus of which has been specifically biomedical and based on poorly researched techniques. However, a more appropriate conclusion would be that it comes as a package of biomedical assessment, intervention and the development of an interpersonal relationship between therapist and patient. The latter develops from an implicit 'psychological' appraisal of the patients' reaction to their condition by the therapist and the way in which the therapist tries to help them deal with it and regain function. Physiotherapy is therefore not a single intervention technique, and success in rehabilitation lies in the way in which people are managed in addition to the techniques used. In this sense the vast majority of physiotherapists actually do adopt a biopsychosocial approach.

Wall (1996) when commenting on the Back Pain in the Workplace report (Fordyce 1995) said that the medical model was a 'strawman…taught in some mythical medical school which claims that all pains are caused by known organic lesions to the exclusion of social and psychological factors…'. I do not believe, based on the evidence I see in most educational establishments, that most teaching is welded to a medical model. Unfortunately, although the importance of social and psychological factors is taught, it is often given a low level of importance and students are rarely given any education on how to assess and manage these factors.

Consequently physiotherapy assessment protocols do not explicitly assess psychosocial factors in the presentation of illness and the response to treatment. Experienced physiotherapists may, through clinical practice, develop an intuitive capacity to identify the influence of such factors. At best this leads to an empathic response from the physiotherapist who then takes time to explain the therapy and the possible outcomes and tries to motivate the patient. At worst a label 'psychological overlay' can be attached to the patient which might serve as a convenient catch-all explanation for the failure of treatment and/or lack or compliance. The accusation of rigid biomedical adherence is justified if the therapist misinterprets the patients' pain-related distress and magnified pain behaviour as a physical sign and then uses physical techniques to change it, an approach that is destined to fail.

The identification and management of psychosocial risk factors had until recently been seen as relevant only in chronic pain presentations. There is now increasing evidence that these psychosocial factors are important in early stages of musculoskeletal pain. Reports into the management of low back pain (LBP) and whiplash associated disorder (WAD) (Spitzer et al 1995) have suggested that early assessment and management of these factors and encouragement to remain active are essential for good outcome (CSAG 1994, Bigos et al 1994, Kendall et al 1997). The Clinical Standards Advisory Group in the UK suggested that a psychosocial assessment 'could be carried out by a doctor or therapist' (CSAG p61).

A sensation of pain is the most common presenting complaint that prompts an individual to seek the help of a therapist. The therapist usually attempts to identify the cause of the pain at initial examination. This is achieved through questioning about the specific characteristics of the pain, its nature, response to movement, and the precipitating and easing factors. This is followed by a physical examination, that includes passive testing, palpation and observation of movement where the reproduction of the pain sensation and/or the identification of abnormality of motion helps to locate the cause and/or sites of increased mechano-sensitivity. This approach serves well for the identification of specific problems or impairments and can help establish a useful baseline for the management of the symptom of pain. However, difficulties arise in the exact location of specific lesions in those patients where the picture is complicated by previous physical interventions (e.g. neurolysis, surgery), secondary tissues changes (muscle weakness and tight structures) and the effects of secondary, central sensitisation.

The examination and questioning about the 'bio' or physical component of the assessment will not only address the identification of possible serious pathology (see Ch. 1) but also be influenced by the school of thought to which the examining therapists adhere and their previous training. It is not the intention of the author to critically appraise the relative merits of all the possible approaches. The reader is encouraged to review available research based evidence to evaluate the validity and efficacy of different modalities. To date there is very little research evidence to demonstrate that examination procedures and measures specific to the commonly used major schools of thought in the management of back pain (e.g. McKenzie, Maitland, Cyriax, or muscle imbalance approaches) have any predictive value in the identification of poor outcome or the development of chronic incapacity.

Musculoskeletal pain alone is not the problem; what is, is the pain and associated disability. Reducing the pain will help people avoid incapacity only if it is translated into a return to their pre-injury/pre-pain activities at the earliest opportunity. Since the late 1980s there has been an increasing move from viewing pain as having a one-to-one relationship with disability to an appreciation that *it is the reaction of the individual to the pain that is most important factor in the development of disability*. This has become popularly known as, the *biopsychosocial* model of disability. At the heart of the biopsychosocial model (Waddell 1987, Waddell 1992) is the assumption of an on-going sensation that is nociceptive in nature or which is perceived by the sufferer as being painful. The behaviour demonstrated by individuals at any time will be a product of their understanding of what the pain means, their beliefs and their emotional response to the pain. This behaviour will be influenced (reinforced or modulated) by the social environment in which it takes place (Waddell 1987, Loeser & Fordyce 1983). To effect outcome physiotherapists must develop a wider initial assessment to investigate these important influences.

At the beginning of this section it was asked if physiotherapy was solely biomedically orientated. Most physiotherapists try to do the best for their patients. The biomedical approach serves us well in cases where the cause is clearly identifiable and it can be used to *manage symptoms* to good effect, but symptom management is only one of the ways in which we can speed up the process of rehabilitation. Since physiotherapy is a rehabilitation profession it

87

is our responsibility to incorporate models of management that offer the most efficient pathway to achieve the rehabilitation goal. Skilled physiotherapists develop an intuitive understanding of their patients' needs and try to individualise the treatments offered; they may call this 'good patient handling skills,' but in effect it is biopsychosocial management. By formalising this process into a structured assessment and management approach, using sound evidence, it can be evaluated, assessed, improved, and taught to others.

Prediction of outcome: what is an outcome measure?

Before looking at the factors that predict outcome, it is important to be clear about what an outcome is and what a desirable outcome might be for the patient group or sub-groups. Outcome measures may be classified into three main areas:

- Patient orientated outcomes
- Clinician orientated outcomes
- Purchaser orientated outcomes.

Patients are most worried about their pain, loss of function, and potential inability to work or perform their usual, enjoyable activities. *Clinicians* may be interested in outcomes that are related to their own training. They will of course wish to see an improvement in the pain and disability, but may, for example, concentrate on the correction of patterns of muscle activity or segmental motion in the belief that this will lead not only to the resolution of symptoms but also the prevention of a recurrence. The *purchaser* will require that the treatment intervention improves the health of the patient and reduces the cost of future healthcare consulting for the condition for which the patient was referred, at the most acceptable cost.

In research into back pain the most commonly used primary outcomes are *reduced disability, reduction in pain,* and *return to work.* The following sections will review the predictive nature of different factors with reference to the three outcomes listed above. It must be emphasised that these outcomes should be viewed as being related but relatively independent. For instance, pain and disability have been shown to be only moderately correlated (Waddell 1987) and the relationship between the level of self report of disability and work will inevitably be influenced by the type of work the subject usually performs and the opportunity for alteration in the work place physical demands.

Factors predicting outcome

Pain report

The physiotherapist routinely asks about the self-report of pain, its intensity, location, and behaviour, primarily as an indication of the nature of the problem and possible underlying structural causes. Can pain self-report also be used as an indication of the likelihood of a poor outcome?

Intensity of pain

In a group of workers suffering acute back pain (within 6 weeks of onset) and using return to work as the outcome criteria, Gatchel et al (1995) used a multiple regression technique to show that high initial pain intensity and high report of disability were important components to predicting poor outcome in a model that incorporated physical and psychosocial factors. In the study, physical examination variables did not help predict the rate of return to work. The influence of high intensity of initial pain in predicting slow return to work for patients consulting early within their back pain history is supported by other researchers (Hazard et al 1996, Klenerman et al 1995, Rose et al 1995). In contrast Coste et al (1994) found no such association between initial pain intensity and slow return to work in a group of patients with recent onset of back pain. Many of the patients in this group (69%) suffered with recurrent back pain. This finding is supported by that of Lehmann et al (1993) who recruited specifically those with pain of between two and six weeks duration. The message from this evidence is that we must treat intensity of pain as a predictor of outcome in pain of recent onset with some caution.

Bendix et al (1998) compared a group of chronic pain patients undergoing functional restoration with a control group of chronic pain patients receiving no rehabilitation intervention. Like some of the research discussed above for acute pain, they too demonstrated a link between initial back pain report, working ability and return to work in both groups. Those with low initial pain report were more likely to return to work, have higher physical function at one year follow up in both groups. Those with a high initial pain report were more likely to progress onto a disability pension. In contrast, Haazen et al (1994) found that initial level of pain did not predict the pain at one year in patients undergoing a cognitive behavioural therapy (CBT) programme. Whether these differences are as a result of the differences in the patient groups (the research was conducted in different European countries) or as a result of the treatment received—CBT or functional restoration, is difficult to determine.

Burton et al (1995) and Main and Burton (1995) in two companion papers looked at the relative predictive value of a number of measures in osteopathic practice. They compared their predictive ability in acute (defined as up to 4 weeks duration) and sub-chronic (greater than 4 weeks duration) back pain. The outcomes assessed were continued disability and continued pain report. They found interesting differences between the two groups. The initial level of pain was not associated with continued disability at one year in the acute group but it was in the sub-chronic group although it explained only 6% of the variance.[1] Continued report of significant pain was not found to be associated with the initial pain report.

Even though the evidence presented above appears contradictory, very high reports of pain do appear to be influential on outcome, at least in those who have had their pain for more than a few weeks. This might be reflected in the fact that pain subsides rapidly in the very early stages (the first two or three weeks).

Site of pain and radiation of pain

The distribution of pain and especially the presence of leg pain has been demonstrated to be related to poor outcome in a number of studies (Bendix et al 1998, Cherkin et al 1996, Burton et al 1995). Burton et al (1995) once again demonstrated differences between acute and sub-chronic subjects. Leg pain was significant in predicting ongoing disability in the acute group (explaining 3% of the variance) but not the sub-chronic. Bendix et al 1998 found that leg pain in chronic pain patients did not predict working ability or return to work, but was predictive of continued pain report. These results suggest that the presence of leg pain predicts outcome only in those whose problem is of recent onset. The reasons for this are unclear but it may be that, with time, patients become accustomed to their leg pain and it ceases to be predictive of outcome.

The problem of the distribution of pain is given a twist by the observation of Frank et al (1996) that doctors may 'overtreat' most patients identified as having symptoms suggestive of spinal root pathology and intervertebral disc problems. This in itself will lead to increased sickness certification, a slower return to work, and an increasing involvement in medical consultations. This observation was also made by Watson et al (1998) who identified a slower return to work by those patients diagnosed as having sciatica or an intervertebral disc problem rather than a non-specific diagnosis of low back pain. The message for the clinician is that great care should be taken with the way in which a diagnosis is given and with the terms used. Clearly, the ability of individuals to return to work during an episode of back pain will depend upon the type of work they do, their ability to vary the work, and their control over the type of work they perform and the working environment. It is easier for a person in a sedentary job where they are able to change position frequently to return to work, than for a bricklayer or a person lifting heavy weights on a production line.

Initial self report of disability

It would appear logical that those who report the greatest disability have further to go to recover and therefore might be expected to have a slower rate of recovery, return to normal activity and work. This has indeed been demonstrated to be the case in many studies. The strongest evidence comes from research into those with sub-chronic and chronic low back pain. Haazen et al (1994), Hildebrandt et al (1997) and Bendix et al (1998) all found that the patient's initial level of self-reported disability was the greatest predictor of activity after a cognitive behavioural intervention programme or functional restoration in chronic back pain. Burton et al (1995) found that the initial level of disability was the single strongest predictor (12% of the variance) of residual disability at one year following osteopathic manipulation in those who had had their pain for 4-52 weeks, i.e. a sub-chronic group.

In those with acute back pain the pattern appears to be less clear; Gatchel et al (1995) and Rose et al (1995) both identified initial level of disability as a significant predictor of future disability in acute low back pain. Coste et al (1994) demonstrated significant influence of initial level of disability on the rate of recovery from symptoms but this was not clearly related to the number of days absent from work due to back pain. This is in contrast to Lehmann et al (1993) who found that there was no relationship of initial levels of disability with return to work or recovery. Burton et al (1995) concur with this finding in those who had their back pain for less than 3 weeks. From these studies we can conclude that the presenting level of disability increases in importance, with respect to outcome, the longer the patient remains disabled. In the acute stage it is less predictive presumably because some patients will get going despite their initial limitations. This is an important lesson for clinical practice: *patients who remain disabled and inactive for prolonged periods do less well.*

The observation about work type and ability to control the work environment to effect changes in posture and position and mechanical stress made in the section on pain are equally relevant to the relationship between disability and work loss.

Beliefs and coping as predictors

As discussed, physical therapy is a package that consists of intervention, motivation and education. No person comes for treatment to an injury or a medical condition without having made some attempt to make sense of the problem themselves, labelling it and giving it meaning (see Ch. 6). Issues that effect the cognitions the patient may have about their condition might usefully be placed in three areas:

- Specific beliefs about back pain and treatment
- Fears regarding hurting and harming or fear-avoidance beliefs
- Coping styles/strategies.

The physiotherapist must find out what the patient understands and believes about their condition and what they are currently doing about it. From this they can then challenge cognitions and behaviours which lead to persistent disability and thereby improve treatment.

Specific beliefs about back pain and treatment

Patients may develop pessimistic or negative beliefs regarding the nature of their pain and injury or disease, and the outcome of treatment. This may be based on previous experience with the healthcare system or may be based upon the 'folk beliefs' of their own cultural environment. They may come to believe, for example, that pain always means harm, that the amount of pain they feel should always guide their physical function, and that further damage and an eventual poor outcome is inevitable. Such beliefs lead not only to demoralisation but also to debilitation. Patients avoid interactions or activities that are expected to elevate pain and/or suffering. Without assessment of and action to correct these beliefs the therapist is unlikely to assure the patient's full participation in a programme of treatment which involves increasing exercise and return to normal physical activity. An obvious example is the patient who has been told that they have progressive degeneration of their spine associated with wear and tear. If they believe they must avoid bending and lifting for fear of further damage they will be unwilling to perform exercises involving such activities. Without identifying these beliefs the physiotherapist might interpret an unwillingness to do certain exercises as non-compliance rather than fear of injury.

Beliefs about the extent to which pain can be controlled would appear to be a powerful determinant of the development of incapacity and compliance with an activity based treatment program. Pain 'locus of control' scales have been developed (Crisson & Keefe 1988, Main & Waddell 1991) which help to identify to what extent patients feel they are able to influence and control their pain and whether they are willing to take responsibility in the management of their own condition. A willingness to accept that they have a role in their own management and that they are not to be a passive recipient of treatment is important in the therapeutic relationship.

> Pain patients who perceive themselves lacking the capacity to acquire self-management skills might be less persistent, more prone to frustration, and more apt to be non-compliant with treatment recommendations. Hence, some patients might demonstrate adequate understanding of a particular treatment rationale, yet be non-compliant due to their perceived inability to produce the behaviour necessary to follow treatment recommendations
> (DeGood & Shutty 1992:221)

DeGood and Shutty (1992) further suggest that patients develop beliefs about pain in the following areas: eitiology of pain, expectations about diagnoses, expectations about treatments and their (the patient's) role in it, and expectations about the outcome of treatment. It is these beliefs which can colour the individuals' response to low back pain and the role they adopt in the management of their condition. It is ultimately these beliefs which determine whether a person with back pain consults a healthcare practitioner about the problem.

The way in which patients respond to their illness and whether they seek treatment and the type of treatment they prefer depends upon their 'locus of control'. Broadly, patients have been classified into those with an 'internalised' locus of control, where individuals seek to manage the problem themselves, and those with an 'externalised' locus of control who are more likely to rely on healthcare workers to cure their problem. Of course the division is not as straight forward and people are not fixed in boxes. Locus of control lies on a continuum and patients lie at a point on that continuum. The way in which we manage patients can move them to be more externalised (reliant on professional help) or internalised (self-reliant and confident) about their ability to manage back pain (Williams & Keefe 1991, Symonds et al 1995).

Many influences that shape the development of beliefs about back pain. Symonds et al (1995, 1996) demonstrated that cultural beliefs about back pain which are present in an industrial setting influence absence from work. They developed a Back Beliefs Questionnaire which assessed a group of workers beliefs about back pain, the treatment of back pain , the progression of the condition and their perceived ability to work. The Questionnaire includes statements about back pain which the patient is asked to score on a scale, for example the limits might range from 'strongly disagree' at one extreme to 'strongly agree' at the other. Negative statements such as: 'Back trouble will eventually stop you from working' and 'Medication is the only way of relieving back trouble' are examples.

In the investigations of Symmonds et al (1995, 1996) an 'intervention' group was given a simple information pamphlet about back pain that challenged negative beliefs and gave indications about self-management. This group demonstrated less sick leave than a control group and was associated with reduction in negative beliefs about back pain and a positive shift in their pain locus of control towards being more 'internalised.'

People with back pain will do better if they believe that they have a role in managing their condition. Those who rely heavily on professional help risk becoming dependent on the physiotherapist. The over medicalisation of back pain, identification of spurious derangements, and encouraging the patient to see the physiotherapist's 'hands on interventions' as the most powerful factor for improvement, all remove the sense of control from the patient. Empowerment of the patients' role in their own management would seem vital.

Fear avoidance beliefs

A particularly powerful influence in the development of chronic incapacity is fear of injury and mistaken beliefs about hurting and harm. Anyone who has an injury will naturally develop at the least a wariness of the activity that caused it. This may develop into a fear and avoidance of activity. This has already been reviewed extensively in the first of the PPA Yearbooks and the reader is directed to this for more detail (Gifford 1998). I will concentrate on the predictive validity of fear-avoidance beliefs.

Letham et al (1983) developed a fear-avoidance model of exaggerated pain perception to help explain the development of disability following an acute onset of pain. They suggested that patients (who they classified as 'confronters' or 'avoiders') respond to the pain by adopting different styles of coping. As the names suggest people may remain active and use activity and distraction as a strategy to cope with pain; whereas others withdraw from activity and use rest as their predominant coping style. At its worst, fear of pain, or fear of causing more damage, may transfer to the avoidance and fear of even the simplest of everyday activities. It is therefore, crucial to recognize the role of fear and avoidance as obstacles to rehabilitation following injury.

A number of questionnaires for the assessment of fear and avoidance have been developed . For example, the Fear-avoidance and Beliefs Questionnaire (FABQ.) (Waddell et al 1993) and the Tampa Scale of Kinesiophobia (TSK) (Kori et al 1990). Increased scores on these instruments have been associated with increased disability and a poor outcome such as increased work loss (Waddell et al 1993, Vlaeyen et al 1995). The FABQ has two sections, the first assesses fears of physical activity, while the second assesses fear beliefs about work. The TSK relates more to the fear of reinjury and increased pain.

What such instruments cannot assess is how patients came to the conclusion that their work is causing harm to their back or that being careful and not moving too much is the best thing to avoid damage. Such fears might develop from information from a combinations of health professionals, family members, or popular culture which influence interpretation of events. Someone who has been told that they have a disc problem which is causing pressure on a nerve is likely to interpret pain as evidence that the disc is damaging the nerve. They will then tend to believe that pain always means further damage and so keeping the back still is the best way to avoid it. They eventually become avoidant of activities they think may lead to further damage. This results in a decrease in activity and a generalised physical deconditioning.

These 'fears' may range from the patient simply complying with well intentioned advice about restricting activity, to the patient who has become phobic about physical activity with accompanying autonomic nervous system manifestations (increased heart and respiratory rate, sweating etc). What is likely is that fear of reinjury and increased pain focuses the attention of the individual on to the problem. The increased attention then leads to increased pain (see Ch. 5) and a change in movement and activity that over time is likely to lead to the deconditioning effects seen.

Physiotherapists will not be successful in their management unless they are able to assess and address these fears. Of course, at its best, physical therapy exercise represents controlled exposure to the fear-inducing stimulus. In this case, exercise, either general (e.g. lifting) or specific (bending), is the stimulus. By exposing the patient to the fear (exercise) in a graded and controlled way (a graded exercise programme) in a safe environment (the clinic) the therapist can help to desensitise the patient and then transfer these successes into the home and work environment. *This is potentially one of the most powerful effects of contact with a physiotherapist.*

Most of the work on fear-avoidance beliefs has identified close relationships between fear of activity-related pain, and reinjury with disability at the time of testing, and previous work loss. People who are very fearful that activity is going to cause them pain and injury are likely to report more pain, be more disabled, have a history of prolonged work loss, and are more likely to remain off work and remain disabled. (Waddell et al 1993, Vlaeyen 1995a, Vlaeyen

1995b). The two most widely used instruments, the FABQ (Waddell et al 1993) and the TSK (Kori et al 1990), have been used to look at this. The Pain and Impairment Relationship Scale (Riley et al 1988) has also demonstrated that the belief that activity will lead to increased pain and possibly damage is strongly related to the extent of physical impairment. Jensen (1991) developed a 'harm' scale that was extracted from the 'Survey of Pain Attitudes' questionnaire. High 'harm' beliefs predicted the level of physical dysfunction in a group of chronic pain patients. It was also able to predict disability levels in back pain patients.

A number of authors have suggested that fear-avoidance is a strong predictor of future disability. Klenerman et al (1995) found in a large group of acute back pain patients that fear-avoidance variables could correctly classify 66% of cases with persistent pain and disability at 12 months. Further to this, initial fear-avoidance variables explained 25% of the variance for pain and disability at 12 months. These findings are supported by the work of Rose et al (1992 & 1995). Burton et al (1995), however, found no association between fear-avoidance variables assessed by the physical activities beliefs component of the FABQ (Waddell et al 1993) in either an acute group or a sub-chronic group of patients. The studies by Rose et al (1992) and Klenerman et al (1995) were conducted in primary care and looked a treatment as usual by GPs. Those studied by Burton received osteopathic manipulation, reassurance and advice on exercise. This may account for the differences in the studies.

In a recent study, Muncey and Watson (1999) demonstrated that fear-avoidance beliefs measured using the TSK were moderately correlated with current disability in a mixed group of back pain patients entering a generalised fitness and education programme for musculoskeletal pain. Fear-avoidance beliefs assessed following the programme showed highly significant correlation between their fear-avoidance beliefs and levels of pain—in other words, patients who still believed that activity was to be avoided or was structurally damaging had higher report of pain after the programme. As might be expected, changes in fear-avoidance beliefs achieved during the programme were found to be the most important predictor of residual disability following the programme. Thus, reduction in fear-avoidance lead to reduced disability, and was of more importance than measures of depression, or initial pain. This is only a small study and does not assess long-term follow up, but it does suggest that fear-avoidance beliefs can be challenged in individuals attending such a programme and that changing these beliefs is of great importance in changing the levels of disability and pain.

Pain coping styles and strategies

People have a range of coping strategies when confronted by pain. Brown and Nicassio (1987) distinguished between active (adaptive) and passive (non-adaptive) coping strategies. Active strategies (e.g. taking exercise, ignoring the pain) require the individual to take a degree of responsibility for pain management by either attempting to control pain or attempting to function despite pain. Passive strategies (e.g. resting, relying on medication) either involve withdrawal or the passing on of responsibility for the control of pain to someone else (for example the therapist as described above).

> Patients who believe they can control their pain, who avoid catastrophising about their condition, and who believe they are not severely disabled appear to function better than those who do not. Such beliefs may mediate some of the relationships between pain severity and adjustment.
>
> Jensen et al (1991)

The Coping Strategies Questionnaire (Rosenstiel & Keefe 1983) is the most frequently used measure of pain coping strategies. It identifies both positive (or adaptive) and negative (or maladaptive) coping strategies. Use of the negative coping strategies such as passive praying/hoping and catastrophising ('fearing the worst') are suggested as predictive of poor response to treatment. In addition to this the questionnaire asks patients to make an assessment of how well they are able to control the pain and decrease the pain as a result of their coping (the effectiveness of their particular strategy). The evidence for the predictive nature of coping strategies in the acute back pain patient is most clearly demonstrated in the work of Burton et al (1995). Here the negative coping strategy of catastrophising accounted for 47% of the variance for continued disability at 12 months follow up. For the whole patient group (acute and sub-chronic) the negative coping strategy of 'praying and hoping' (that the pain will go away) accounted for 23 % of the variance. However in the sub-chronic group alone coping strategies did not appear to be important in disability. Klenerman et al (1995) also found that negative coping was associated with poor outcome. When looking at the continued report of pain rather than disability as an outcome measure, then both catastrophising and praying and hoping were predictive of a poor outcome in a mixed group of low back pain patients (Main & Burton 1995). It is interesting to note that, although the negative coping strategies were predictive of poor outcome, the positive coping strategies have not been reported to have a significant predictive value.

Allied to coping is the relative optimism of an ability to return to work or normal activity. This can be seen as the antithesis of catastrophising; those who feel that they will be able to return to work or their normal occupation have been demonstrated to have a much better outcome than those who fear they will not be working in the near future. This has been demonstrated in patients throughout the range of pain duration from acute to chronic.

Psychological distress

Psychological distress is the term that has come to relate to the following features in those who go on to develop chronic incapacity:

- Exaggerated attention to bodily symptoms
- Anxiety
- Anger
- The development of depression.

Depression can be anywhere in a wide spectrum of emotions ranging from the slightly demoralised or fed-up to the suicidal. Pain patients frequently seem to be demoralised or depressed and the similarities between chronic pain patients and depressed patients has led to a vigorous debate about the nature of depression in pain patients. For physiotherapists it is therefore important to be able to distinguish between the more benign dysphoric mood associated with the ongoing problem and the relatively serious depressive *illness* for which there are clear diagnostic criteria.

In the past there has been an assumption that depressed individuals develop pain secondary to their depression. This has been challenged by a number of good studies (von Korff et al, 1993, Hassenbring et al 1994, Hansen et al 1995, Averill et al 1996) which suggest that depression is a consequence rather than an antecedent to back pain. However, whether patients consult a health professional for their pain problem may be influenced by their current mood (Croft et al 1995, Papageorgiou et al 1997).

The initial reaction to a painful injury is usually recognised in terms of anxiety, shock and fear rather than depression. However, with the passage of time, and the failure of treatment, a patient's coping skills can become exhausted and depression or anger can become evident. If it is possible to avoid painful activities or compensate successfully by changing activities and routines, then patients are unlikely to become depressed (even with persistence of pain). If however the pain is sufficiently severe, cannot be controlled, and as such has a widespread effect on a patient's life, then depression is much more likely.

Pain-associated depression is often best viewed as a form of 'learned helplessness' which can develop after many different types of chronic unresolved stress, including health-related problems. In the context of the development of chronic pain it is best understood as a psychological consequence of the persistence of pain and its incapacitating effects. Learned helpessness should not be viewed as a pejorative term. As a person withdraws from activities and social interactions these roles are often taken over by other family members. This reinforces the patient's inactivity and sick role. Depressed mood makes re-establishment of social roles difficult to achieve and so the patient remains in a more dependant role.

The predictive ability of mood and somatic anxiety has been well documented in a number of studies (Main & Waddell 1984, Main et al 1992). Somatic anxiety is a form of distress manifest by an increased preoccupation with bodily sensations. Pain or illness in the absence of a clearly identifiable cause or which has proved resistant to treatment heightens bodily concern and anxiety (see also Ch. 5).

Main et al (1992) developed the Distress Risk Assessment Method (DRAM) which is a combination of two questionnaires: the Modified Zung Depression Questionnaire, and the Modified Somatic Perception Questionnaire (MSPQ) (Main 1983). Since its publication this questionnaire has received widespread use because it is easy to administer and can predict treatment intervention outcomes. The patient's responses to the questionnaire can be classified by cut off scores into different categories: DD is distressed and depressed, DS is depressed and somatically anxious, and R are those who are at risk. Normal subjects (N), i.e. those with low risk of a poor outcome, acted as the reference group in these studies and the results were expressed in terms of relative risk of a poor outcome compared to this group. In a study of low back pain patients of various duration it demonstrated that those in the R or the DD/DS groups had 2.0-3.5 times the risk of having the same or worse *pain* at follow up. With respect to disability the R group were at 1.9 times greater risk of remaining *disabled* or getting worse, and the DD/DS groups were at 5.2 times greater risk.

These findings have been replicated in other studies in secondary care (Greenough 1993) and primary care (Burton et al 1995). In primary care the MSPQ in particular appears to be predictive of the residual disability at one year, depression appears to be less important in the acute and sub-chronic group.

Of particular interest to the physiotherapist are the findings of Williams et al (1995). In this study of 261 patients with chronic low back pain (greater than 3 months) referred to a McKenzie rehabilitation programme were investigated. The main outcome measures used were disability, pain report and receipt of wages compensation. The group were followed up one year after completion of the programme. Not only were the researchers able to demonstrate the same cut off scores for the four categories (N, R, DD & DS), for the DRAM they found similar predictive power. DD/DS subjects were 3.3-8.1 times more likely to have a poor outcome; R patients were 2.4-5.0 times more likely to have a poor outcome. This demonstrated that those who are psychologically distressed on the DRAM are at increased risk of a poor outcome if managed by the McKenzie approach alone.

Pain

Pain behaviour is defined as 'any and all outputs that a reasonable observer would characterise as pain' (Loeser & Fordyce 1983).

In physiotherapy we depend upon the description of pain, its intensity, location and nature and an observation of the patient's movement in coming to a clinical diagnosis. Sometimes our findings and reasoning do not concur with the degree of behaviour demonstrated by the individual. For example, a patient is capable of normal walking but an examination of quadriceps muscle strength demonstrates profound weakness. It is then that we might suggest that the pain behaviour is exaggerated or inappropriate to the condition.

High self-report of pain has already been reviewed as a risk factor for the development of chronic pain and self-report of pain is in itself an example of pain . Systematic observations of non-verbal (observational) pain behaviour have been developed (Keefe & Block 1982, Richards et al 1982). These tend to rely on either videotaped performance of standardised exercises or serial observations. One criticism of these tests is that they may not be sufficiently challenging to elicit pain behaviour in some individuals (Keefe & Dunsmore 1992). For example, patients may restrict their activities in order to avoid pain, therefore observing them go about routine activities may not elicit observable pain responses. Some pain behaviour measures require the patient to perform very simple tasks such as walking sitting and standing. These may be insufficiently sensitive to pick up pain related behaviours in some patients.

Watson and Poulter (1997) developed a functional and task orientated measure of pain behaviour to overcome this objection. In it subjects were required to perform more challenging tasks such as lifting and carrying a weight, climbing stairs and getting onto and off the floor.

It does seem that high levels of pain behaviour are related to increased disability and poor outcome and this has been shown to be the case in many studies (Keefe & Block 1982, Richards et al 1982, Watson & Poulter 1997). There does not appear to be any additional benefit from designing more complex and stressful measures of pain behaviour to improve prediction of outcome. This may be because it is those who demonstrate high levels of pain behaviour in the simplest tasks who are at the greatest risk of poor outcome.

One of the most commonly used and researched assessments of pain behaviour with respect to prediction of outcome are the non-organic signs, often referred to as the 'Waddell' signs (Waddell et al 1980, Waddell et al 1984). These are a series of simple examination tests designed to elicit behavioural responses to examination and assist in the identification of illness (pain) behaviour (Main & Waddell 1998). They have since been used (and in the opinion of the original authors occasionally misused, Main & Waddell 1998) as predictors of outcome from treatment. The originators of these signs have suggested that they should be understood as a reflection of psychological distress and fear in the context of recovery from injury and not as evidence of malingering or a willingness to mislead the health professional (Main & Waddell 1998).

Although most of the research performed using these tests has been on outcomes from medical and surgical intervention rather than rehabilitation, it has demonstrated a link between the presence of non-organic signs and poor outcome (Dzioba & Doxey 1984, Waddell et al 1986: Atlas et al 1996).

The non-organic signs have been demonstrated both to predict (Lancourt & Kettlehut 1992, Ohlund et al 1994, Kummel 1996) and to have no association with return to work (Brandish et al 1988). Some of the confusion in the research may be because of the inappropriate use of the suggested cut off scores (originally suggested to be 3 or more) or an assumption that the non-organic signs are proof of psychological distress rather than *an indication of the need for investigation of distress and fear* (Main & Waddell 1998). Gaines & Hegmann (1999) performed a prospective study of 55 acute back pain patients (free of back pain in the previous year, present pain of less than 10 weeks duration) and found that those patients (n=14) who demonstrated one or more of these signs (see above) had a much slower rate of return to work. They found that these patients used 'more physical therapy and more lumbar computed axial tomography'. This is a strange observation; surely it is a clinician who decides whether to treat or perform imaging studies? These results are better viewed as a tendency of clinicians to over treat or over investigate those with increased levels of pain behaviour.

It is better to view these signs as an additional screen in the context of a physical examination assisting the clinician to identify the need for a more broad assessment to identify psychological distress and fear of injury or harm in the examination. These measures must not be used in isolation and they should never be used to make decisions about access to treatment. In the author's personal experience many people have been unnecessarily stigmatised as 'magnifying' their condition following the uninformed use of these tests.

Socioeconomic factors

The role of socioeconomic factors in the development of disability has engaged much opinion and has generated a lot of debate. There still appears to be an assumption that financial gain is an important force in the development of disability. If this is so then the following must follow:

- Long term back pain related incapacity rates will be higher in those social systems where there are more generous allowances for disability due to back pain.
- Workers are more likely to be absent from work where wages compensation most closely approximate wages.
- Absences are likely to be greater where there is no (or a short) delay between first absence and the receipt of wages compensation.
- Changes in entitlement to wages compensation benefits and levels of such benefits will affect absence from work and long term incapacity.
- Those engaged in litigation or benefits appeals will remain off work longer.
- The level of incapacity of claimants in litigation claims will improve on the completion of their case and receipt of compensation.

It is not the purpose of this chapter to review this information in great detail because of the complexity of the arguments and the lack of convincing evidence. Indeed the argument in this area appears to have generated a lot of heat and not much light.

Nachemson (1992) related the high levels of back pain related incapacity in Sweden to the generous levels of wages compensation and the relative ease with which disability benefits can be claimed. Recent changes in the benefits system in Sweden have been accompanied by a fall in the claims for incapacity for back pain. According to the same source, the amount of work lost and wages compensation claims for long term incapacity due to back pain continues to climb in the United Kingdom, but has stabilised or is not climbing as fast in other European countries (Waddell 1998a).

The UK does not have generous wages compensation rate for such benefits. The first 28 weeks of sickness benefit (wages compensation) is paid by the employer and the rate of compensation may vary depending on local agreements. The state wage compensation (incapacity) benefit is paid at a flat rate and does not relate to the individual's previous income. In a study by Watson et al (1998) in Jersey, all wages compensation was paid by the State at a flat rate, was very low and was unrelated to earnings, but return to work rates were comparable with the findings of the CSAG report (1994) for the

UK mainland, where the compensation rates are more generous. Although the overall level of work loss and long-term incapacity were lower than suggested by CSAG it was little different to a comparable, rural area of the UK mainland (Walsh et al 1992). This calls into doubt the role of level of wage compensation in the UK, although it in no way represents anything more than an observation. As the authors point out, factors such as the level of unemployment (virtually full employment in Jersey), the local economy, and type of work available will also contribute.

Do patients really benefit from absence from work due to back pain? Waddell (1998 & b) states that less than half of the people on benefits receive less than 50% of their previous net earnings, only 1 in 8 received more than 80% of their previous net earnings, and only 5% are better off on benefits than working. This suggests that many individuals are worse off on benefits than when working.

Most of the evidence for the role of 'compensation' in back pain absence comes from North America and in particular from the Workers' Compensation Schemes. To qualify for access to wages compensation and medical treatment under these schemes it must be adjudged that the person suffers from back pain as a result of their work. Comparisons have frequently been made between those who qualify for treatment under this scheme and those who do not. Some results have demonstrated a relationship between those who are compensated under this system and delayed return to work and increased healthcare costs (Cats-Baril & Frymoyer 1991). Rohling et al (1995), reviewed a large number of studies and concluded that there was indeed an effect for compensation in delaying recovery and increasing health care costs. In contrast to this Volinn et al (1991) and Hadler (1995) found no such association and the latter found no evidence for a relationship between the wages compensation and the claimants' normal wage. Gallagher et al (1995) found that compensation status was only significant in those with an external locus of control and who were more likely to consult healthcare practitioners.

After a review of much of the evidence Waddell (1998b) concludes that there is a relationship between wages compensation, increased work absence, poor surgical outcome and poor rehabilitation outcome. He adds that most people on wages compensation get better and that it is only one of many social influences and must be seen in that context.

Fishbain et al (1995) reviewed a large series of papers relating to litigation and compensation claims for chronic pain and could find no evidence that settlement of the claim led to a resolution or improvement in the patients' condition or a return to work. Greenough (1993) found that seeking lump sum compensation claims (medicolegal claims) was related to poor outcome from low back pain and psychological disturbance (greater distress). Settlement of these lump sum compensations did not influence employment status or resolution of the psychological disturbance at one year or five-year follow up. Main and Watson (1995) also found that engagement in previous litigation was a risk factor for poor outcome from rehabilitation in chronic back pain patients with a history of prolonged unemployment. It would therefore appear that involvement in litigation is an important factor, but we must not assume that all litigants are likely to have a poor outcome. Once again the influences are many and complex. Litigants in the UK legal system may spend years pursuing a claim and be required to demonstrate residual incapacity on many occasions during that time. A return to work is likely to reduce the amount of the final settlement and, furthermore, involvement in the medico-legal system may contribute to the general level of psychological distress.

Other variables

Gender

Although females have a higher incidence of back pain and are more likely to consult a general practitioner than males (Croft et al 1998) the predictive validity of sex is unclear. In many studies in the acute, sub-chronic or chronic stages of the condition and for most treatment interventions there has been no observed effect (Coste et al 1994, Burton et al 1995, Klenermann 1995, Main & Burton 1995, Hazard et al 1996: Linton & Hallden 1998). Contrary to this, the work of Polatin et al (1989) and Bendix et al (1998) did demonstrate a higher return to work for female patients. Bendix et al (1998) demonstrated that this effect was independent of the treatment given but may relate to the type of work under taken by females in the studies, which is not reported.

Age

Similarly, the evidence for age is a poor predictor of outcome in some studies of acute and sub-chronic back pain (Lehman et al 1993, Burton et al 1995, Klennerman et al 1995, Main and Burton 1995). In studies from Denmark, the age of chronic low back pain patients has been demonstrated to affect outcome with a greater progression onto disability pension in the older worker and a lower return to work (Bendix et al 1998). There is evidence of an increased move towards early retirement in those with persistent back pain (Waddell 1998b). The trend towards earlier retirement is a phenomenon of the last decade; the number of people over the age of 55 in employment has fallen, in some cases sharply, in every country in Western Europe (Waddell 1998a). It is tempting to speculate that the poor outcome related to age (Bendix et al 1998) is the product of society's complicity in allowing early access to retirement benefits.

Work

Despite the technological advances in the Western society, the decline of heavy industries, and a general reduction in the physical nature of work over the past three decades, there are still some occupations that place the employee in a position where their body is subjected to stresses which make them more prone to injury (Halpern 1992).

Satisfaction with work, relationships between the injured worker and the employer, the worker's perception of safety in the workplace, and the worker's perception of workplace stress, monotony and physical demands of the workplace have all been demonstrated to be influential in workplace absence and the rate of return to work. In an early investigation into the relationship between ergonomic, fitness and psychological variables satisfaction with work was identified as a highly significant predictor (Bigos et al 1991). Cats-Baril and Frymoyer (1991) studied subjects with acute back pain and demonstrated 4 main areas of risk for long term work absence:

1 Job characteristics, which included work status at the time of onset of pain.
2 Past work history and type of occupation.
3 Job satisfaction factors, including local retirement policies and wages compensation benefits.
4 Perceptions of job safety and employer liability for injury.
5 Previous hospitalisations for any cause, and educational level of the injured worker were other important, but lesser, factors.

Other evidence for the nature of the occupation were identified by Bongers et al 1993. They found that *perceived* monotony, high physical demand or high work load and time pressure were predictive of the development of musculoskeletal pain and prolonged work absence. In addition musculoskeletal pain was more prevalent in those who perceived they had low job control and poor support from colleagues.

The perception of the employer's interest in the well being of the injured employee was studied by Wood (1987). In a study conducted in a nursing home, a simple telephone call from a line manager to the worker inquiring after their welfare, offering support and expressing concern, significantly reduced the length of work absence.

We can see from this brief overview that the influences of work on the development of incapacity and work loss are many. They depend not only on the physical and ergonomic demands of the work but also on the subject's perception of the intensity of those demands. Those who perceive their work as monotonous, believe their employer is uncaring, and who perceive a lack of safety in the workplace, are more likely to absent themselves from work and remain absent for longer than those subjects without these perceptions.

Multidimensional questionnaires

In recent years there has been an attempt to combine those factors thought to be most predictive of the development of chronic incapacity into a single questionnaire which may be used as a screening tool in clinical practice. This is an attractive idea. There are currently two questionnaires gaining in popularity. It should be emphasised that, at the time of going to press, neither of these has been validated in the UK healthcare system and both were developed in the occupational health setting.

The Vermont Disability Prediction Questionnaire (VDPQ) (Hazard et al 1996) was developed on a series of 166 persons with low back pain who completed the initial questionnaire. All respondents were working and reported their onset of back pain as a work-related injury. The work status at 3 months following the initial incidence of back pain was assessed by telephone contact.

There was no attempt to control the treatment received. The eleven questions on the form ask primarily about back pain history, current pain, perception of job demands, perception of ability to perform their job in the future, and marital status.

The VDPQ has been demonstrated to have a high degree of sensitivity and specificity in identifying those who were at risk of remaining off work for longer than 3 months. This would appear to be an attractive and simple prediction tool for use in an acute occupational setting where injuries are associated with work. However, it may not be an appropriate tool for use in a different setting.

Linton and Hallden (1997, 1998) developed a screening questionnaire to identify those who were likely to accumulate absence from work 6 months following an episode of back or neck pain, whether it was directly attributed to work or not. The authors followed up 137 people absenting from work. The interesting part about this study is that subjects were included if they had been pain free in the previous 4 months, and also included those with pain in more than one site because they felt *'this best reflects the usual patients seeking primary health care for back and neck pain'*. There was no attempt to control the treatment received by the patients.

The questionnaire was derived from a number of previously validated questionnaires which had been demonstrated to have predictive validity in identifying those likely to have a poor outcome from musculoskeletal pain. It had acceptable intra-subject test-retest reliability over one week.

The authors developed a range of cut off scores to identify: no absence from work during the 6 month follow up; low absence rates (<than 30 days); and high absence rates (>30 days) sickness absence. A score of 105 points on the questionnaire demonstrated correct identification of 86 % of those absent for 1–30 days and 88% correct classification of those absent for more than 30 days. There was also 75% correct classification of those not-absenting from work. These cut off scores may only be specific for this group and in this setting. Work in New Zealand (Kendall, personal communication) suggests a cut off score of 90 is more appropriate for their low back pain patient group. Linton and Hallden (1997, 1998) suggest that the questionnaire may be used not only to identify risk of poor outcome, but also to identify the need to assess the individual more specifically in problem areas; a suggestion that is taken up by Kendall et al (1997) in forming the basis of a systematic screening protocol (see Ch. 3). There appears to be merit in using a psychosocial screening tool not only to predict poor outcome, but also to assist in identifying the treatment options most appropriate for the individual (see Ch. 3).

Conclusion

We have discussed the many variables that predict outcomes from a variety of treatment interventions such as functional rehabilitation, osteopathic manipulation, McKenzie physiotherapy and non-standardised treatments. The evidence indicates that there is a commonality of risk factors that appear to predict poor outcome from management of low back pain. However, research has not been sufficiently comprehensive to indicate the relative importance of *all* the indicators of good or poor outcome in *all* treatment approaches at different points in the development of chronic incapacity. Neither do we have a clear picture of how those important variables change in a way to influence a positive outcome *during* physiotherapy interventions. We therefore have to synthesise an approach gained from the best evidence available and incorporate this into physiotherapy practice. Chapter 3 suggests a structured framework for the assessment, identification and remediation of barriers to successful rehabilitation.

REFERENCES

Atlas SJ, Deyo RA, Keller RB, Chapin AM, Patrick DL, Long JM, Singer DE 1996 The main lumbar spine study, part 2: 1-year outcomes of surgical and nonsurgical management of sciatica. Spine 21:1777–1786

Averill PM, Novy DM, Nelson DV, Berry LA 1996 Correlates of depression in chronic pain patients: a comprehensive examination. Pain 65(1):93–100

Bendix AF, Bendix T, Haestrup C 1998 Can it be predicted which patients with chronic low back pain should be offered tertiary rehabilitation in a functional restoration program? Spine 23(16):1775–1784

Bigos SJ, Battie MC, Spengler DM, Fisher LD, Fordyce WE, Hanson T, Nachemson AL, Zeh J 1991 A prospective study of work perceptions and psychosocial factors affecting the report of back injury. Spine 16:1–6

Bigos S, Bowyer O, Braen GR, Brown K, Deyo R, Haldemann S et al 1994 Acute low back problems in adults: Clinical Practice Guideline No. 14. AHCPR Publication No. 95-0642. Rockville, MD: Agency for Health Care Policy and Research, Public Health Service, U.S. Department of Health and Human Services

Bongers PM, de Winter CR, Kompier MAJ, Hildebrandt VH 1993 Psychosocial factors at work and musculoskeletal disease. Scandinavian Journal of Work and Environmental Health. 19:297–312

Brandish CF, Lloyd GJ, Adams CH, Abert J, Dyson P, Doxey NS, Mitson GL, 1988 Do non-organic signs help predict the return to activity of patients with low back pain? Spine13:557–560

Brown GK, Nicassio PM 1987 The development of a questionnaire for the assessment of active and passive coping strategies in chronic pain patients. Pain 31:53–65

Burton AK, Tillotson KM, Main CJ, Hollis S 1995 Psychological Predictors of Outcome in Acute and Subchronic Low Back Trouble. Spine 20:722–728

Cats-Baril WL, Frymoyer JW 1991 Identifying patients at risk of becoming disabled because of low-back pain: the Vermont Engineering Center predictive model. Spine 16:605–607

Cherkin DC, Deyo RA, Street JH, Barlow W 1996 Predicting poor outcomes for back pain seen in primary care using patients' own criteria. Spine 21:2900–2907

Coste J, Delecoeuillerie G, Cohen de Lara A, Le Parc JM, Paolaggi JB 1994 Clinical course and prognostic factors in acute low back pain: an inception cohort study in primary care practice. British Medical Journal 308:577–580

Crisson JE, Keefe FJ 1988 The relationship of locus of control to pain coping strategies and psychological distress in chronic pain patients. Pain. 35:147–154

Croft PR, Papageorgiou AC, Ferry S, Thomas E, Jayson MIV, Silman AJ 1995 Psychologic distress and low back pain: evidence from a prospective study in the general population. Spine 20:2731–2737

Croft PR, Macfarlane GJ, Papageorgiou AC, Thomas E, Silman AJ 1998 Outcome of low back pain in general practice: a prospective study. British Medical Journal. 316:1356–1359

Clinical Standards Advisory Group Epidemiology Review 1994 The epidemiology and cost of back pain. The Annex to the Clinical Standards Advisory Group's Report on Back Pain, London: HMSO: 1–72

Clinical Standards Advisory Group Back Pain 1994 Report of a CSAG committee on back pain, London: HMSO: 1–89

DeGood DE, Shutty MS 1992 Assessment of pain beliefs, coping and self efficacy. In: Turk DC, Melzack R (eds), Handbook of pain assessment. Guildford Press, New York: 221

Dzioba RB, Doxey NC 1984 A prospective investigation into the orthopaedic and psychologic predictors of outcome of first lumbar surgery following industrial injury. Spine 9(6):614–23

Faas A 1996 Exercises: which ones are worth trying, for which patients, and when? Spine 21:2874–2879

Fishbain DA, Rosomoff HL, Cutler RB, Rosomoff RS 1995 Secondary gain concept: a review of the scientific evidence. Clinical Journal of Pain 11:6–21

Fordyce WE, 1995. Task force on pain in the workplace back pain in the workplace: management of disability in nonspecific conditions. IASP Press, Seattle 1–75

Frank JW, Brooker A, DeMaio SE, Kerr MS, Maetzel A, Shannon HS et al 1996 Disability resulting from occupational low back pain—Part II: What do we know about secondary prevention? A review of the scientific evidence on prevention after disability begins. Spine 21:2918–2929

Gaines WG, Hegmann KT 1999 Effectiveness of Wadell's non-organic signs in predicting a delayed return to regular work in patients experiencing acute occupational low back pain. Spine 24:396–401

Gallagher RM, Williams RA, Skelly J, Haugh LD, Rauh V, Milhous R, Frymoyer JD 1995 Workers compensation and return to work in low back pain. Pain 6:299–307

Gatchel RJ, Polatin PB, Mayer TG 1995 The dominant role of psychosocial risk factors in the development of chronic low back pain disability. Spine 20(24):2702–2709

Gifford L S (Ed) 1998 Physiotherapy Pain Association Yearbook 1998-1999 Topical issues in pain. Whiplash—science and management. Fear-avoidance beliefs and behaviour. CNS Press, Falmouth

Greenough CG 1993 Recovery from low back pain. 1–5 year follow-up of 287 injury-related cases. Acta Orthopaedica.Scandinavia. Suppl. 254:1–34

Haazen IWCJ, Vlaeyen JWS, Kole-Snijders AMK, van Eek FD, van Es FD 1994 Behavioural rehabilitation of chronic low back pain: searching for predictors of treatment outcome. Journal of Rehabilitation Science 7:34–43

Hadler NM 1995 The disabling backache: an international perspective. Spine 20:640–649

Halpern M 1992 Prevention of low back pain: basic ergonomics in the workplace and clinic. Balliere's Clinical Rheumatology 6:705-730

Hansen FR, Biering Sorensen F, Schroll M 1995 Minnesota Multiphasic Personality inventory profiles in persons with or without low back pain. A 20-year follow-up study. Spine 20(24):2716–2720

Hassenbring M, Marienfeld G, Kuhlendahl D, Soyka D 1994 Risk factors of chronicity in lumbar disc patients. A prospective investigation of biologic, psychologic, and social predictors of therapy outcome. Spine 19(24):2759–2765

Hazard RG, Haugh LD, Reid S, Preble JB, MacDonald L 1996 Early prediction of chronic disability after occupational low back injury. Spine 21:945–951

Hildebrandt J, Pfingsten M, Saur P, Jansen J 1997 Prediction of success from a multidisciplinary treatment programme for chronic low back pain. Spine 22:990–1001

Jensen MP, Turner JA Romano JM 1991 Self efficacy and outcome expectancies: relationship to chronic pain coping strategies and adjustment. Pain 44:263–269

Jensen MP,Turner JA, Romano JM, Strom SE 1995 The Chronic Pain Coping Inventory: development and preliminary validation. Pain 60(2):203–16

Keefe FJ, Block AR 1982 Development of an observational method for assessing pain behaviour in chronic low back pain. Behaviour Therapy 13:363–375

Keefe FJ, Dunsmore J 1992 Pain behaviour: concepts and controversies, American Pain Society Journal. 1:92–100

Kendall NAS, Linton SJ, Main CJ 1997 Guide to assessing psychosocial Yellow Flags in acute low back pain: risk factors for long-term disability and work loss, Wellington, New Zealand:Accident Rehabilitation & Compensation Insurance Corporation of New Zealand, and the National Health Committee, Ministry of Health. 1–22

Klenerman L, Slade PD, Stanley IM, Pennie B, Reilly JP, Atchison LE, Troup JD, Rose MJ 1995 The prediction of chronicity in patients with an acute attack of low back pain in a general practice setting. Spine. 20:478--84

Koes BW, Bouter LM, Beckerman H, van der Heijden GJMG, Knipschild PG 1991 Physiotherapy exercises and back pain: a blinded review. British Medical Journal 302:1572–1576

Koes BW, van Tulder MW, van der Windt AWM, Bouter LM 1994 The efficacy of back schools: a reveiw of randomized clinical trials. Journal of Clinical Epidemiology. 47:851–862

Koes BW, Assendelft WJJ, van der Heijden GJMG, Bouter LM 1996 Spinal manipulation for low back pain: an updated systematic review of randomized clinical trials. Spine 21:2860–2873

Kori SH, Miller RP, Todd DD 1990 Kinesiophobia: a new view of chronic pain behaviour. Pain Management Jan/feb: 35–43

Kummel BM 1996 Nonorganic signs of significance in low back pain. Spine 21(9):1077–81

Lancourt J, Kettelhut M 1992 Predicting return to work for lower back patients receiving worker's compensation. Spine 17:629–640

Lehmann TR, Spratt KF, Lehmann KK 1993 Predicting long-term disability in low back injured workers presenting to a spine consultant. Spine 18:1103–1112

Lethem J, Slade PD, Troup JDG, Bentley G 1983 Outline of a fear-avoidance model of exaggerated pain perception-1. Behaviour Research and Therapy 21:401–408

Linton SJ, Hallden K 1997 Risk factors and the natural course of acute and recurrent musculoskeletal pain: developing a screening instrument. In: Jensen TS, Turner JA, Wiesenfeld-Hallin Z (Eds) Proceedings of the 8th world congress on pain, progress in pain research and management, Vol. 8, IASP Press, Seattle. 527–536

Linton SJ, Hallden K 1998 Can we screen for problematic back pain? A screening questionnaire for predicting outcome in acute and subacute back pain. Clinical. Journal of Pain. 14:209–215

Loeser JD, Fordyce WE 1983 Chronic pain. In: Carr JE, Dengerik HA (eds), Behavioural science in the practice of medicine. Elsevier, Amsterdam

Main CJ 1983 The Modified Somatic Perception Questionnaire (MSPQ). Journal of Psychosomatic Research. 27:503–514

Main CJ, Burton AK 1995 The patient with low back pain: who or what are we assessing? An experimental investigation of a clinical puzzle. Pain Reviews 2:203–209

Main CJ, Waddell G 1984 The detection of psychological abnormality in chronic low back pain using four simple scales. Current Concepts in Pain 2(1):10–15

Main CJ, Waddell G 1991 A comparison of cognitive measures in low back pain: statistical structure and clinical validity at initial assessment. Pain 46(3):287–98

Main CJ, Waddell G 1998 Behavioural responses to examination. A reappraisal of the interpretation of 'nonorganic signs'. Spine 23(21):2367–2371

Main CJ, Wood PLR, Hollis S, Spanswick CC, Waddell G 1992 The Distress and Risk Assesment Method: a simple patient classification to identify distress and evaluate the risk of poor outcome. Spine 17:42–52

Main CJ, Watson PJ 1995 Screening for patients at risk of developing chronic incapacity. Journal of Occupational Rehabilitation 5: 207-217

Muncey H, Watson PJ 1999 Efficacy of a Unidisciplinary Outpatient approach for patients with muscluloskeletal pain. Abstracts, Annual Scientific Meeting of The Pain Society, Edinburgh

Nachemson AL 1992 Newest knowledge of low back pain: a critical look. Clinical Orthopaedics and Related Research. 279:8–20

Ohlund C, Lindstrom I, Areskoug B, Eek C, Peterson L, Nachemson A 1994 Pain behaviour in industrial subacute low back pain. Part I. Reliability, concurrent validity and predictive validity of pain behaviour assessments. Pain 58:201-209

Papageorgiou AC, Macfarlane GJ, Thomas E, Croft PR, Jayson MIV, Silman AJ 1997 Psychosocial factors in the workplace—do they predict new episodes of low back pain? Spine 22:1137–1142

Polatin PB, Gatchel RJ, Barnes D, Mayer H, Arens C, Mayer TGA 1989 Psychosociomedical prediction model of response to treatment by chronically disabled workers with low-back pain. Spine 14(9):956–961

Richards JS, Nepomuceno C, Riles M, Suer Z 1982 Assessing pain : the UAB pain behaviour scale. Pain 12:393–398

Riley JF, Ahern DK, Follick MJ 1988 Chronic pain and functional impairment: assessing beliefs about their relationship. Archives of Physical Medicine and Rehabilitation 69:579–582

Rohling ML, Binder LM, Langhinrichsen-Rohling J 1995 Money matters: A meta-analytical review of the association between financial compensation and the experience and treatment of chronic pain. Health Psychology 14:537–547

Rose MJ, Reilly JP, Slade PD, Dewey M 1995 A comparative analysis of psychological and physical models of low back pain experience. Physiotherapy 81:710–716

Rose MJ, Klenerman L, Atchison L, Slade PD 1992 An application of the fear avoidance model to three chronic pain problems. Behaviour Research and Therapy 30:359–365

Rosenstiel AK, Keefe FJ 1983 The use of coping strategies in chronic low back pain patients: relationship to patient characteristics and current adjustment. Pain 17:33–44

Spitzer WO, Skovron ML, Salmi LR, Cassidy JD, Duranceau J, Suissa S, Zeiss E et al 1995 Scientific monograph of the Quebec Task Force on whiplash-associated disorders: redefining 'whiplash' and its management. Spine 20(8 Suppl):1S-73S

Symonds TL, Burton AK, Tillotson KM, Main CJ 1995 Absence resulting from low back trouble can be reduced by psychosocial intervention at the work place. Spine 20:2738–2745

Symonds TL, Burton AK, Tillotson KM, Main CJ 1996 Do attitudes and beliefs influence work loss due to low back trouble? Occupational Medicine 46:25–32

Van der Heijden GJ, Beurskens AJ, Koes BW, Assendelft WJ, de Vet HC, Bouter LM 1995 The efficacy of traction for back and neck pain: a systematic, blinded review of randomized clinical trial methods. Physical Therapy 75(2):93–104

Vlaeyen JWS, Kole-Snijders AMJ, Rotteveel AM, Ruesink R, Heuts PHTG 1995 The role of fear of movement/(re)injury in pain disability. Journal of Occupupational Rehabilitation 5:235–252

Vlaeyen JWS, Kole-Snijders AMJ, Boeren RGB, Van Eek H 1995 Fear of movement/ (re)injury in chronic low back pain and its relation to behavioural performance. Pain 62:363–372

Volinn E, Van Koevering D, Loeser JD 1991 back sprain in industry: the role of socioeconomic factors in chronicity. Spine 16:542–548

Von Korff M, Le Resche L, Dworkin SF 1993 First onset of common pain symptoms: a prospective study of depression as a risk factor. Pain 55:251–258

Waddell G 1987 A new clinical model for the treatment of low-back pain. Spine 12:632–644

Waddell G 1992 Biopsychosocial analysis of low back pain. Clinical Rheumatology 6:523–557

Waddell G 1998a Social policy influences in low back pain disability. Presented at 3rd International Primary Care Forum on Low Back Pain, Manchester

Waddell G 1998b The back pain revolution. Churchill Livingstone, Edinburgh

Waddell G, McCulloch JA, Kummel E, Venner RM 1980 Nonorganic physical signs in low-back pain. Spine 5:117–125

Waddell G, Bircher M, Finlayson D, Main CJ 1984 Symptoms and signs: physical disease or illness? British Medical Journal 289:739–741

Waddell G, Morris EW, Di Paola MP, Bircher M, Finlayson D 1986 A concept of illness tested as an improved basis for surgical decisions in low-back disorders. Spine 11:712–719

Waddell G, Newton M, Somerville D, Main CJ 1993 A Fear-Avoidance Beliefs Questionnaire (FABQ) and the role of fear-avoidance beliefs in chronic low back pain and disability. Pain 52:157–168

Wall PD 1996 Editorial Comment: Back pain in the workplace.I. Pain 65:5

Walsh K, Cruddas M, Coggon D 1992 Low back pain in eight areas in Britain. Journal of Epidemiology and Community Health 46:227–230

Watson PJ, Poulter ME 1997 The development of a functional task orientated measure of pain behaviour in chronic low back pain patients. Journal of Back and Musculoskeletal Rehabilitation. 9:57–59

Watson PJ, Main CJ, Waddell G, Gales TF, Purcell-Jones G 1998 Medically certified work loss, recurrence and cost of wages compensation for back pain: A follow up study of the working population of Jersey. British Journal of Rheumatology 37(1): 83–86

Williams DA, Keefe FJ 1991 Pain beliefs and the use of cognitive-behavioural coping strategies. Pain 46(2):185–90

Williams MM, Grant RN, Main CJ 1995 The Distress Risk Assessment Method (DRAM) as a predictor of outcome in chronically disabled workers attending a physical rehabilitation. Abstracts International Society for the study of the lumber spine, Helsinki, Finland p 46

Wood DJ 1987 Design and evaluation of a back injury prevention programme within a geriatric hospital. Spine 12:77–82

NOTES

1   Regression techniques try to explain how variables in research relate to each other. The statistic used is not important here but the concept is. For example, in a population tall people are generally heavier that short people. This is by no means true for all. Increase in height explains 50% of the variance for increase in weight; the rest is explained by increased muscle (10%), increased fat (10%), and others factors (water content, bone density). Eventually you might explain 100% of the variation in weight. This is rare in multiply-determined things like disability.

109

3

Assessing psychosocial yellow flags

PAUL WATSON, NICHOLAS KENDALL

The previous chapter set out the case for the assessment of psychosocial factors in the management of low back pain. It demonstrated that psychosocial factors have greater influence on outcome, what ever the outcome is, than physical factors alone. The authors stress that physiotherapists must continue to perform standardised physical assessments and endeavour to research and investigate the diagnostic and predictive value of their own repertoire of assessment skills and integrate these into a fully biopsychosocial assessment. Furthermore, therapists must develop management strategies in musculoskeletal pain that address those factors which prevent successful rehabilitation.

There has been a widespread proliferation of interventions based on theoretical assumptions about the cause of symptoms. It is our contention that this has occurred for a number of reasons. First, therapists always wish to do well for their patients and constantly wish to improve their clinical practice. Secondly, there is a cultural impetus in physiotherapy to grasp change and embrace the new (which is often introduced into practice before efficacy is established). Thirdly, treatment failure can often lead to self-doubt in the physiotherapist which makes them question their current skills. These factors stimulate therapists to attend more and more courses, to gain more and more skills of unproven scientific merit, from charismatic leaders or the acolytes of such leaders (Kendall 1997, Cole et al 1995). These persons may also reinforce the therapist's self-perception of lack of competence.

Western societies currently provide more manual therapy and healthcare for musculoskeletal disorders than at anytime in their histories, but the problem of chronic disability continues to worsen. As a result of this observation attempts have been made to delineate those treatments that are effective from those that are ineffective (Deyo 1993, Deyo 1983). Evidence has accumulated that in patients who are experiencing long term disability and who are treated with a biomedical focus (i.e. as if they had an acute episode that is going to be amenable to a 'curative' technique) the treatment may actually contribute to the ongoing disability.

Agencies that fund and purchase health care are under increasing budgetary constraint. It is understandable therefore that they are now choosing more frequently to exercise their right of asking what value they get from the provision of treatments to this group of patients. One response to these circumstances has been the publication of several major task force reports and guideline documents (Spitzer et al 1987, CSAG 1994a, CSAG 1994b, Bigos et al 1994: Fordyce 1995: Waddell et al 1996).

Additionally, over the last decade there has been a fundamental shift in our understanding of back pain. It has been recognised that the adoption of a dualistic approach separating mind and body has failed to assist in the resolution of one of the most pressing problems facing modern healthcare—the development of widespread disability due to back pain *without evidence of any increase in the prevalence of the condition*. It is important to realise that what has happened is not a change in back pain but a change in the disability due to back pain (Waddell 1997).

Assumptions underlying the yellow flags approach

In 1997 the Accident Rehabilitation and Compensation Insurance Corporation of New Zealand and the National Advisory Committee and Health and Disability launched an initiative to manage low back pain more effectively. At the time it was clear that, although treatment providers in New Zealand acknowledged the relevance of psychosocial factors in the continued incapacity from back pain, they had a near universal lack of confidence to assess and manage psychosocial issues—a situation that is mirrored in the UK today.

The key goal for the Yellow Flags project was to provide primary care treatment providers involved in low back care with:

- A systematic approach to identifying and quantifying the risk of psychosocial factors contributing to long term disability.
- Suggestions for improved early behavioural management of acute LBP patients that may prevent the development of long-term problems.

The authors wish the reader to note that at the present time there are few, if any indications that the prevention of chronic pain per se is a viable goal. However, there is evidence from randomised controlled trials that cognitive-behavioural interventions applied to the sub-acute and chronic population are effective in improving outcome and reducing chronic disability.

The role of multidisciplinary or interdisciplinary approaches to the rehabilitation of chronic pain patients has been established and has been reviewed elsewhere (Hazard et al 1989, Flor et al 1992, Bendix et al 1998, Watson 1999). The consensus of opinion is that these approaches are successful in tackling many of the psychosocial barriers to improvement as well as enabling patients to improve their physical fitness and functioning. In recent years there has been an increasing body of evidence that similar approaches can be used earlier in the patients' musculoskeletal pain history to improve outcome and hence prevent the decline into chronic incapacity.

In addition we have evidence that simple interventions using psychological strategies are effective when delivered by primary care treatment providers. Such strategies include reassurance, active encouragement, advice to remain active and graded return to work. Linton et al (1993) give an excellent example. Using a randomised controlled trial patients with acute musculoskeletal pain were assigned to either an early activation programme using a cognitive-behavioural approach, or a control group who received analgesia and advice to rest on an 'as needed' basis. The results demonstrated that the number of subjects developing chronic incapacity (defined as greater than 200 days work loss) was *eight times higher in the group given analgesia and advice to rest*. Linton et al (1989) and Linton and Bradley (1992) also demonstrated that a cognitive behavioural approach to the management of sub-acute musculoskeletal pain was successful in reducing work loss, reducing pain report and improving mood.

Linstrom (1992) demonstrated that an early activation programme based on an operant conditioning approach to the management of patients with sub-acute low back pain (defined as absence from work for eight weeks) reduced sickness absence. The activation programme consisted of education and an individualised exercise programme. The control group received treatment 'as usual'. At long term follow up (1 year) *those who received treatment as usual were four times more likely to remain absent from work than those in the early activation group*. Hence the prevention of long tem disability associated with common musculoskeletal pain problems such as LBP, is considered to be an attainable goal.

Who should be assessed and when?

Should we assess all patients attending for physiotherapy for yellow flags? At what point in the patient's pain history would screening be most effective? Reports into the management of acute low back pain have suggested that patients should receive such an assessment after 2-4 weeks (Kendall et al 1997) or 6 weeks (CSAG 1994), from initial presentation if they are still consulting and particularly if they are still unable to return to work. The guidelines issued in the USA were less clear on this subject (Bigos et al 1994) but still advocate such an assessment if routine advice and symptomatic treatment fail. Before implementing a psychosocial screening and intervention programme the service manager is wise to ask how many patients will need it and what it will cost to implement. To make any estimation of this we need to understand the referral patterns to physiotherapy.

There is little research into the referral patterns to physiotherapy for low back pain in the UK. Data from Mason (1994) states that of all patients consulting their GP with back pain, only 12% were referred to a physiotherapist. In the South Manchester Study only 2% of patients attending for their first consultation for back pain received physiotherapy within 3 months (Croft et al 1994). Waddell (1998) concludes from his review of the evidence that patients will probably be referred to physiotherapy if their pain persists for more than a few months. This accords with the experience of most physiotherapists, -that the majority referrals are for those patients who have suffered back pain for a considerable time and few can be considered to be acute. In a recent study of patients referred to a fitness programme for low back pain at a large hospital-based physiotherapy department (Muncey & Watson 1999) 50% of patients reported having their back pain for greater than six months and only 30% reported having it for less than three months (acute or sub-chronic).

The evidence is clear, few patients are referred to a physiotherapist within a short time frame. (Although there is little evidence available at the time of writing to establish the speed of referral of people with back pain in private practice.) This leads us to conclude that most patients attending a physio-therapist in the UK will have had their current episode of back pain for a substantial period and the majority can be considered to be at least sub-acute in terms of time. One can conclude from this that *all physiotherapy departments should have access to staff trained in psychosocial screening and assessment, and all specialist staff managing back pain patients should be able to devise treatment interventions to address these problems.*

In the experience of the authors, simple screening questionnaires take no more than a few minutes to complete, and can be done in the waiting room and so need not involve physiotherapy time. Scoring of questionnaires is relatively quick and simple once the staff have been trained and are used to doing it.

We can conclude that screening is appropriate in:

- All those with low back pain where the symptoms have significantly interfered with or prevented normal activities, including work, for more than 4 weeks.
- Those patients who are not making expected progress within 2-4 weeks of onset of treatment for an acute low back pain problem.

Screening for poor outcome

The Yellow Flags approach is based on five important assumptions and these are listed in Box 1 below. We should recognise that in the same way that not every patient has red flags, we cannot assume that they all have significant psychosocial yellow flags. However, care needs to be taken to ensure that psychological factors are not missed since their omission may be more detrimental than their over-identification. The significance of a particular factor is relative. Immediate notice should be taken if an important red flag is present, and careful consideration given to the appropriate response. The same is true for yellow flags. The presence of yellow flags should cause consideration to be given to the behavioural aspects of management, tailored to meet the needs of the individual. Put another way, the identification of the risk factors should lead to an appropriate intervention. red flags should lead to appropriate medical intervention; yellow flags should lead to appropriate cognitive and behavioural management. Red and yellow flags are not mutually exclusive—an individual patient may require intervention in both areas concurrently.

Box 1 Assumptions of the psychosocial Yellow Flags approach (Kendall et al 1997)

---

1 Impairment, pain and disability are conceptually related, but are also distinct.
2 Impairments (such as disc prolapse) are not caused by psychosocial factors, whereas the perception of pain is always subjective and is readily influenced by such factors.
3 The report of injuries and pain, and seeking healthcare, is usually mediated by the complex interaction of medical, work-related beliefs and behaviours, and other psychosocial factors.
4 Disability, including work-loss and reductions in activity is commonly influenced by a diverse range of psychosocial factors. These include attitudes and beliefs held by the patient; behaviours; compensation and litigation issues; diagnosis and the behaviour of treatment providers; emotions, such as fear or low mood; family members behaviour, such as a solicitous spouse; and work factors.
5 The presence of a specific disease does not mean that the psychosocial factors are unimportant.

What should be assessed at interview varies with the timing of the assessment. If the patient presents within days of an initial injury or onset of pain then the most important consideration is the presence of red flags, although the presence of any yellow flags should be noted. However, as time goes by the potential of psychosocial yellow flags to be salient increases. One should always remember that an uncomplicated episode of acute back pain, of recent onset, has a very good recovery rate, even without (or despite) the intervention of the healthcare professions.

The assessment of yellow flags emphasises the identification of beliefs, emotions and behaviours in the individual and significant others that interact with the pain problem; it is important to determine whether they are contributing to the perpetuation, or worsening, of the situation. Health professionals are encouraged to remember that the key question is always: 'What can be done to help this person experience less distress and disability at this time?' This does not mean that we do not try to reduce the patient's pain intensity but the focus of the treatment is on reducing the pain-associated distress and disability. We must continue to use pain-relieving modalities of *proven* efficacy and integrate psychosocial assessment and management into practice.

The number of psychosocial factors that might contribute to the development of long-term disability is large and it would prove time consuming to perform a psychosocial interview on all LBP patients presenting to physiotherapy. In the development of the New Zealand guidelines a brief 24 item screening questionnaire (Linton & Hallden 1997) was provided to quantify the probability of the individual with low back pain being at risk of long term disability and time off work. It is recommended that this questionnaire is used as a screening tool to determine the need for a further psychosocial interview. It should not be used to determine who gets access to treatment or the type of treatment the patient should get at that point.

Results of questionnaires should alert the clinician to the possibility of psychosocial barriers to recovery or improvement in function. These factors can then be explored in the clinical setting with an interview. The important issues in the clinical interview can be encapsulated in the mnemonic ABCDEFW—they relate to:

- **A**ttitudes and beliefs about back pain
- **B**ehaviours
- **C**ompensation issues
- **D**iagnosis and treatment issues
- **E**motions
- **F**amily
- **W**ork.

They are not in any particular order of importance.

Linton & Hallden (1998) concluded that the following factors were most important and consistently predicted poor outcomes:

a) The presence of a belief that pain is harmful or potentially severely disabling.
b) Fear-avoidance behaviour (avoiding movement or activity due to misplaced anticipation of pain) and reduced activity levels.
c) Tendency to low mood and withdrawal from social interaction.
d) An expectation that passive treatments rather than active participation in therapy would help.

Some simple key questions appear in Box 2. They can easily be phrased in the clinician's own words.

Box 2 Key Yellow Flags interview questions

- Have you had time off in the past with back pain?

- What do you understand is the cause of your back pain?

- What are you expecting will help you?

- How is your employer (co-workers, family) responding to your back pain?

- What do you currently do to help you cope with your back pain?

- Do you think you will be able to return to work (your usual levels of activity)? When?

Clinical assessment of yellow flags involves judgement about the relative importance of factors for the individual. The list of factors provided here is not exhaustive and for a particular individual the order of importance may vary.

A word of caution: some factors may appear to be mutually exclusive, but are not in fact. For example, partners can alternate between being socially punitive (ignoring the problem or expressing annoyance/frustration) to being over-protective in a well intentioned way (and inadvertently encouraging extended rest and withdrawal from activity, or excessive treatment seeking). In other words, both factors may be pertinent. A patient's partner may repeatedly pressure the patient get their back 'fixed' so they can get back to work, but at the same time be critical of the patient's attempts to become more active because of the risk of aggravating the problem.

Assessing the presence of psychosocial yellow flags should produce two key outcomes. The first is the decision as to whether a more detailed assessment is needed; the second is the identification of any salient factors that can become the subject of a specific intervention, thus saving time and helping to concentrate the use of health care resources. There would be little point in referring the patient to an intensive rehabilitation programme to address fears and distorted beliefs if they were not present in the individual. Likewise there is potential risk in offering a programme of passive treatment to patients who do not demonstrate any willingness to take responsibility for increasing their own activity.

It must be emphasised that the presence of psychosocial yellow flags *in no way* indicates the likelihood of malingering. Rather, they should be interpreted as individual, employment and system factors that may interfere with the recovery potential. It is hoped that treatment providers will explore the benefits of this approach within their regular clinical practice, and that this is done in a manner that results in improved quality of life for those with low back problems.

The identification of yellow flags raises important question with respect to changing the way we treat patients. It suggests that a range of generic skills are needed by clinicians treating musculoskeletal pain to change the patient's beliefs and behaviours, and these will lead to improved early management of patients.

Physiotherapists are practised in identifying musculoskeletal pain problems in the individual, and understand that rarely are the problem and the precipitating circumstance identical. The resolution of the problems requires an individualised problem solving approach. It is hoped that, with appropriate training, physiotherapists can identify the psychosocial barriers to improvement and likewise develop the same approach to the resolution of these barriers to full recovery. The identification of a minority of problems should lead to the provision of appropriate psychosocial intervention of support for the individual, since they are unlikely to be greatly influenced by the application of biomedical treatments.

What screening questionnaires can and cannot do

There are two major methods that are used in the identification of psychosocial yellow flags: clinical assessment and structured questionnaires. We can also use a combination of both. The methods you will use depend on your setting, and your confidence at assessing these issues yourself. The authors strongly suggest that clinical assessment is the most useful and powerful method, providing the individual has received appropriate training. The advantages and disadvantages of each method are given in Table 3.1.

Note that the yellow flags questionnaire does not provide a 'diagnosis', or a definitive classification of risk. Higher scores on questionnaires ought to be interpreted to mean that you should look for reasons *not to* consider the patient to be at risk of long-term disability. This means carrying out further assessment. The results from questionnaires should be used to identify 'relative risk' of poor outcome.

For this reason we advocate the use of a clinical interview to determine the nature of the barriers to improvement. For example on questionnaires which assess fear-avoidance beliefs we might identify that the patient appears to be fearful of re-injury on movement, but it will not tell us *why* they are fearful or *how* they came to develop these beliefs.

The individual items on the questionnaires may be used to identify which ones are contributing most to the risk score. On the Linton and Hallden questionnaire (Linton & Hallden 1998) we can see that there are questions on pain, disability, fear, and catastophising (see Ch. 4). By examination of the areas scored most highly (catastrophising, for example) we can identify the areas of greatest concern and at most significant risk of poor outcome. These would then form the basis of further assessment and may be the subject of intervention. Remember, just as in musculoskeletal clinical diagnosis, you cannot intervene effectively until you have assessed thoroughly!

The Yellow Flags interview

In the UK we must be cautious about the interpretation of the results from questionnaires used in other healthcare systems. To date we do not have published data on the use and interpretation of the yellow flags screening questionnaire.

In the opinion of the authors basic physiotherapy training does not give the therapist the skills necessary to perform a good psychosocial assessment; additional training is required. Some physiotherapists may have undertaken training in communication skills and counselling; although elements of these approaches are transferable to psychosocial assessment, specific training is still indicated.

The Yellow Flags approach was intended for the management of people with acute low back pain in a specific primary care setting where the emphasis was on the reduction of workloss. There are lessons that may be learned for

Table 3.1 Advantages and disadvantages of various methods of yellow flag assessment

Method	Advantages	Disadvantages
Questionnaire	Quick to administer	Requires time to score, need to check for missing information
	Useful for screening large numbers	Unsuitable for those with reading problems
	Little skill needed	May not be applicable to all members of a community (ethnic group differences)
	Interpretation is usually unequivocal	May predict only one outcome (work loss but not pain)
	Can be statistically based on evidence	May be sensitive to time of measurement (influenced by duration of symptoms)
		Susceptible to confounds such as social desirability. People may tell you what they think you want to hear
Clinical Interview	Clinician can readily adapt to the characteristics of the individual	Potentially time consuming
	Incorporates clinical experience	May result in confused picture unless interviewing skill is adequate
	Facilitates establishing goals for potential intervention	Possibility of observer bias, or prejudice
	Less susceptible to confounds such as social desirability	Requires training
	Judgements about severity can be made	
Questionnaire with Clinical Interview	Improved accuracy	Requires more time and resources
	Clinician can integrate quantitative information and interview data	Requires organisational change
	Can use a two-stage process with questionnaire as first stage to target clinical interview	Requires training
		More time needed (potential for delays)

the management of other musculoskeletal pains of longer duration. The suggested yellow flags which can be identified in the clinical interview are particularly relevant. These are given in the boxes below. The simple mnemonic **ABCDEFW** was developed to simplify the system and is repeated here. These have been adapted slightly from the original to make them more representative of the UK health system.

A   Attitudes and beliefs about back pain

- Belief that pain is harmful or disabling results in fear-avoidance behaviour e.g. the development of guarding and fear of movement.

- Belief that all pain must be abolished before attempting to return to work or normal activity.

- Expectation of increased pain with activity or work, lack of ability to predict capability.

- Catastrophic thinking, fearing the worse, misinterpreting bodily symptoms.

- Belief that pain is uncontrollable.

- Passive attitude to rehabilitation; it is the health professional's role to fix the problem.

It is in this section that the therapist can do so much that is positive to change patients' perception of their condition, and improve their physical confidence as well as their vision of the future. Physiotherapists must be vigilant not to provide or reinforce beliefs that are unhelpful and which are ultimately detrimental to treatment outcome. Physiotherapists are rarely taught to ask patients what *they* think is wrong with them. Until you have understood the patient's own concept of their condition you will not be able to understand their behaviour (see Rose 1998).

In giving any advice to patients we need to know what they currently understand and believe. Even the most seemingly innocuous information can be wildly misunderstood. A patient who believes they have a serious degenerative condition of the spine and who is told by a surgeon that they have 'a degenerative condition and an operation will not help' may believe 'my condition is so bad even an operation cannot cure it'. Most of us would be thankful that we did not need an operation!

A patient who is fearful of moving and as a consequence is very tense may feel increased discomfort after exercise. If they are told by the physiotherapist 'my exercises only seem to be making you worse so I am discharging you' this not only reinforces their fear of movement, it also creates a link between movement and a worsening of the condition.

Similarly we need to understand what the patients' expectations of physiotherapy are. Do they expect passive treatment (and are unlikely to adhere to a self exercise programme)? Are they looking for advice and a self-directed treatment programme (willing to develop a self management strategy)?

B Behaviours

- Use of extended rest of disproportionate 'downtime' (long periods of reclining/resting.)
- Reduced activity level and withdrawal from activities of daily living.
- Irregular participation in or poor compliance with physical exercise, tendency to be in a boom bust cycle.
- Avoidance of normal activity and progressive substitution of lifestyle away from productive activity.
- Report of extremely high intensity of pain (always 10/10 or even 11/10 on VAS or VRS.)
- Excessive reliance on the use of aids of appliances.
- Poor/reduced sleep quality since onset of back pain.
- High intake of alcohol or other substances since onset of pain.
- Smoking.

When interviewing patients about their behaviours we are trying to build up a picture of what they are doing, or not doing, as a result of the pain. This gives an insight into the patient's current coping and their ability to pace exercise. As was described in the previous chapters passive coping strategies have been demonstrated to be predictive of poor outcomes. Reducing activity, reliance on medication, including prescription medication and self-medication, and the absence of positive coping such as gradually increasing activity are suggestive of poor outcome. Self-medication also includes the use of substances such as alcohol, street drugs and increased tobacco consumption.

We are very familiar with the patient who avoids activity due to pain but we must be alert to those who fail to regulate activity appropriately. It is equally maladaptive to completely ignore a significant injury and to continue activities that may risk further injury. Many individuals are unaware that they fail to regulate activity. A typical example is a housewife who must complete vacuuming the house despite the effect on her pain and the consequences (reduced activity for the next few days due to increased pain).

It is important that the interview identifies not only the way the patient behaves as a result of the pain but also whether they have insight into their current behaviour. Do they realise, for example, that they are unable to pace their activities?

Once the patient has insight into how they are behaving, the therapist must try to find out what is fueling that behaviour. Has the patient withdrawn from a particular activity because they fear that it will cause further injury or degeneration? Does the person who cannot pace work activities fail to do so because they fear they may loose their job if they under perform, or is it because their own self-image depends on being able to do more work than others around them?

We can only change the behaviour if the patient is aware of it, understands why they are doing it, and is willing to change in the short term for improvement in the long term.

C	Compensation issues

- Lack of financial incentive to return to work.
- Disputes over access to benefits.
- History of claims due to other injuries.
- History of back pain with previous receipt of sickness benefits.
- Participation in medico-legal claim.

The previous chapter demonstrated that the association between financial compensation and chronic disability is complex and inextricably linked with the healthcare system and access to other benefits including retirement pensions. The difficulty for the physiotherapist is in making a judgement whether an ongoing claim or dispute represents a barrier to rehabilitation.

Contrast these two cases.

John is 29, married with two children. He was injured at work when the forklift truck he was driving fell into an unmarked excavation on a poorly lit yard in the early hours of the morning. John was absent from work for four months due to soft tissue injuries to his spine. He returned to work and experienced difficulties with his ability to do his former job and has been offered a new job with retraining on the same money, provided he can get back to work. John is suing the company on the advice of his union. The company admitted responsibility and was prosecuted by the Health and Safety executive. John was previously very happy with the firm and looks forward to his new job. He is of the opinion that he will eventually reach settlement with the litigation but believes that keeping his job is more important in the long term.

Harold is a 59 year old labourer for a company which lays and maintains gas pipelines. His job is very physical, he has no other qualifications or skills. He has had repeated episodes of back pain with increasing absence from work. In addition he has osteoarthritis of both knees and has been finding it increasingly difficult climbing in and out of trenches and in carrying heavy equipment. He also is being treated for high blood pressure and mild diabetes. He has now been off work for five months and has investigated the possibility of retirement on medical grounds with the occupational physician. The occupational physician wants Harold to try physical rehabilitation before he comes to any decision. Harold has worked for the same firm for 25 years and, he believes, will be eligible for a large redundancy payment.

These cases illustrate that the presence of compensation issues, per se, are not always indicators of poor outcome. The importance of the compensation issue to the individual needs to be assessed. The physiotherapist should also be candid with the patient and outline the effects the treatment may have on their condition and claim. These too can be complex: for example, failure to comply with or complete therapy may be seen in a poor light by those assessing the veracity of the claim. There still may be cases where patients cannot see a future at work and they may be unwilling to participate fully in the rehabilitation process if improvement would results in loss of benefits or the loss of an early pension.

D Diagnosis and treatment issues

- Health professionals sanctioning disability, not providing interventions geared towards improvement of function.

- Experience of conflicting diagnoses or explanations for back pain, resulting in patient confusion.

- Unfamiliar diagnostic language leading to catastrophisation (fearing inevitable poor outcome.)

- Dramatisation of back pain problem by health professions leading to dependency on treatment.

- Continued receipt of passive treatment.

- Expectations of quick and easy cure.

- Lack of satisfaction with previous treatments for back pain.

- Advice from professionals to change or withdraw from job.

Until the production of the CSAG report in 1994, and in many cases since that time, the routine advice for those with back pain was to rest and take analgesia. This had been the received wisdom for many tens of years and had been sanctioned by all health professions. There was even an expectation in many patients that the general practitioner would give them a sick note exempting them from work until the pain resolved. In the past few years there has been a sea change to recommending early return to work with minimal, if any, time off. This may lead to confusion in the sufferer who at one time goes to the doctor with a bad back and is told to rest, and a few years later presents with the same symptoms only to be given the opposite advice.

The more professionals the patient sees the more attributions he/she may be given for the cause of the pain. This becomes particularly unhelpful if the attribution given by the professional is purely a way to justify the intervention they (the professional) favour. This leads to confusion in the patient and, in those who are apt to catastrophise, increases distress and reinforces fear-avoidance beliefs.

The clinical interview should identify not only what the patient has been told about their condition but also what they *understand* by the explanations they have been given and how this has affected what they do. Mis-understandings are common, what we say to patients and what they believe we said can be very different.

What people understand about investigations can be problematic. A patient presented to the chronic pain centre with a full report of the results of his

MRI scan and X-rays given to him following a private consultation. These reported degenerative changes in the discs at three levels with accompanying arthritic changes in the facet joints. This he thought was evidence of severe degeneration of his spine. He was very surprised to learn that these are relatively normal findings in the spine of a 60 year old male.

We know from the literature on the natural history of back pain that the symptoms continue for some time after the initial event, even in those with a first episode (Croft et al 1998). It is therefore disingenuous to give patients the impression that back pain is caused by a single identifiable source and can be cured easily and permanently by, for example, a single manipulation or course of manipulations. Symptomatic management is not rehabilitation and so cannot be expected to address the wider issues in disability.

Patients should be asked about their previous treatments and also about the type of treatments they think are appropriate to their condition—what do they expect of your service? An over-reliance on passive therapies in the past and an expectation of more in the future does not bode well for an approach that focuses on self management and increased activation and this needs to be addressed early on.

E Emotions

- Fear of increased pain with increased activity.
- Depression (especially long-term low mood), loss of enjoyment.
- More irritable than usual.
- Anxiety about and heightened awareness of body sensations.
- Feeling under stress and unable to maintain sense of control.
- Presence of social anxiety or disinterested in social activity.
- Feeling useless and not needed.

The reasons for assessing the effect that the pain problem has on the individual have been addressed in Chapter 2, and discussed in PPA Yearbook Volume 1 (Gifford 1998). The yellow flags interview identifies risk factors and tries to use a problem solving approach to manage these factors in the intervention. Fear of pain and further injury is a powerful agent in the development of disability. It is essential that fears about pain and injury are identified but the physiotherapist should try to identify how those fears arose and what maintains them. Some people are told they have crumbling spines or that their discs are wearing away, this might translate into reduced activity because of a fear of further damage.

Fear of pain and injury can be addressed through information and progressive reactivation via graded return to normal activity, including work. Pacing return to work and normal activity will help the patient develop a sense of control over the condition and help them achieve more.

Depression, or more accurately low mood, is a common feature of prolonged incapacity and is a normal reaction. Reduction in incapacity and resumption of rewarding activities will assist in resolving this. However, low mood may be as a result of factors not directly connected with the incapacity (marriage breakdown, unresolved grief). Physiotherapists should distinguish between low mood that is a result of pain and related incapacity, which is their responsibility, and that which is as a result of other factors in the patients' life (marriage break-up, financial worries). The latter is not the responsibility of the physiotherapist but they should give the patient time to express their problem and listen to them. If the patient then requires help in addressing it, the physiotherapist can refer them to a specialist practitioner.

F Family

- Over-protective partner/spouse, reinforcing fear of harm or encouraging catastrophisation.

- Solicitous behaviour from spouse (taking over tasks).

- Socially punitive responses from spouse (ignoring, expression of frustration).

- Extent to which family members support return to work/normal activity.

- Lack of person to talk to about problem. (See Chapters 6 & 7)

It might be unusual for the therapist to see the relatives of a patient with low back pain. However, an assessment of their attitude to the person's back pain is important. The physiotherapist will have a very difficult time encouraging compliance with an activity based programme if the patient's spouse or significant other person continually reinforces the message that activity is potentially harmful and encourages the patient to seek passive treatment and rest.

If patients are to maintain improvement following physiotherapy intervention they must quickly regain activities and duties they may have relinquished to other family members. The family must be willing to allow them to do this and to have the confidence in a good outcome.

Even with the reduction in heavy industry in an increasingly technological society, there are still occupations which require physical effort or which expose the body to an environment that is known to represent physiological risk to those recovering from an episode of back pain. This must be considered when planning treatment, particularly with reference to the degree of physical fitness required to do the job (the level of physical capacity that the patient needs to attain before being discharged from management if physiotherapy is to be successful) and the possibilities that exist for graded return to work. The physiotherapist should be sure about the type of physical tasks that are performed and whether the patient can be returned to them gradually.

W Work

- History of manual work (forestry, farming, construction, truck driving, labouring, nursing).
- Repetitive or boring work.
- Previous work history, frequent job changes, experiencing stress at work, job dissatisfaction, and poor relationships with peers or supervisors.
- Belief that work is harmful, that to do it will cause damage or be dangerous.
- Unsupportive or unhappy current work environment.
- Low educational background, low socioeconomic status.
- Job involves significant biomechanical demands, such as heavy or frequent lifting, manually handling heavy items, extended period in static postures (sitting or standing, driving), whole body vibration, constrained postures, inflexible work schedules preventing appropriate breaks.
- Minimal availability of selected duties to facilitate graded return to work.
- Negative experience of workplace management of back pain (e.g. absence of reporting system, discouragement to report, punitive responses from supervisors and management).
- Absence of interest from employer.

There are additional non-physiological risks which make early return to work less likely. These are often given the generic term *job satisfaction*. Satisfaction with work is only one component of this. Many patients may feel pressure at work if their performance falls below what they perceive is expected of them. Unsympathetic employers, supervisors, or co-workers may not be willing to understand or sanction reduced performance and productivity.

Currently there is a general reluctance as well as a lack of a mechanism for physiotherapists in primary and secondary settings to become involved in the patients' workplace. This is much easier for physiotherapists employed in industry. If we are to complete the rehabilitation of people back into society this must include returning them to work.

Conclusion

The authors are optimistic that, with appropriate training, physiotherapists in the UK can take on the role of psychosocial assessment of those with low back pain. The CSAG (1994b) report suggested that a psychosocial assessment 'could be performed by the patient's family doctor or therapist' (p61); we believe that the physiotherapist in the UK is in a unique position to perform this service and to affect the outcome from low back pain nationally. Box 3 contains our recommendations to achieve a quality outcome for patients and therapists.

Box 3   Recommendations

- All physiotherapists treating patients with low back pain should receive a basic training in psychosocial assessment and management approaches.

- All physiotherapists operating as sole practitioners, those supervising junior staff, and those specialising in the management of low back pain should receive specialist training in psychosocial assessment and management of back pain.

- Psychosocial assessment and management should be included in the curriculum of studies for physiotherapy undergraduate students.

- Psychosocial assessment and behavioural management must not be separated, but should be *integrated* into routine physiotherapy management of those with low back pain.

- Psychosocial Screening Questionnaires must only be used to identify areas of concern for a psychosocial interview.

- Normative data and 'cut off' scores for a UK back pain population should be established.

- Clinicians should audit the referral of back pain patients to determine the profile of their caseload with respect to duration of symptoms and risk of developing chronic incapacity. (The results will inform the manager of the resources required to develop an integrated approach to the management of low back pain).

- Further research needs to be performed to establish the reliability and normal values for screening questionnaires and the development of appropriate cut off scores based on duration of symptoms.

REFERENCES

Bendix AF, Bendix T, Haestrup C 1998 Can it be predicted which patients with chronic low back pain should be offered tertiary rehabilitation in a functional restoration program? Spine 23(16):1775–1784

Bigos S, Bowyer O, Braen GR, Brown K, Deyo R, Haldemann S, et al 1994 Acute low back problems in adults: clinical practice guideline No. 14. AHCPR Publication No. 95–0642. Rockville, MD: Agency for Health Care Policy and Research, Public Health Service, U.S. Department of Health and Human Services

Clinical Standards Advisory Group 1994a Epidemiology review: the epidemiology and cost of back pain. The Annex to the Clinical Standards Advisory Group's Report on Back Pain. HMSO, London

Clinical Standards Advisory Group (1994b) Back pain: report of a CSAG committee on back pain. HMSO, London

Cole B, Finch E, Gowland C, Mayo N 1995 Physical rehabilitation outcome measures. Williams & Wilkins, Baltimore

Croft P, Joseph S 1994 Low back pain in the community and in hospitals. A report to the CSAG of the Department of Health. Arthritis and Rheumatism Research Council Epidemiological Research Unit, University of Manchester

Croft PR, Macfarlane GJ, Papageorgiou AC, Thomas E, Silman AJ 1998 Outcome of low back pain in general practice: a prospective study. British Medical Journal 316:1356-1359

Deyo RA 1983 Conservative therapy for low back pain: distinguishing useful from useless therapy. Journal of the American Medical Association 250:1057–1062

Deyo RA 1993 Practice variations, treatment fads, rising disability: do we need a new clinical research paradigm? Spine 18: 2153–2162

Flor H, Fydrich T, Turk DC 1992 Efficacy of multidisciplinary pain treatment centers: a meta-analytical review. Pain 49:221–230

Fordyce WE 1995 Report of the task force on pain in the workplace. Back pain in the workplace: management of disability in non-specific conditions. IASP Press, Seattle

Gifford L S (Ed) 1998 Physiotherapy Pain Association yearbook 1998–1999. Topical issues in pain. Whiplash—science and management. Fear-avoidance beliefs and behaviour. CNS Press, Falmouth

Hazard RG, Fenwick JW, Kalisch SM, Redmond J, Reeves V, Reid S, Frymoyer JW 1989 Funtional restoration with behavioural support: a one-year prospective study of patients with chronic low back pain. Spine 14:157–161

Kendall NAS 1997 developing outcome assessments: a step-by-step approach. NZ Journal of Physiotherapy 25:11–17

Kendall NAS, Linton SJ, Main CJ 1997 Guide to assessing psychosocial yellow flags in acute low back pain: risk factors for long–term disability and work loss.: Accident Rehabilitation & Compensation Insurance Corporation of New Zealand and the National Health Committee, Ministry of Health, Wellington

Lindstrom I, Ohlund C, Eek C, Wallin L, Peterson LE, Fordyce WE, Nachemson AL 1992 The effect of graded activity on patients with subacute low back pain: a randomized prospective clinical study with an operant–conditioning behavioural approach. Physical Therapy 72:279–293

Linton SJ, Bradley LA, Jensen I, Spangfort E, Sundell L 1989 The secondary prevention of low back pain: a controlled study with follow up. Pain 36: 197-207

Linton SJ, Bradley LA 1992 An 18-month follow-up of a secondary prevention programme for back pain: help and hindrance factors related to outcome maintenance. The Clinical Journal of Pain 8: 227–236

Linton SJ, Hellsing A, Andersson D 1993 A controlled study of the effects of an early intervention on acute musculoskeletal pain problems. Pain 54:353–359

Linton SJ, Hallden K 1997 Risk factors and the natural course of acute and recurrent musculoskeletal pain: developing a screening instrument. In: Jensen TS, Turner JA, Wiesenfeld–Hallin Z (Eds) Proceedings of the 8th world congress on pain, progress in pain research and management, Vol 8. IASP Press, Seattle 527–536

Linton SJ, Hallden K 1998 Can we screen for problematic back pain? A screening questionnaire for predicting outcome in acute and subacute back pain. Clinical Journal of Pain 14:209 –215

Mason V 1994 The prevalence of back pain in Great Britain. Office of Population Censuses and Surveys, Social Surveys Division, HMSO, London

Muncey H, Watson PJ 1999 Efficacy of a unidisciplinary outpatient fitness programme for patients with musculoskeletal pain. Abstracts of Annual Scientific Meeting of The Pain Society, Edinburgh

Rose M J 1998 Iatrogenic disability and back pain rehabilitation. In: Gifford L S (Ed) Physiotherapy Pain Association Yearbook 1998–1999. Topical issues in pain. Whiplash—science and management. Fear avoidance behaviour and beliefs. CNS Press, Falmouth 167–172

Spitzer WO, LeBlanc FE, Dupuis M, Abenhaim L, Bloch R, Bomardier C, et al 1987 Scientific approach to the assessment and management of activity-related spinal disorders: a monograph for clinicians. Report of the Quebec Task Force on Spinal Disorders. Spine 12:S4–S59

Waddell G, Feder G, McIntosh A, Lewis M, Hutchinson A 1996 Low back pain evidence review. Royal College of General Practitioners, London

Waddell G 1997 Low back pain: a twentieth-century health care enigma. In: Jensen TS, Turner JA, Wisenfeld-Hallin Z (Eds), Proceedings of the 8th world congress on pain, progress in pain research and management Vol 8. IASP Press, Seattle: 101–112

Waddell G 1998 The back pain revolution. Churchill Livingstone, Edinburgh

Watson PJ 2000 Interdisciplinary pain management in fibromyalgia. In: Chaitow L (ed) Fibromyalgia syndrome: a practitioners guide to treatment. Ch 7. Churchill Livingstone, Edinburgh: 91-109

4

Identifying psychosocial yellow flags and modifying management

NICHOLAS KENDALL, PAUL WATSON

Identifying yellow flags

Consider the following hypothetical case study. You are the therapist who is going to treat this young woman with low back pain.

Presenting problem

Helen is a 19-year-old woman who presented with an 8-week history of recurrent pain arising from the region of her low back. She attributed the problem to her work as an assistant cook. Helen said that the onset of her problem began gradually with a heavy sensation in her back. She was unable to say when she had begun to experience pain. She also emphasised that it was 'sore' rather than painful.

Helen said that at the time of onset she was seeing Dr Smith as her GP but decided to see a different doctor in the group practice, Dr Jones. She reported that she stopped work as an assistant cook 4 weeks previously, was referred to a manual therapist at that time, and has received treatment eight times so far. She has been treated with heat, manipulation, ultrasound, and a specific exercise prescription of extension exercises. It was also suggested to her that she wear a lumbar support if she wanted. Helen has not performed her usual activities, such as housework, for several weeks. In fact, she has been avoiding nearly all activity, preferring to 'take it easy'. She acknowledges that her muscles are weaker than they were.

Work history

Helen said that she left full time education aged 17 and immediately began work in a small supermarket. She took a job in another supermarket for about one year, and then started her current job as an assistant cook. She emphasised that she had 'dropped CVs off everywhere' at supermarkets.

Current presentation

No Red Flag conditions are present. She has no medical history of note and no history of psychological health problems. She does not currently take any prescribed or over-the-counter medication. She has never engaged regularly in exercise or sporting activity. She lives with her boyfriend, who works full time as a mechanic. She described him as 'supportive', although unhelpful with domestic chores. Her mother previously worked in the same assistant cooks job that she is now employed. She has modified her lifestyle since stopping work and reports that she 'stays up late, and sleeps in'.

Administration of the Acute Low Back Pain Screening Questionnaire yielded a score of 144 (see Fig 4.1, pp. 134–5) which indicates the probability of high risk for long-term disability and the need for further assessment (Kendall et al 1997, Linton & Hallden 1997 & 1998). Information about some key issues is needed.

What would you ask Helen? There are at least nine straightforward questions that are relevant to ask.

1 Why did she initially seek health care, and what was she expecting?
2 Why did she consult with another GP?
3 What are her expectations of the treatment, and the treatment provider?
4 What response has she had to treatment so far, has she adhered to treatment?
5 What does she believe is the cause of her pain?
6 Why did she leave her first two jobs working in supermarkets, and does she enjoy her current job?
7 What role does her mother play?
8 How is her employer responding to her back pain?
9 What are her plans regarding lifestyle, activity, and work?

Note that this information could be readily elicited during the course of her next treatment session. Features that are particularly important to identify are:

• the belief that her back pain is harmful or potentially disabling;
• any tendency to avoid movement or activity due to fear that it might hurt;
• any tendency for low mood, or wanting to stay away from being with other people; and
• an expectation that her problem will be simply fixed by passive treatments.

Let us look at this case again, but this time incorporate the details from the answers to the nine questions outlined and then consider the potential for long-term disability and the need to modify her ongoing management.

Presenting problem

Helen is a 19-year-old woman who presented with work-disability, and an 8-week history of recurrent pain arising from the region of her low back. She attributed the problem to her work as an assistant cook. Helen said that the onset of her problem began gradually with a heavy sensation in her back. She was unable to say when she had begun to experience pain, and was very vague about the history of onset and concluded that it began 8 weeks ago. She also emphasised that it was 'sore' rather than painful.

Helen said that at the time of onset she was seeing Dr Smith as her GP but decided to change to another GP in the practice, Dr Jones who is her mother's GP, and complained that 'Dr Smith wasn't doing anything about it, he told me that it was nothing and did not sign me off work'. She explained that Dr Jones 'put me off work and sent me to the physiotherapist'. That is, she gave the clear impression that she expected to be put off work, and this was the main reason she went to see her mother's doctor. With regard to beliefs about the cause of her pain Helen outlined that 'all my muscles are inflamed', and also used the terms 'torn', 'pinched nerve', and added, 'my back goes out'.

Helen stopped work as an assistant cook 4 weeks previously, and was referred to a physiotherapist at that time, and has received eight treatment sessions to date. She has been treated with heat, manipulation, ultrasound, and a specific extension exercise prescription. It was also suggested to her that she wear a lumbar brace for support if she wanted. Helen has not noticed any beneficial effect from this treatment so far, although she admitted that she did not want to say this because she hoped that it might still help her one day soon. When asked about the specific exercises she had been told to do she was able to demonstrate three different movements, and said, 'I try to do them twice a day'. She demonstrated a lack of interest in these exercises, and gave the impression that she was marginally compliant with instructions about specific exercises at best.

She had picked up on the suggestion that wearing some form of lumbar support may be helpful and said that she now wore a brace pretty much constantly, and that other people thought that this was a good idea. She emphasised that her level of discomfort was '0/10' when she had lumbar support. When asked to demonstrate her exercises without the brace on she also said there was no pain or discomfort until she went into forward flexion. She was unwilling to lift any objects, and said that she would not even consider lifting something like a small bag of groceries. Helen has not performed usual activities, such as housework, for several weeks. In fact, she has been avoiding nearly all activity, preferring to 'take it easy' instead. She acknowledges that her muscles are weaker than they were.

Work history

Helen said that she left fulltime education aged 17, and immediately began work in a small supermarket. This job involved quite a lot of lifting, but she did not experience any back pain problems. She enjoyed her job, and had a good relationship with her boss, and only left because she was made redundant. She then took a job in another supermarket for about one year. She said that this boss 'went through a lot of workers', and that she left because she 'wasn't getting on with the boss'. She then started her current job as an assistant cook, which was arranged by her mother who works as a cook at the same restaurant. She initially took this job as an interim measure, intending to get another supermarket job. She emphasised that she had 'dropped CVs off everywhere' at supermarkets.

Physiotherapy Service Back Pain Initial Questionnaire

1. Where do you have pain? Tick boxes for all sites.   (2x sites)
Neck ☐   Shoulders☐   Lower back☐✓   Leg☐   2

2. How many days of work have you missed because of your pain in the past 18 months?
Tick one only   (n)
0 days☐[1]   1-2 days☐[2]   3-7 days☐[3]   8-14 days☐[4]   15-30 days☐[5]   6
1mth☐✓[6]   2 mths☐[7]   3-6 mths☐[8]   6-12 mths☐[9]   over 1 year☐[10]

3. How long have you had your current problem? Tick one only   (n)
0-1 wk☐[1]   1-2 wks☐[2]   2-3 wks☐[3]   4-5 wks☐[4]   6-8 wks☐[5]   6
9-11wks☐✓[6]   3-6 mths☐[7]   6-9 mths☐[8]   9-12mths☐[9]   over 1 year☐[10]

Please circle one number from 0-10 which best describes your answer to the following questions:

4. Is your work heavy or monotonous. Circle the best alternative.
   0   1   2   3   4   5   6   7   (8)   9   10   (n)
   Not at all   *Extremely*   8

5. How would you rate the pain that you have had in the past week?
   0   1   2   (3)   4   5   6   7   8   9   10   (n)
   No Pain   *Pain as bad*   3
                                                 as it could be

6. In the past three months. on average, how bad was your pain?
   0   1   2   (3)   4   5   6   7   8   9   10   (n)
   No Pain   *Pain as bad*   3
                                                 as it could be

7. How often would you say you have experienced pain episodes, on average, during the past 3 months?   (n)
   0   1   2   3   4   5   (6)   7   8   9   10   6
   Never   *Always*

8. Based on all things you do to cope or deal with your pain, on an average day how much are you able to decrease it?
   0   (1)   2   3   4   5   6   7   8   9   10   (10-n)
   Can't decrease   *Can decrease it*   9
   it at all   *completely*

9. How tense and anxious have you felt in the past week?
   0   1   2   3   (4)   5   6   7   8   9   10   (n)
Absolutely calm   *As tense and anxious*   4
and relaxed   *as I've ever felt*

10. How much have you been bothered by feeling depressed in the past week?
   0   1   2   (3)   4   5   6   7   8   9   10   (n)
   Not at all   *Extremely*   9

11. In your view, how large is the risk that your current pain may become persistent?
   0   1   2   3   4   5   6   7   8   (9)   10   (n)
   No risk   *Very large risk*   9

12. In your estimation, what are the chances that you will be working or back to your usual activity in 6 months?
   0   1   (2)   3   4   5   6   7   8   9   10   (10-n)
No chance   *Very large chance*   8

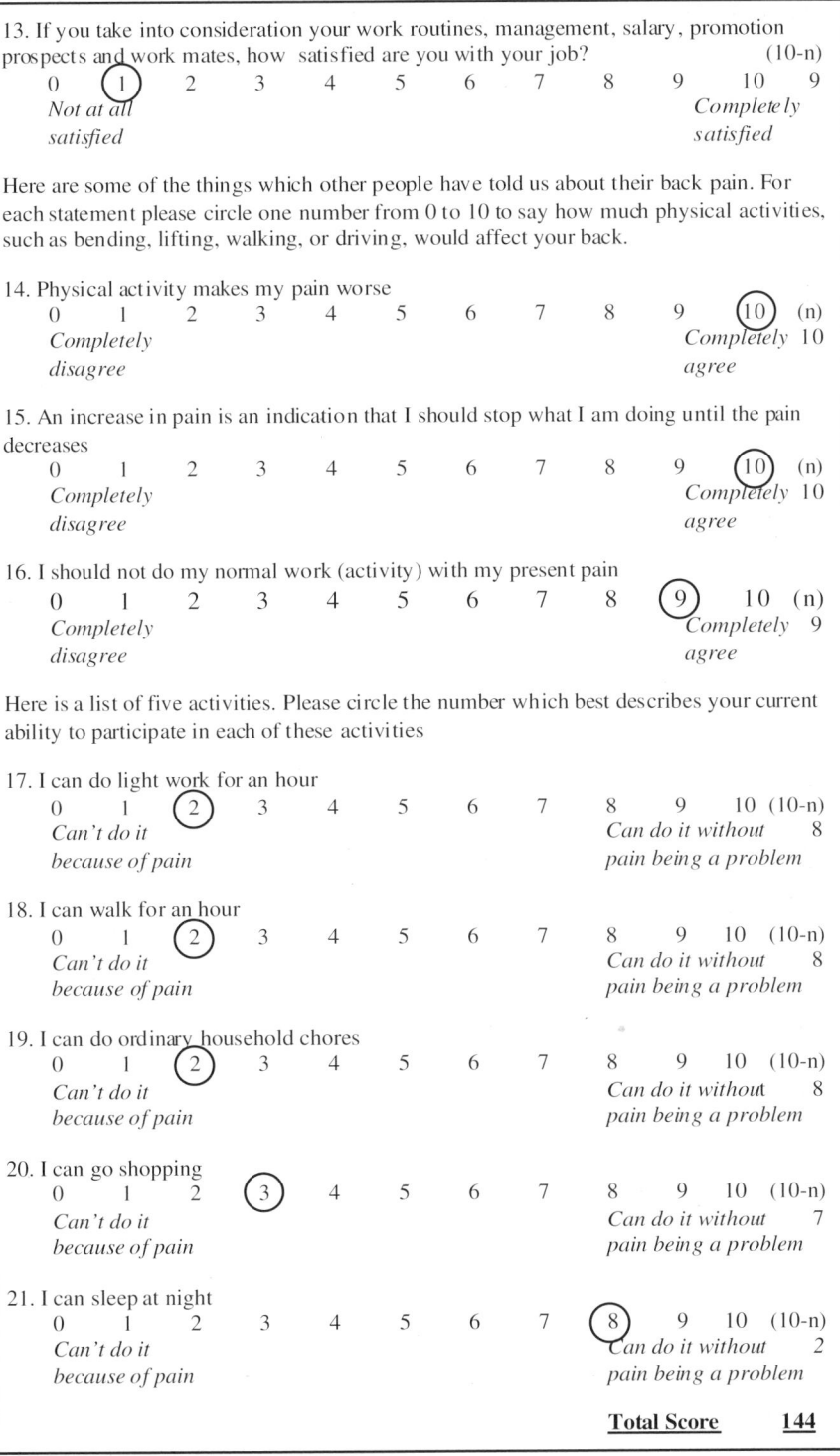

13. If you take into consideration your work routines, management, salary, promotion prospects and work mates, how satisfied are you with your job? (10-n)

0 (1) 2 3 4 5 6 7 8 9 10   9
Not at all   *Completely*
satisfied   *satisfied*

Here are some of the things which other people have told us about their back pain. For each statement please circle one number from 0 to 10 to say how much physical activities, such as bending, lifting, walking, or driving, would affect your back.

14. Physical activity makes my pain worse

0 1 2 3 4 5 6 7 8 9 (10) (n)
Completely   *Completely* 10
disagree   *agree*

15. An increase in pain is an indication that I should stop what I am doing until the pain decreases

0 1 2 3 4 5 6 7 8 9 (10) (n)
Completely   *Completely* 10
disagree   *agree*

16. I should not do my normal work (activity) with my present pain

0 1 2 3 4 5 6 7 8 (9) 10 (n)
Completely   *Completely* 9
disagree   *agree*

Here is a list of five activities. Please circle the number which best describes your current ability to participate in each of these activities

17. I can do light work for an hour

0 1 (2) 3 4 5 6 7 8 9 10 (10-n)
Can't do it   *Can do it without*   8
because of pain   *pain being a problem*

18. I can walk for an hour

0 1 (2) 3 4 5 6 7 8 9 10 (10-n)
Can't do it   *Can do it without*   8
because of pain   *pain being a problem*

19. I can do ordinary household chores

0 1 (2) 3 4 5 6 7 8 9 10 (10-n)
Can't do it   *Can do it without*   8
because of pain   *pain being a problem*

20. I can go shopping

0 1 2 (3) 4 5 6 7 8 9 10 (10-n)
Can't do it   *Can do it without*   7
because of pain   *pain being a problem*

21. I can sleep at night

0 1 2 3 4 5 6 7 (8) 9 10 (10-n)
Can't do it   *Can do it without*   2
because of pain   *pain being a problem*

Total Score   **144**

Fig. 4.1 Helen's responses to the Acute Low Back Pain Screening Questionnaire (Linton and Halden 1998)

However, she has not been actively seeking work to date and has not made any follow-up calls to prospective employers, instead passively waiting for them to phone her and say there is a job.

Current presentation

She presented as passive, and sub-assertive. She described herself as a hard worker, and said that she 'goes hard at it' when she is at work. She said strongly that she does not enjoy her job. No Red Flag conditions are present. She has no medical history of note and no history of psychological health problems. She does not currently take any prescribed or over-the-counter medication. She has never engaged regularly in exercise or sporting activity. She lives with her boyfriend, who works full time as a mechanic. She described him as 'supportive', although unhelpful with domestic chores. She has modified her lifestyle since stopping work, including 'staying up late, and sleeping in'. She said that she has been regularly sleeping in until 10 am. Her mother previously worked in the role as assistant cook in which she is currently employed and 10 years ago 'she got a bad back as well', and had back surgery with a very good outcome; it was Dr Jones who arranged for her mother to have surgery. Helen perceives that this helped her mother, and both she and her mother are wondering if Helen is going to need surgery also. Her mother continues to work as the senior cook in the same restaurant as Helen.

Potential for long-term disability

When her Acute Low Back Pain Screening Questionnaire is reviewed (see Fig. 4.1) it is noticed that she endorsed strong agreement with the items that indicate fear-avoidance: *Physical activity makes my pain worse*; *An increase in pain is an indication that I should stop what I am doing until the pain decreases*; and, *I should not do my normal work with my present pain*. Endorsement of these items may reflect either biomechanical limitations, or learned behaviour involving fear of movement due to the apprehension that pain might occur, or a mixture of both. As a therapist you must judge the relative contribution of each. In considering the potential for long-term disability we might conclude that Helen is of at least moderate risk, unless she is soon returned to her usual activities and participation in work. She has developed beliefs about her musculoskeletal system that are contributing to avoidant behaviour. She has also developed limited lifestyle substitution as a result of being off work, and is exhibiting some loss of work habits. Her style of working probably places her at risk of excessive biomechanical strain on her musculoskeletal system.

Modifying management

For this hypothetical case a number of possibilities arise. The following would be worthy of consideration:

1   Address her beliefs about her musculoskeletal system. It is important that she believes her discomfort will almost certainly go away, and that it is both manageable and controllable.

2   Modify her behaviour so that she stops guarding her lower back. She needs the consequences of long term disuse explained to her clearly. A graduated increase in activity is indicated at this stage, based on the principle ***Do no more on good days, and no less on bad ones***. That is, her activity increase should be on a quota basis, and not contingent on her subjective experience of pain or discomfort. She should set goals for increased activity and these must be monitored.

3   Recognise her potential to place excessive strain on her musculoskeletal system, by failing to pace herself when working or doing activities such as housework. She should be encouraged to perform work and activities with a smoother level of participation, and not a 'boom-bust' approach going from high levels to little or nothing. Her co-workers or supervisors may be able to assist with this. Her mother is the cook in charge of the kitchen and allocates tasks.

4   Her return to work should be carefully managed, but instituted as soon as possible in order to negate the potential for lifestyle substitution that has already begun. Important goals will be to increase her workload gradually, but not to allow the increase to level out at a plateau below her usual level. Failure to achieve either of these will increase the probability of long-term work loss. Any graded return to normal activity must be *time limited*. Helen must set dates for when she will return to *all* usual work tasks.

5   She should be encouraged to actively seek the type of work that she has identified as most enjoyable to her. Her present approach is relatively passive, and unlikely to be successful in the current labour market unless she is very lucky.

6   The expectation of a full recovery within a limited period of time without the need for ongoing support from the sickness benefits system, should be outlined to her. She should be strongly encouraged to adopt a self-management approach, and aim for full independence as soon as possible.

7   Helen should be encouraged to set goals in her social and domestic activities and re-engage with her usual lifestyle in the same way as she is encouraged to return to work.

Note that each one of these suggested management strategies is fully compatible with the provision of ongoing manual therapy, if that is judged to be necessary. However, if she continued to report little symptom modification following treatment its value may rapidly become questionable—other than as a means to motivate her to increase her activity levels.

Outcome

Helen agreed an action plan (see Box 1) with her therapist. In addition to the plan below she outlined specific goals for her work, social activity and specific exercises and kept a record of her progress. She agreed with her supervisor that she would return to work half-time for four weeks and progress to full time after this. However, she also agreed that for the time remaining before returning to work she would increase her activity and look for another job.

The aim of this was to reintroduce a period of activity of similar length to a working day. At the end of the four week period she returned to work but soon after handed in her notice and started work in a supermarket.

Box 1 Helen's action plan

My plan for return to work and normal activity

It is essential that you develop your own action plan to help you return to your normal lifestyle. Fill in this Action Plan with the help of your physiotherapist.

Home

I have difficulties with the following activities:

Hoovering, Carrying heavy bags

While I am improving I can make these activities easier by:

Pacing the hoovering; only doing half a room going on to one room at a time. Carrying smaller bags–getting my boyfriend to come shopping with me!

As I build myself up I will measure progress by:

1. Being able to go shopping.
2. Doing all my own housework.
3. Going out to the pub.
4. Getting back to work part-time then back to work full-time without help with the lifting.

Workplace

Parts of my job I may have difficulties with:

Lifting heavy pans (10-12Kg); Lifting heavy bags of food (up to 20kg) from floor to work heights.
Standing for long periods preparing food.

Ways I can get around these difficulties:

Ask others to lift pans until I feel strong enough and confident enough to lift again.
Take 'mini-breaks' to do stretches, or take breaks from standing still and walk around kitchen.
Break up large bags of food into manageable sizes for lifting and carrying. Use trolley to move bags.

How can the physio help me?

Show me how to lift properly in physiotherapy with heavier and heavier weights.
Help with back strengthening exercises.
Help me to get fitter.
Tell me what to do if it happens again.

Things I need to talk to my boss or supervisor about:

Getting help with lifting for the first four weeks after my getting back to work. By the end of this time I will be back to my normal lifting.

Other problems at work that I need to deal with, how I can solve them and who I need to talk to about them:

I do not like the work I am doing. I will drop off CVs at supermarkets personally and follow this up with a phone call to the manager. I will try to get a different job.

Things I enjoy about my work:

It gets me out of the house.
I get paid for it.
Talking to other people and having a laugh.

Comment

We acknowledge that in the UK physiotherapists are not normally involved in the work activities of their patients. Indeed many people who are referred to physiotherapy departments may not be employed. The authors feel strongly that unless the rehabilitation of the individual includes plans for a return to all normal activities, rehabilitation has not been achieved. Symptom management, a reduction in pain, is not rehabilitation and physiotherapists should rehabilitate.

From this brief case study you can see that the aim of the yellow flags assessment is to integrate the psychosocial assessment into a rehabilitation plan that is individualised and relevant to the patient. Group work can be useful in managing patients but **all** patients require an individual plan of action with appropriate, relevant, personal goals and individual monitoring of progress if rehabilitation is to be successful.

REFERENCES

Kendall NAS, Linton SJ, Main CJ 1997 Guide to assessing psychosocial yellow flags in acute low back pain: risk factors for the development of long-term disability and work loss. Wellington, New Zealand: Accident and Compensation Insurance Corporation of New Zealand, and the National Health Committee, Ministry of Health

Linton SJ, Hallden K 1997 Risk factors and the natural course of acute and recurrent musculoskeletal pain: development of a screening instrument. In: Jensen TS, Turner JA, Weisenfeld-Hallin Z (Eds). Proceedings of the 8th world congress on pain, progress on pain research and management. IASP Press, Seattle

Linton SJ, Hallden K 1998 Can we screen for problematic back pain? A screening questionnaire for predicting outcome in acute and sub-acute back pain. The Clinical Journal Of Pain 14:209–215

5

Pain: perception and attitudes

JENNIFER KLABER MOFFETT

The way in which pain is perceived by individuals, their attitude to and understanding of it, needs to be considered carefully by all health care professionals dealing with musculoskeletal pain. Therapists and other clinicians could improve their effectiveness if psychological influences were always taken into account.

Past and present experience

Childhood

Childhood experiences may contribute to how an individual deals with pain. The influence will be through both social modelling and social conditioning as discussed below. Role models in childhood, like our parents and peers, play an important part in shaping our behaviour. Parents' attitudes and behaviour towards pain or injury may be either stoical, ignoring pain, or at the other extreme very cautious—at the least sign of a headache the need for rest and a darkened room become apparent; or commonly, a child is allowed to stay away from school with a minor ailment. This may lead to over solicitous behaviour in later life towards themselves, offspring and other members of the family, friends, and colleagues. It could in part explain why some people when confronted with pain are very passive and use rest a lot. Also these people may express excessive sympathy in response to minor illnesses and injuries in others. People who have been brought up by parents with a more stoical attitude are in turn likely to expect more stoical behaviour from themselves and others in later life.

Social modelling

Observational learning is one of the main ways in which new patterns of behaviour are acquired (Bandura 1986), and is also relevant to pain behaviour. In the literature this type of learning it is referred to as social modelling. If an individual is exposed to someone else displaying intense and prolonged pain complaints anomalous patterns of pain behaviour may develop (Craig 1986). Conversely, observation of toleration of pain and stoical behaviour may reduce an individual's reaction to pain.

Experiments

A number of interesting experiments (which would not now get through ethical approval) have been reported in the psychological literature. For example, Craig demonstrated experimentally, using shock-induced pain, that observation of a tolerant model can greatly increase an individual's tolerance levels (Craig and Weiss 1971). In this study, subjects were prepared to tolerate a much stronger electric shock if they had observed 'another subject' (who was actually an actor) apparently tolerating a strong shock well. Conversely, subjects who had observed 'another subject' tolerating much less were themselves prepared to tolerate a weaker shock. The difference in tolerance demonstrated by this experiment was almost twofold (9.93 mA compared with 5.43 mA). Both the sensory and affective components of pain could be influenced in this way. Craig (1989) showed in further experiments that social modelling was more influential than personality variables, but the two can interact. The message seems to be that we are all prone to social modelling. Our own behaviour and attitudes are likely to influence those of other people around us including our patients.

Clinical setting

In the clinical setting other patients will also become role models. Therapists can take advantage of this by introducing their patients to someone who has been through a similar process and responded in a positive way. Allowing them to hear about the experiences of a treatment such as surgery or intensive rehabilitation can be useful prior to their undergoing it themselves. It could reduce the likelihood of an extreme reaction and be reassuring, especially for a more nervous individual or for a child.

Social conditioning

Both in childhood and throughout our adult life our behaviour is shaped or conditioned depending on the response received. For example, a parent who always over-responds to a child's crying following a very minor graze or bump will condition the child to expect attention for this behaviour and reinforce the behaviour. This is probably especially true where this is the only way in which the child can get attention from the parent. These and other social influences in early childhood, especially if extreme, can in part explain aberrant response to pain in later life, and should be taken into consideration by the health professional. Social influences continue throughout life to have an impact on our behaviour.

A partner's reaction to complaints of musculoskeletal pain are important factors to consider (see Chs 3, 6 & 7). Over sympathetic response to pain reports can markedly increase levels of pain reporting and in particular lead to disability through inactivity and disuse in more extreme cases. There is a case for involving the family in any programme of treatment if at all possible. The effect of repeatedly rewarding a person complaining of pain with sympathy or attention may be to inadvertently reinforce the problem. Even encouraging rest or a reduction in activity may condition the person to behave more like an ill person.

The physiotherapist may also inadvertently condition individuals to expect pain and encourage them to respond to it. Unless the physiotherapist is quite clear and explains to the patient that *hurt* is not the same as *harm* the impression may be gained that the person should be guided by the pain. This approach is important, particularly in chronic pain. It may also be important, even in more acute presentations of pain, to take into consideration the individual's attitude to pain. The therapist by focussing repeatedly on the pain and the 'pain behaviour' may heighten the patients' awareness of their problem. Unintentionally, it can be a form of conditioning which is probably very common in many therapist-patient encounters. It is counterproductive, if not iatrogenic (see Rose 1998). In order to avoid this, therapists would do well to concentrate more on improving function.

The influence of emotions on pain perception

Pain perception may be modulated through anxiety, depression, anger and other emotions via the autonomic nervous system (ANS) (Craig 1989). A raised ANS response may increase activity in the viscera and in the skeletal muscles.

Stress, anxiety and muscle tension

An increase in muscle tension may be an important factor in perpetuating a vicious cycle of pain with stress and anxiety leading to further increases in muscle tension. The relationship between pain, stress, and hyperactivity is complex and is still the subject of much discussion (e.g. Ohrbach & McCall 1996, Flor & Turk 1996). Central plastic changes may be mediators of this process. In chronic pain patients, increases in muscle tension caused by stress or pain become associated with neutral stimuli and 'memories for pain' are laid down through classical conditioning. However, high levels of muscle tension which increase chronic pain may be protective in acute pain. This may then become a learned response. According to Flor and Birbaumer (1991) chronic pain patients may interpret increased muscle tension as painful stimuli, although there is evidence to show that they cannot distinguish between levels of muscle tension as well as non-pain patients. Patients with chronic pain may become preoccupied with physical symptoms. Anxiety and somatic complaints, according to McCreary et al (1980), are the most important predictors of chronicity (but see Chs 2 & 3). Also, studies of EMG on chronic back pain patients (Flor et al 1985) provide evidence for a relationship between anxiety (as measured by the state form of the State-Trait Anxiety Inventory (Spielberger 1970)) reported pain, and spinal immobility.

Depression and somatisation

Depression can be considered to be the result of cognitive schema (thought patterns) leading to a negative view of the self, the world, and the future (Beck 1967). It has sometimes been considered in terms of a learned helplessness model (e.g. Seligman 1972). Every clinician will at times encounter patients who appear to be reluctant to help themselves. They are passive and dependent in their attitude and may have learned to think in a very negative way. These patients may be difficult to work with and fail to respond to advice or treatment. Often these people's thoughts are focussed on their bodily symptoms which in turn may become exaggerated. There is some evidence that depression and somatisation in back pain patients can be predictive of poor outcome (Main et al 1992) (see Ch. 2).

Somatisation or paying undue attention to bodily function can also be considered from another theoretical framework, and will now be discussed under the heading of thought processes or cognitions.

Cognitions

Selective attention

An individual is, during waking hours, constantly assailed with information which has to be processed to decide which of the information needs to be attended to. This process which controls the perception of external stimuli, is referred to as selective attention (Keele & Neill 1978, Triesman 1966). There is much evidence to show that the same processes control the perception of internal stimuli, i.e. physical symptoms such as pain (Pennebaker 1982, Chapman 1978, Weinman 1987). The nervous system is constantly being bombarded with a barrage of sensory signals. These multiple messages are integrated at a higher level of the nervous system to provide the individual with an organised meaningful message (Chapman 1978). The perception of pain depends on selective attention and the filtering of relevant messages. According to Chapman (1978), the probability of noticing internal bodily cues can be expressed as a function of the ratio of the strength or salience of internal information over external stimuli. If a patient is asked to concentrate on and report any pain experienced whilst a physiotherapist is examining and handling anatomical structures such as muscles and joints, an exaggerated pain response may result. By contrast, the same individual may be able to reduce pain by means of distraction, if they are absorbed in some demanding or enjoyable activity (Barsky 1986).

Melzack and Wall's widely documented gate theory of pain (Melzack & Wall 1965), although not totally substantiated, is conceptually useful in explaining the complexity of these processes. The theory, which has been restated to include more up to date neurophysiological findings, has generated an enormous quantity of research (Melzack & Wall 1996). It provides a basis for understanding that pain experienced is not necessarily directly related to tissue damage. Nociceptive input is modulated by means of a gating mechanism situated in the dorsal horn cells of the spinal cord. Sensory messages pass along two different types of nerve fibre. The first are the small diameter, unmyelinated (A-delta and C) nerve fibres along which impulses pass facilitating the opening of the gating system, allowing synaptic transmission to T-cells that convey rostrally. The other type of sensory nerve fibre is the large diameter (A-beta) nerve fibres which carry impulses that in the first moments after injury tend to close the gate and prevent nociceptive impulses passing from synapses in the spinal cord to the brain to be processed as pain. Local interneurones and descending nerve fibre tracts from the brain also impact on the activity of the T-cell and can thus facilitate or inhibit activity too (Fields & Basbaum 1994) . Since the gate theory included this 'connection' to higher brain centres it is especially useful in explaining the role of central modulating mechanisms such as affective and cognitive processes which influence the perception of pain.

Thus the 'gate' can be opened and closed via psychophysiological pathways descending to the dorsal horn and to other areas of the brain involved in selective attention. A person's thoughts, emotions, beliefs, and attention may have a profound influence on the gating mechanism directly affecting the pain experienced.

Vigilance

The awareness of an internal sensation depends on a number of factors. Pennebaker (1982) carried out a large number of controlled experiments mainly on normal subjects. He concluded that reporting of physical symptoms and pain depend on:

1 The magnitude of the internal receptor stimulus;
2 The amount of available information (in which a good clinician may play a vital role in defusing a situation perceived by the patient as threatening);
3 The individual's beliefs that may cause him to selectively attend to internal states, in the context of the pain;
4 A tendency to attend to internal sensations.

Vigilance plays an important role in the perception of pain. Attention to self increases the likelihood of psychological and physiological symptoms and negative evaluation (Barsky 1979, Mechanic 1986). Those who have heightened self awareness, termed 'perceivers', are very ready to respond to weak and infrequent sensory signals (Mackworth 1976).

Pennebaker (1982) reported an experiment carried out by the biologist Adams (1980) which demonstrated that sensations are constantly being processed by an individual although they do not necessarily reach conscious levels of awareness. The experiment showed how through learning and attention these processes could be perceived. A small rubber balloon on the end of a tube was inserted into the small intestine of an experimental subject, a common procedure for examination of the jejunum or duodenum. While it was inflated and deflated electroencephalogram (EEG) readings were taken from the brain. These showed that the activity had registered in the brain, but the subject had no awareness of the activity. In the second part of the experiment the subject was trained by means of feedback to become aware of a sensation in his intestine when the balloon was being deflated and inflated. He learnt to be aware of an internal sensation to which he had previously been oblivious, and was able to identify correctly when inflation was taking place without any external cues. Attentional processes operate in conjunction with the memory system (Weinmann 1987). It seems that learning and the filtering of relevant messages can play an important role in the perception of physical symptoms especially pain (Fordyce 1976).

There is some evidence that selective attention and vigilance are influenced by beliefs, attitudes and expectations (Pennebaker 1982). Therefore, when a clinician examines or palpates the spine and asks the patient to say if it hurts the chances of a positive response are high. 'Let me know if you feel anything apart from pressure, while I find out how your joints are moving' might produce a different response. Selective monitoring of physical symptoms not only affects the quality and severity of perceived pain, but these are also dependent on the subject's cognitive schema and experience. The pain experienced may be influenced by polarisation of attitudes, for example in the clinical setting suggestion of benefit of treatment, or the reassurance that can be provided following history taking and a physical examination. If patients are informed that ligaments, bones and muscles are strong and that they all benefit from movement even in the presence of pain, they are more likely to respond positively to an active management strategy. The importance of thought processes in reporting symptoms are illustrated in an experiment carried out by Pennebaker (1982). Subjects were asked to run or walk on the spot for two minutes. Half had had their attention drawn to 'flu bugs being around'. The control group (to whom flu had not been mentioned) described any sensation such as raised temperature, sweating, fatigue, or aching muscles in terms of arousal related to the activity (rather than sickening for flu). The subjects who had the idea of flu in their heads were more likely to report these sensations as flu symptoms.

According to Skelton and Pennebaker (1982), once an individual is aware of a bodily sensation, selective monitoring occurs, and he will adopt an explanatory hypothesis that is based on past experience or knowledge (see Ch. 6). It seems that the individual then searches for verification of the process. It may be possible for a therapist to modify the patients' interpretation of their pain, by providing appropriate information. However, an established set or cognitive schema may be difficult to alter (Flor et al 1990). Individuals need not only to alter their hypothesis, but also to actively encode the new information within the restructured hypothesis (Massad et al 1979).

Suggestion, faith and credibility

There is, however, evidence that suggestion and faith can play an important role in pain relief (Plotkin 1985). They can provide a powerful tool in the clinical setting encouraging patients to expect a positive outcome of the treatment they are undergoing. Langley and colleagues (1984) carried out an ingenious experiment to test the analgesic effect of transcutaneous nerve stimulation (TNS). Importantly, they made sure that all the subjects had not previously experienced TNS and for the placebo control group they used suggestion by providing sham visual 'feedback'. Here, the subjects were apparently wired up to an oscilloscope on which they could see a pattern of pulsed waves suggesting the current that they expected to receive, but this was in fact fake as the subjects did not receive any input. This increased the credibility of the placebo and provided distraction. The result was that there was no difference in response between the active and placebo groups.

The placebo effect is strongly related to a positive expectation of recovery or pain reduction. Individuals then will behave as a 'well person' and may perceive themselves as 'cured'. This practical application of a psychological process is used intuitively by physiotherapists and other health professionals.

The meaning of the pain

It is important for people to understand that when pain accompanies activity, harm is not automatically implied. It does not necessarily mean that they are damaging themselves. Once this is understood pain perception is likely to be less distressing. Following exercise programmes for back pain, especially if cognitive behavioural principles are used, a decrease in *distressing* pain is often reported, although the *intensity* of the pain is unaffected (Klaber Moffett et al 1999) or changes less (Frost et al 1995). Great care should be taken by the therapist to be sure that misconceptions have not led the individuals to believe that they have a sinister or progressive disease. Misunderstandings may commonly occur and an improvement in communication can also result in a significantly better outcome in treatment.

Influence of the therapist-patient relationship

Perceived control

Perceived control and self efficacy both play an important role in pain management, as well as in rehabilitation and health care generally (Partridge & Johnston 1989, O'Leary 1985). Partridge has shown that perceived control can be increased simply through writing to patients on a waiting list for physiotherapy to inform them that their recovery would depend on their own efforts during the rehabilitation process. Dependence on health care professionals is not advantageous for the patient. Active participation in their treatment is likely to be a prerequisite to long term success enabling the individuals to feel that they can cope on their own (see Ch. 2).

Self efficacy expectancy

A self-efficacy expectancy has been defined as 'a belief about one's ability to perform a specific behaviour' (Jensen et al 1991). How individuals cope with pain can in part be explained by social learning theory. This suggests that people engage in coping activities that they believe are within their capability and which they believe will lead to a successful outcome. Learning through observing others, verbal persuasion, and performance attainments can all influence a person's self-efficacy expectancy (Bandura 1986). However, successful attainment of a desired behaviour (e.g. carrying out a physical activity) is an especially powerful tool for increasing self-efficacy expectancies and has been shown to be an important factor in exercise programmes (Dolce et al 1986, Council et al 1988).

Chronic back pain patients who attended an exercise programme designed to increase confidence in using the spine normally increased their reported self-efficacy for coping with pain (Frost et al 1995). A self help management programme for chronic arthritis patients which was developed over a twelve year period has been demonstrated to be more effective when measures to enhance self-efficacy were included (Lorig & Gonzalez 1992). Therefore self-efficacy is an important concept in the management of patients with chronic musculoskeletal pain.

Clinical implications

All the processes discussed above may influence individuals' perception of pain and their attitude towards it. The processes are complex and overlap but for convenience are presented in summary in Box 1.

Most important is that the clinician should appreciate that the perception of pain is not closely related to tissue damage. It is much more strongly influenced by thoughts, feelings and attitudes, all of which can be modified by the way in which the clinician talks to and interacts with the patient. The choice of words which the practitioner uses and the way in which they are interpreted can be very powerful in either aiding or hindering recovery (see Harding 1998). It may be useful for the physiotherapist to think of most patients' pain problem being due to dysfunction rather than damage (Waddell 1998). This is then the basis for encouraging movement and return to normal activities and facilitate active rehabilitation.

The key seems to be to enable patients to become individuals who know they can help themselves overcome their problem.

Box 1 Influences on pain perception and attitudes

- Social modelling
  - In childhood
  - At home and socially
  - In the clinical setting—other patients

- Social conditioning
  - In childhood
  - At home and socially
  - In the clinical setting—doctors, therapists and nurses

- Affective states
  - Anxiety
  - Depression
  - Somatic concern

- Cognitions
  - Selective attention and vigilance
  - Expectations: suggestion, faith, credibility
  - Meaning of the pain

- Influence of the therapist-patient relationship should:
  - Encourage self-efficacy and a sense of self control
  - Encourage positive but realistic expectations
  - Avoid reinforcing pain behaviour or fear of movement.

REFERENCES

Bandura A 1986 Social foundations of thought and action. Prentice-Hall, New Jersey

Barsky A 1979 Patients who amplify bodily sensations. Annals of Internal Medicine 91(1):63–70

Barsky A 1986 Palliation and symptomatic relief. Archives of Internal Medicine 146:905–909

Beck A 1967 Depression. Harper & Rowe, New York

Chapman C 1978 Pain: perception of noxious events. In: Sternbach R (Ed) The psychology of pain. Raven Press, New York

Council J, Ahern D, Follick M, Kline C 1988 Expectancies and functional impairment in chronic low back pain. Pain 33:323–331

Craig K, Weiss S 1971 Vicarious influences on pain-threshold determinations. Journal of Personality and Social Psychology 19:53–59

Craig K 1986 Social modeling influences; pain in context. In: Sternbach R (Ed) Psychology of Pain 2nd edn. Raven Press, New York

Craig K 1989 Emotional aspects of pain. In: Wall P, Melzack R (Eds) Textbook of pain. Churchill Livingstone 220–230

Dolce J, Crocker M, Moletierre C, Doleys D 1986 Exercise quotas, anticipatory concern and self-efficacy expectations in chronic pain: a preliminary report. Pain 24:365–372

Fields H L, Basbaum A I 1994 Central nervous system mechanisms of pain modulation. In: Wall P D, Melzack R (Eds) Textbook of pain 3rd edn. Churchill Livingstone, Edinburgh 243–257

Flor H, Turk D, Birbaumer N 1985 Assessment of stress-related psychophysiological reactions in chronic back pain patients. Journal of Consulting and Clinical Psychology 53:354–364

Flor H, Birbaumer N 1988 Stress related responses in chronic pain patients. Annual Meeting of the Society of Psychophysiological Research, San Francisco

Flor H, Birbaumer N, Turk D 1990 The psychobiology of chronic pain. Advances in Behavioural Research and Therapy 12:47–84

Flor H, Birbaumer N 1991 Comprehensive assessment and treatment of chronic back pain patients without physical disabilities. In: Bond M, Charlton J, Woolf C (Eds) Proceedings of World Congress in Pain, Adelaide, Australia. Elsevier, Amsterdam 229–234

Flor H, Turk D C 1996 Integrating central and peripheral mechanisms in chronic muscular pain. An initial step on a long road. Pain Forum 5(1):74–76

Fordyce W 1976 Behavioral methods for chronic pain and illness. CV Mosby, St Louis

Frost H, Klaber Moffett J, Moser J, Fairbank J 1995 Evaluation of a fitness programme for patients with chronic low back pain. British Medical Journal 310:151–154

Harding V 1998 Are we being patientist? In: Gifford L S (ed) Physiotherapy Pain Association Yearbook 1998-1999. Topical issues in pain: Whiplash science and management. Fear avoidance beliefs and behaviour. CNS press, Falmouth 193–198

Jensen M, Turner J, Romano J, Karoly P 1991 Coping with chronic pain: a critical review of the literature. Pain 47:249–283

Keele S, Neill W 1978 Mechanisms of attention. In: Carterette E, Friedman M (Eds). Handbook of Perceptions: Academic Press, New York

Klaber Moffett J, Torgerson D, Bell-Syer S, Jackson D, Llewelyn Phillips H, Farrin A, et al 1999 A randomised trial of exercise for primary care back pain patients: Clinical outcomes, costs and preferences. British Medical Journal 319:279–283

Langley G, Sheppeard H, Johnson M, Wigley R 1984 The analgesic effects of transcutaneous electrical nerve stimulation and placebo in chronic pain patients. Rheumatology International 4:119–123

Lorig K, Gonzalez V 1992 The integration of theory with practice: a 12-year case study. Health Education Quarterly 19(3):355–368

Mackworth J 1976 Development of attention. In: Hamilton V, Vernon M (Eds) The development of cognitive processes. Academic Press, London

McCreary C, Turner J, Dawson E 1980 Emotional disturbance and chronic low back pain. Journal of Clinical Psychology 36(3):709–715

Main C, Wood P, Hollis S, Spanswick C, Waddell G 1992 The distress and risk assessment method. A simple patient classification to identify distress and evaluate the risk of poor outcome. Spine 17(1):42–52

Massad C, Hubbard M, Newtson D 1979 Selective perception of events. Journal of Experimental Social Psychology 15:513–532

Mechanic D 1986 Illness behaviour: an overview. In: McHugh S, Vallis T (Eds) Illness Behavior. Plenum Press, New York

Melzack R, Wall P 1965 Pain mechanisms: a new theory. Science 150:971–979

Melzack R, Wall P D 1996 The challenge of pain. Penguin, Harmondsworth

Ohrbach R, McCall W D 1996 The stress-hyperactivity pain theory of myogenic pain. Proposal for a revised theory. Pain Forum 5(1):51–66

O'Leary A 1985 Self-efficacy and health. Behavior Research and Therapy 23(4):437–451

150

Partridge C, Johnston M 1989 Perceived control of recovery from physical disability: measurement and prediction. British Journal of Clinical Psychology 28:53–59

Pennebaker J 1982 The psychology of physical symptoms. Springer-Verlag, New York

Plotkin W 1985 A psychological approach to placebo: the role of faith in therapy and treatment. In: White L, Tursky B, Schwartz G (Eds) Placebo: theory, research, and mechanisms. Guildford Press, Oxford 237–254

Rose M J 1998 Iatrogenic disability and back pain rehabilitation. In: Gifford LS (ed) Topical issues in Pain. Whiplash—science and management. Fear avoidance behaviour and beliefs. Physiotherapy Pain Association Yearbook 1998–1999 CNS Press, Falmouth 167–172

Seligman M 1972 Learned helplessness. Annual Review of Medicine 23:407–412

Skelton J, Pennebaker J 1982 The psychology of physical symptoms and sensations. In: Sanders G, Suls J (Eds) Social psychology of health and illness. Lawrence Erlbaum Associates, New Jersey

Spielberger C, Gorsuch R, Lushene R 1970 Manual for the State-Trait Anxiety Inventory. Consulting Psychologists Press, Palo Alto

Triesman A 1966 Human attention. In: Foss B (Ed) New horizons in psychology. Penguin, Harmondsworth

Waddell G 1998 The back pain revolution. Churchill Livingstone, Edinburgh

Weinman J 1987 An outline of psychology as applied to medicine 2nd edn. Wright, London

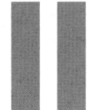

Relationships and pain

6

Pain 'stories'

HAZEL O'DOWD

Fellowship is heaven, and lack of fellowship is hell:
Fellowship is life, and lack of fellowship is death...
William Morris, A Dream of John Ball (1888)

Relationships have a critical bearing on our mental and physical health (Martin 1997). However, relationships, be they with partners, family, friends, colleagues or professionals, can be a two-edged sword. An essential feature of human life, they can be a source of succour or a source of stress. They can enhance or encumber how an individual copes with any health problem.

In this chapter, the way in which relationships contribute to the genesis and maintenance of the pain experience, and how they can affect management, will be reviewed through a relatively new field of the psychological sciences—the use of narrative.

Narrative psychology (Epston & White 1990) is a branch of academic psychology that looks in detail at the theories or, in their terms, the 'stories' people develop to explain what is happening to them. In challenging the notion of linear causality (derived from Newtonian physics), narrative psychology posits that the understanding or meaning any of us attributes to events in our lives is shaped by the context in which they occur. Human sense organs, for example, can only detect change or difference. This automatically includes a temporal (time related) dimension; how things were, compared to how they are now. Time is essential for the perception of difference.

In describing any problem, the patient will use a temporal perspective that maps the 'career' of the presenting difficulty. This is presented in the form of a story, with a clear beginning, middle, end, and prospective future. The way people make sense of their lives is by narrating their own stories and listening to the stories of others. More than that, we are also surrounded by popular cultural stories in the media, novels, films and television.

Some stories appear more frequently than others and are experienced by the majority. For example, the dominant story regarding pain is the acute model. As a result, what people hear (and expect) is that pain signifies damage, and that with time and adequate medical care it will diminish.

Of course other explanations or stories also exist to explain pain, but they are heard less frequently and lie outside of the linear causality paradigm, so dominant in many health care models. As a result, they are unfamiliar to people and are misheard and misunderstood.

Often our colleagues, clients and their families will hold their different stories quite strongly and consequently find it difficult to hear and act upon alternatives. In physiotherapy practice this frequently presents as either clients, family or colleagues assuming that if no cause can be found, then the pain cannot exist. The consequences of adopting this story are lowered self-esteem in the client, and accusations of malingering in the wider social network.

The biopsychosocial model refutes this story of a linear causality and instead tells a tale of a more complex, interacting sub-system. The links in this sub-system are mediated by relationships.

There are three types of relationship relevant to the pain sufferer:

1   Relationships with the pain itself
2   Relationships with family, friends and the wider social world
3   Relationships with professionals.

The purpose of any intervention, therefore, must be to alter one or all of these relationships. Through this process, unhelpful beliefs can be altered and problem stories can be edited and 're-authored' (McLeod 1998).

However, this change fails to take place through the simple delivery of facts alone. In order to bring about change, more recent research and theoretical literature is now making the distinction between process and outcome.

Outcome refers to the benefit to the patient at the end of any intervention. Process, on the other hand, refers to what actually happens during the intervention, the interaction between the therapist and the client. The interaction is dynamic and temporal. Through the process, a new meaning can be co-created. The new meaning or understanding leads to change. 'Process' is what produces 'outcome' in any type of relationship.

The three key relationships identified above will now be considered in more detail.

Relationships with the pain

One problem in working with pain is the variation in how it is experienced, and the inadequacy of the language we have to describe it in ourselves and in others. Pain is a multifactorial construct which includes sensory and affective qualities as well as degrees of intensity etc. There is some evidence that doctors and patients may not attribute the same meanings to the often metaphorical, common pain terms such as 'sore', 'burning' or 'sharp' (Melzack & Torgerson 1971).

Helman (1990) states that:

> How pain is described is influenced by a number of factors, including language facility, familiarity with medical terms, individual experiences of pain, and lay beliefs about the structure and function of the body. ... The use of the technical terms borrowed from medicine to describe pain may also confuse the clinician: the patient who says 'I've had another migraine doctor' may be using the term to describe a wide variety of head pains.

The events we are describing may not always reflect a joint understanding. Our own somewhat idiosyncratic use of language is a product of our own learning experiences and if inadequately explored, can give rise to mis-understandings.

In order to help illustrate this point, an extract from a clinical situation has been included (see Box 1). The therapist was attempting to discover the limitations the individual was experiencing in activities of daily living. It is clear from the extract that although the client believes he is talking about pain, the real meaning of his comments are about the experience of fear. Early in the conversation the therapist could have been satisfied with his explanation 'it hurts' and moved on, but further exploration revealed that Bob was really experiencing fear, not pain.

As the interview continued, another familiar misunderstanding regarding language is highlighted, the difference between the medical use of the term 'degeneration' and the dramatically different understanding that a layperson attributes to this term.

Box 1 Extract from clinical interview with chronic pain sufferer

Bob:	Well, I don't do jobs that involve bending or lifting now.
Therapist:	Because…?
Bob:	It hurts, obviously.
Therapist:	Tell me about that hurt.
Bob:	I can't bend from the waist, it's difficult, I don't want to risk it.
Therapist:	How bad is the hurt when you do that?
Bob:	Well, not as bad as sometimes, not as bad as when it really hurts, but you know it's there…
Therapist:	There?
Bob:	There to remind me, you know, oh ho, don't do that.
Therapist:	Why is it reminding you?
Bob:	Of my spine, its degenerating, you know, crumbling away, so you know, bending and things will just make it worse.

The experience of pain, often described as 'being ill', represents a serious disruption in the life-narrative of the person suffering. Most people will describe their own life-story in terms of a continuum, encompassing past, present, and

157

future. The experience of pain can radically alter this story for some people, not only regarding their future, but also their past, for example, by attributing causality to earlier activities, accidents or lifestyle. Often the pain experience must fit into previous narratives; for example, someone who has learnt to mistrust authority may come to explain pain as medical negligence. A person who explains their life in religious terms may believe the pain is a punishment and yet someone else for whom control is a dominant theme may feel responsible for the pain and therefore crushed by their inability to over-ride it.

In addition to using past experiences to make sense of the current experience, the person must also consider what lies ahead. Future hopes may have to be vanquished and often the future is compressed into a terrifyingly short time scale, with thoughts of a rapid and painful demise intruding and interfering with the current day. Establishing new expectations about the future and re-authoring the past in order to find a meaning, or reason why this has happened can take some time and it is fundamentally a shattering experience.

If, as it has been suggested (Stacey 1996), the dominant cultural story is one of medical triumph over adversity, personal bravery defeating physical ill-health, the explanations for the chronic pain population become very limited. They find themselves living outside of the popular frame, with no medical triumph looming. The consequences may be two-fold, anger with the professionals and/or anger with themselves. Either way, the result is usually reduced motivation and mood, with their own sense of control severely diminished. Previously held beliefs are now in jeopardy and the re-appraisal process takes some time.

The impact on their view of themselves can be profound: what does it mean to be a person who has no legitimate cultural explanation for pain? Are you a malingerer or have you not had adequate care? Both are equally unpleasant and likely to encourage an atmosphere of defensiveness and hostility in both the professional and the sufferer and the resultant relationship will be characterised by negative emotions and difficulties.

Relationships with family, friends and the social world

It is not simply professionals who can hold alternative stories to sufferers; so too can families and friends. Social relationships are seldom the first things that spring to mind when we think of pain or disease, but they undoubtedly have a major impact. Turk and Okifuji (1998) have identified a significant subgroup of pain sufferers for whom the disruption to their interpersonal relationships is the primary problem. In his studies, Turk has consistently found that 18% of sufferers, irrespective of the medical diagnosis, report feeling unsupported by their significant others. However, earlier work by Moore and Chaney (1985) found that including the spouse in the pain management programme did not alter the efficacy of the treatment. Turk has suggested that this is because this treatment approach was not matched to the clients interpersonal characteristics (see also Ch. 7).

Although subgroups exist in which interpersonal difficulties have been identified as particularly problematic, both pain patients and their families or partners generally fare better if effective social support is experienced (Jamison & Virts 1990). The psychological and emotional benefits gained from social support can exert a powerful influence on how they cope. For example, relationships have an influential role in mediating depression, which in turn influences the pain experience. One of the most striking experiences of depression is of isolation, feeling alone and misunderstood:

> The black dog I always hope to resist, and in time to drive, though I am deprived of almost all those that used to help me...When I rise my breakfast is solitary, the black dog waits to share it, from breakfast to dinner he continues barking, except that Dr Brocklesby for a little keeps him at a distance. Night comes at last, and some hours of restlessness and confusion bring me again to a day of solitude. What shall exclude the black dog from a habitation like this?

> Samuel Johnson 1783

The experience of meeting just one other, who shows some understanding for the story and experience, can bring about immense relief. However, even if there is some misunderstanding, the evidence shows that it is still better, healthwise, to be in, rather than out, of a long-term relationship (House 1988). As medical risk factors go, social isolation is fairly substantial. Martin's (1997) review of the research indicates that social isolation generally pre-dates illness, suggesting it is causative not a consequence of ill health.

The way relationships impinge on our health is through mediating variables such as our immune system, our perceptions and our behaviour. For example, other people can help us form accurate and objective perceptions about our own state of health. They can provide a counter-balance to the fear that often accompanies pain and a reminder that a flare-up of pain does not herald something worse. Discussing these anxieties reduces the impact of changing symptomatology and provides an informal second opinion. This can reduce the tendency to seek medical care thereby reducing the focus on pain symptomatology and anxiety. This of course, relies on the partner or friend having been involved in the consultation process previously. Often, all that is really needed is reassurance.

Relationships also foster healthy behaviour. Exercise for example, is easier to initiate in the presence of another. They can also be powerful 'co-therapists' in a programme of graded return of function, for example. Unhelpful behaviours like inactivity, deconditioning, drinking, and medication misuse, can also be reduced through pressure from those in our social world—but only if we understand and share the same treatment rationale or story.

In the next clinical extract it can be seen how Eric and his wife hold different stories regarding achievement (Box 2). Although they both agree that positive reinforcement helps maintain behaviour, they hold different ideas about what this means and how to achieve it. Simply stating that praise is reinforcing at the beginning of the interview would have alienated Eric and would have been unlikely to initiate any change in the behaviours.

159

Box 2 Extract from clinical interview with spouse

Eric:	My wife complains I don't praise her enough when she does the exercises and that…but I believe you should always push for more from people, you know, really motivate them to change and achieve…I shouldn't be praising her should I?
Therapist:	It depends maybe, on what you mean by praise…
Eric:	Well all that softly softly stuff 'There, there, that's enough, you may as well stop now' … That won't help, it's not what I was taught in the marines about training…
Therapist:	Is that what your wife wants, do you think?
Eric:	Oh no, I can't believe she does, she's such a fighter really.
Therapist	So what do you think she's asking for when she wants praise?
Eric:	Maybe its just being seen, well, noticed for what she's doing, she thinks I don't see it, I think.
Therapist:	So could you notice things more for her?
Eric:	Yes, oh yes I could do that.

In order to reap the benefits of relationships, the significant other must be involved in the consultation and education process. This may be even more important in chronic pain, where one experiences the self as 'unwell' but often with no 'legitimate' illness. This affects how family and friends behave toward the sufferer, and much psychological pain and pain behaviour results from such misunderstandings. As pain is a private unobservable behaviour, often the sufferer is forced to rely on observable behaviours (for example: sighing, rubbing, taking medication) in order to demonstrate that the pain is real.

These public expressions, both verbal and non-verbal will be influenced by the individual and by the culture but are ultimately an attempt at communication. Thus the link between internal and external factors is mediated by social factors and learnt behaviour. We are taught culturally to take tablets, rest ,and seek medical opinion when experiencing pain. So we should not be surprised when people in chronic pain continue to do so and find it hard to embrace alternative stories regarding self-management.

'Staying healthy' or 'getting better' is not all about personal responsibility: it relies on the care of others, often unpaid family members. Families and friends can act as a resource, enhancing coping and determining compliance with the treatment process.

Relationships with professionals

Health professionals are trained to adopt a scientific, objective perspective on the symptoms and complaints of patients. In essence, they are trained to develop a hypothesis about the genesis and maintenance of the pain. The development of this diagnostic and treatment approach is usually achieved through many years of training, and often several more of experience.

Families and sufferers, meanwhile, develop their own theories about the pain, often also developed and honed over many years, through previous experiences and in conversation with those around them. Often, the two explanations are disparate.

In recent years, more detailed understanding of the way in which these two accounts can differ, and more importantly how this can affect the course of the treatment, have become manifest. However, the experienced professional will recognise that sometimes it is simply not enough to give the client a more accurate story; they seem not to hear it and may continue to act in their old ways.

In order to improve this process of 're-editing', collaboration between the health professional and the patient must be enhanced. Better communication and mutual understanding pave the way. Allowing the patient to describe fully their own story, i.e. 'What caused the pain' and 'How I think I will get better', can in itself reduce the psychological impact of the illness and have direct effects on health status (Pennebaker 1993).

Katz and Shotter (1996) suggest some ways in which health professionals can start to encourage the expression of the patient's personal story. They argue that a story, or set of beliefs about a given problem, cannot be altered until it has been fully explained. Editing, or the provision of a different view, cannot be achieved until the story has been heard in its entirety. Asking directly for more information about patients' lives and the meaning that they attribute to the events can elicit material more rich than simple symptoms and complaints. Ideas about illness and pain are often invisible in an enquiry restricted to the genesis of symptoms alone.

This final clinical extract illustrates how pervasive the dominant cultural story is about pain (Box 3). Once it is disclosed and understood, patients are able to look at alternative viewpoints and explanations for their difficulties.

Box 3 Extract from clinical interview with chronic pain sufferer

Sally:	The pain's so bad really, I don't know what to do.
Therapist:	What to do?
Sally:	Well I feel so alone in this, why aren't they fixing it?
Therapist:	Why do you think they aren't?
Sally:	I don't think they believe me—if they believed me, they'd fix it.
Therapist:	Is there another reason they might not be fixing it?
Sally:	Well I suppose they might not be able to, perhaps they don't know how…but that's hard to believe…

The extract demonstrates the unquestioning belief in the health professionals, but rather than explain this directly, the therapist allows Sally to try developing another story, another explanation for what is happening. The process of allowing Sally to develop this is ultimately more helpful in bringing about change than simply giving her advice or explanations. Often in healthcare, the professionals hold the power in the relationship so that theirs is the only story that is heard. Not surprisingly people do not drop their own stories just because they hear another one, especially if it does not fit their own experience. Thus it becomes important to encourage clients to 'tell it their way'.

However, Nichols (1991) has argued that health professionals can allow their patients to open up only when they themselves feel sufficiently supported to allow this process to take place. Changes in the broader system can help support therapists in adopting new approaches. Facilitating individuals to tell their stories and enabling them to feel heard and understood should be a priority in enabling effective health-care.

Summary

Humans naturally and instinctively work to make sense of the world they are in. New experiences are understood and ascribed meaning in the context of 'an other'. Our internal and external worlds are dominated by relationships with others. Through these interactions we develop stories about what has happened to us. Such stories describe our past, guide our present and present possible futures to us. These stories form the basis of our interactions. Often we share similar stories and ideas about the world, but when they differ, the consequences can be serious.

This chapter has attempted to review the critical relationships in the pain sufferer in light of the dominant cultural story about pain. It is hoped that through a greater understanding of the stories of others and through the process of listening to and shaping these, we can help our clients find a beneficial outcome.

REFERENCES

Epston D, White M 1990 Narrative means to therapeutic ends. Norton, London
Helman CG 1990 Culture health and illness: an introduction for health professionals 2nd edn. Butterworth-Heinemann, Oxford
House JS 1988 Social relationships and health. Science 241, 550
Jamison RN, Virts KL 1990 The influence of family support on chronic pain. Behaviour Research Therapy 28:283–287
Johnson S 1783 In Martin P 1997 The sickening mind. Flamingo Press, London
Katz AM, Shotter J 1996 Hearing the patients voice: toward a social poetics in diagnostic interview. Social Science and Medicine 43(6):919–931
Martin P 1997 The sickening mind. Flamingo Press, London
McLeod J 1998 Listening to stories about illness and health: applying the lessons of narrative psychology. In: Bayne R, Nicholson P, Norton I (eds) Counselling and communication skills for medical and health practitioners. BPS books, Leicester

Melzack R, Torgerson TS 1971 On the language of pain. Anesthesiology 34:50–56

Moore JE, Chaney EF 1985 Outpatient group treatment of chronic pain: effects of spouse involvement. Journal of Consulting and Clinical Psychology 153:326–334

Nichols KA 1991 Counselling and renal failure. In: Davis H, Fallowfield L (Eds) Counselling and communication in health care. Wiley, Chichester

Pennebaker JW 1993 Putting stress into words: health linguistic and therapeutic implications. Behaviour research therapy 31:539–548

Stacey J 1996 Conquering heroes: the politics of cancer narratives. In: Duncker P, Wilson V (Eds) Cancer: through the eyes of ten women. Pandora, London

Turk DC, Okifuji A 1998 Directions in prescriptive chronic pain management based on diagnostic characteristics of the patient. American Pain Society Bulletin Sept/Oct: 5–11

7

When helping does not help: responding to pain behaviours

TOBY NEWTON-JOHN

Psychological theories of chronic pain have long recognised that the family of a chronic pain patient, and in particular the spouse of the patient, can be highly influential in terms of the level of disability experienced by the patient and the extent to which the patient copes with his or her condition overall (Wall 1994). For over 20 years, writers from as diverse schools of psychology as family systems theory (Meissner 1966) and operant conditioning theory (Fordyce 1976) have highlighted the relevance of spouse or significant other interactions in the development and maintenance of chronic pain problems. Despite a considerable amount of research in this area, our level of understanding of these interactions remains superficial. The result has been minimal progress in terms of improved treatment effect from having spouses included in the treatment protocol (Moore & Chaney 1986). The aim of this chapter, therefore, is to provide physiotherapists with background to the two main theoretical models in this area, and an overview of the research literature which pertains to these models. Suggestions for physiotherapists working with chronic pain patients in this context will then be provided, incorporating some new research findings. Throughout the chapter the term spouse is used in a generic sense, and applies to an adult (of either sex) with whom the pain patient is currently involved in a primary relationship.

Psychological models of family factors in chronic pain

1. Family systems approach

The family systems approach to chronic illness revolves around the central concept of 'homeostasis' or equilibrium, within the family or relationship (Meissner 1966). Homeostasis is poorly defined operationally within this model

(Turk et al 1987), however it essentially refers to a balance or stability of emotion within each member of the family (or within the couple) which is derived directly from interactions with other members of the family unit or dyad. Waring (1977) coined the term 'sick role homeostasis' to refer to the mutual benefits that are conferred upon couples or families as a result of one of the family members being ill. The benefit is usually conceptualised in terms of conflict avoidance, an escape mechanism which has a great deal of value in a family where the expression of negative emotion is seen as excessively threatening and distressing.

An example of sick role homeostasis within a couple is as follows: a husband with chronic headaches states that he is terribly sorry, but he is unable to visit his mother-in-law (with whom he does not get on well) because of his terrible headache. His wife, (who feels trapped in the house all day with her demanding husband) does not quibble with this, but reports that she is 'duty bound to visit her poor mother' and, after much enquiry about her husband's ability to manage on his own, then escapes the house for several hours—to get some peace and emotional support from her mother. Both members of the dyad therefore benefit from the husband's illness (husband avoids the mother-in-law, wife has time away from the demanding husband) without having to actually confront the precipitating problems: the husband's relationship with the mother-in-law, and the wife's frustration with her husband's demanding behaviours. A more common example of illness-derived homeostasis is a mother who says to her unruly children, 'If you don't keep quiet/stop pestering me/do what you are told, you will upset your father—and he has a bad back.' Here discipline is brought to the children via the father's pain problem, rather than as a result of appropriate parental rules and limits.

Family systems writers refer to such relationships as 'overenmeshed', prone to 'colluding' with the symptoms, and suffering from an 'undesirable mutuality' in their beliefs about the illness (Roy 1985; Swanson & Maruta 1980). As thought-provoking as some of these ideas are, and as familiar as some of the scenarios may be in clinical practice, there is little empirical support for the systemic model of chronic pain beyond case studies and small scale research reports (Roy 1994; Watson et al 1992). The difficulty in operationalising terms such as 'homeostasis' and 'overenmeshed' is partly responsible for this lack of quantitative research evidence (Turk et al 1987). However at a clinical level, it is often useful to consider the family systems model when hypothesising about factors that are maintaining or perpetuating a chronic pain problem— there are many parallels with the operant behaviour model of pain which does have a strong research basis.

2. Operant conditioning approach

In contrast to the family systems model, the operant conditioning paradigm advanced by Fordyce (1976) has generated a substantial empirical literature (see Gamsa 1994). Fordyce (1976) was one of the first researchers to place the social environment of the chronic pain patient within a scientific context, and this catalysed much of the research in the area. Briefly, the operant

166

conditioning model states that pain behaviours—those behavioural manifestations of suffering or discomfort such as moaning, limping or taking medication—are subject to the same laws of conditioning as any other forms of behaviour. Therefore if, upon sighing and holding his lower back, a patient receives a gentle, pain-relieving massage from his partner (in this case, a positively reinforcing response), he is more likely to display the pain behaviour in the future. Furthermore, if upon sighing and holding his lower back, the patient's partner says, 'Don't you worry about taking out the rubbish/putting the kids to bed/washing up—I'll do it, you go and rest' (in this case, a negatively reinforcing response), he is more likely to display the pain behaviour in the future. Fordyce (1976) also argued that as spouses and other family members rarely encourage (positively reinforce) healthy behaviours from the patient, such as exercise or attempting new activities, there is a greater emphasis upon positive reinforcement for illness behaviours.

There is now a considerable body of evidence to indicate that spouses who respond to pain behaviours in a 'solicitous' manner, such as taking over duties, encouraging rest, and expressing a great deal of sympathy and concern, tend to be married to patients who report higher levels of pain, greater functional disability and lower levels of overall activity (Flor et al 1989; Turk et al 1992; Romano et al 1995). Using a patient-spouse observational methodology, Romano et al (1992) were able to demonstrate quantitatively that a sequential relationship can exist between patient pain behaviours and spouse solicitous behaviours. They found that the presence of a highly solicitous spouse can act as a discriminative stimulus for eliciting pain behaviours—in other words, a solicitous spouse can act as a cue for pain behaviours being displayed. To further support this hypothesis Lousberg et al (1992) found that patients reported more pain, and walked for a shorter duration on a treadmill test when in the presence of a solicitous spouse than when the test was carried out in the absence of the spouse. However, causality is notoriously difficult to establish in this research area. Perhaps rather than solicitousness increasing patient disability, as is generally hypothesised, it is simply the fact that the more disabled patients require greater instrumental help from their spouses. Flor et al (1987) addressed this question from the spouse's perspective, and found it not to be the case. Their results indicated that the spouse's ratings of the patient's pain level, and beliefs about the extent to which pain interfered in the patient's day to day life, were not associated with the amount of solicitous behaviour that they reported themselves as engaging in. Clearly, Fordyce's (1976) operant conditioning paradigm encapsulates a type of interaction between certain patients and their spouses which has far reaching effects upon patient functioning.

Limitations in the operant conditioning model

The treatment implications of the research cited above are clear: by teaching spouses to stop reinforcing pain behaviours, and start reinforcing healthy behaviours, there will be a reversal of patient functioning. The behavioural approach therefore instructs spouses to remove eye contact from a patient

167

who is talking about their pain (or groaning or sighing or bracing themselves) and wait until they are engaged in some functional activity, such as doing their exercise programme—at which time they should be given a great deal of praise and encouraged to continue (Fordyce 1976). Spouses are now strongly urged to take part in pain management programmes, particularly those conducted on an inpatient basis, in order that they may be taught these behavioural principles (Kerns 1995). It is of major importance that patient changes achieved in treatment are generalised to the home environment, in order to promote long-term maintenance. Spouses are seen as the main agents of influence in this generalisation.

Unfortunately, the few controlled research studies which have included the spouse in treatment in an attempt to utilise these behavioural methods have not been greatly successful. In a carefully designed, well-controlled comparative study, Moore and Chaney (1986) randomised patients into three groups: an individually-based cognitive behavioural pain management group; a couples-based group, where the spouses of the patients were also included in treatment and given training in behavioural methods; and a waiting list control group. Both the individual and the couples groups made significant improvements relative to the no-treatment control group, however the inclusion of the spouses in the treatment did not significantly improve outcome.

More recently, Keefe et al (1996) compared a spouse-assisted pain management programme with a patient-only cognitive behavioural intervention for patients suffering from osteoarthritis of the knee. In the spouse-assisted condition, spouses attended all the patient sessions, and were given specific training in the prompting and reinforcing of coping skills, which the patient was being taught to use in the pain programme. At the end of treatment, Keefe et al (1996) found that the spouse-assisted patients improved more than patients given an arthritis education intervention alone; however, they did not significantly differ from the patients given the individual cognitive behavioural programme. Langelier and Gallagher (1989) reported good results from their behavioural group programme for patients and their partners; however, as this study was uncontrolled, any significant improvements in patient functioning cannot be directly attributed to the intervention alone.

As there is a wealth of research evidence to support the validity of the operant behavioural model, the failure to translate these principles into effective treatment strategies is especially disappointing. However a further examination of the research in this area may provide some explanation for the poor treatment results.

Quantifying solicitousness

The measurement of spousal solicitousness is most commonly carried out using the Significant Other scale of the Multidimensional Pain Inventory (MPI) (Kerns et al 1985). This is either a patient-rated or spouse-rated, self-report instrument assessing spouse responses to patient pain behaviours. The MPI is actually comprised of 3 factor-analytically derived scales of spouse response: Solicitous, Punishing (or Negative), and Distracting. The Punishing scale refers to the spouse expressing frustration or annoyance towards the patient when they are in pain, whilst the Distracting scale represents spousal attempts to divert the patient's attention away from their pain and onto a hobby or other interest. The Solicitous scale is, as mentioned, concerned with the expression of sympathy towards the patient or the provision of a pain-relieving act by the spouse. On the basis of responses to this questionnaire, spouses are categorised as being either Solicitous, Punishing or Distracting types.

As stated, a reliable finding within this literature is that those spouses reporting high levels of solicitous behaviour tend to be married to patients complaining of high levels of pain and disability. However a number of studies have also examined these MPI categories in relation to marital satisfaction scores reported by chronic pain patients and their spouses, and an interesting pattern begins to emerge. Taken collectively, the data from studies by a number of different authors (e.g. Flor et al 1989; Lousberg et al 1992; Romano et al 1995; Schwartz et al 1996) demonstrate that patients with highly solicitous spouses report higher levels of disability and higher levels of pain (as predicted by the operant model)—but also report higher levels of marital satisfaction. Often the marital satisfaction scores are equal with, if not superior to, norms for the healthy population. This stands in direct contrast with the popular view of chronic pain marriages suffering from significant distress (Payne & Norfleet 1986). Conversely, patients whose spouses are categorised as punishing report less pain and disability—but less marital satisfaction also. This contrast is depicted graphically in Figure 7.1.

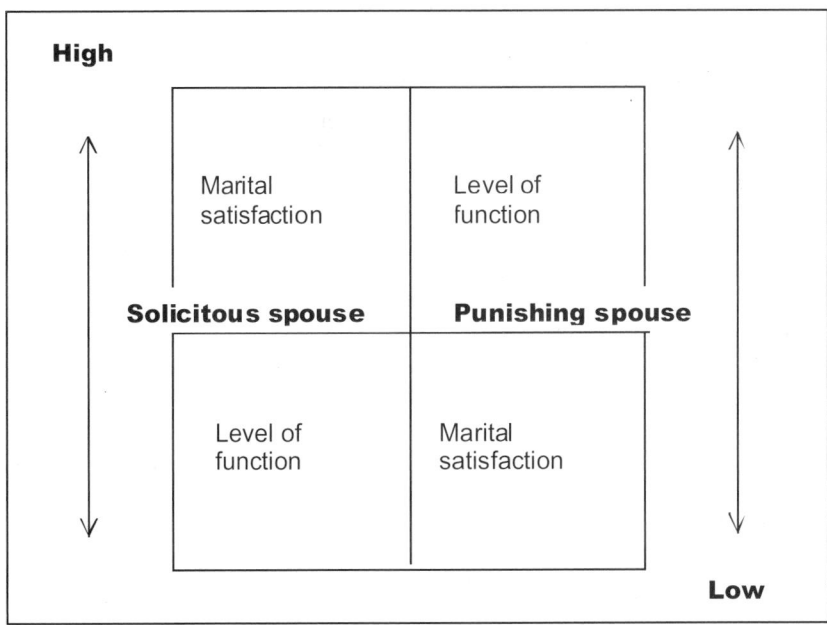

Fig. 7.1 Interaction between solicitous/punishing spouse responses and marital satisfaction/level of disability in patients with chronic pain

Beyond the behavioural model

When considered in the context of marital adjustment issues, these data suggest that solicitousness by a spouse represents something more than simply a behavioural response to a patient expression of pain. At a superficial level, it is difficult to comprehend how patients who are becoming progressively more disabled, and in more pain, with lower levels of functional activity, might be reporting high levels of satisfaction with their relationships. However if we analyse what the act of solicitousness might convey to a patient with chronic pain, interpreting these results becomes clearer.

Pain behaviour has been conceptualised as a communication of the subjective sensation of pain or discomfort to the outside world (Sanders 1996). When a spouse expresses sympathy towards the patient's pain, or when he or she provides a back rub, or offers to take over a chore, that spouse is doing more than just reinforcing pain behaviour. He or she is communicating a number of important messages to the patient. First, in responding solicitously, the spouse is indirectly confirming belief that the patient's pain is real and genuine. A spouse who did not believe in the reality of a partner's pain is less likely to offer to relieve it in some way. It has been well documented that one of the major problems confronting chronic pain patients without identifiable organic pathology is the lack of credibility that is associated with 'not having a diagnosis' (Hanson & Gerber 1990), and therefore partner belief in the validity of the pain is very important.

Secondly, a solicitous response indicates that the spouse cares for the patient. Solicitous behaviours are also expressions of care and concern, and the marital therapy literature informs us that these are important communications within any relationship (Boland & Follingstad 1987). Finally, a solicitous spouse is also signalling an intention to help if required. The provision of social support is known to have positive effects upon mood, morbidity and even mortality rates (Burman & Margolin 1992). When reviewed from this perspective, a solicitous response from a spouse has an impact at a level beyond that of pain and disability. It is addressing several primary relationship factors, and this gives rise to the data indicating high levels of marital satisfaction in this group of patients.

A note should be made at this point about the notion of patient 'secondary gain'. It is now an accepted term within many medical circles that chronically ill patients derive some personal satisfaction from the attention or rewards that their illness brings them. Solicitous responses from a spouse may also be seen in this light—the patient receives attention as well as physical assistance from a spouse behaving solicitously. However secondary gain is not an empirical construct (Fishbain et al 1995), and a recent study by Newton-John (1998) disproved the notion that patients uniformly enjoy being responded to in a solicitous manner. In this study, 81 chronic pain patients were asked to give their affective reaction to different kinds of responses that they received from their spouse/partner when they were in pain. Using qualitative methodology, the responses were coded into 12 categories which included solicitous response categories (such as Offering Help and Providing Help) as well as other types of response (for example, Problem-Solving and Expressing Frustration).

With the exception of the Expressing Frustration category, the Solicitous categories were rated as resulting in the most negative affective reaction for patients. Most commonly, patients reported that solicitous behaviours made them feel that they were a burden to their families, or were useless, or simply made them feel guilty for receiving the help being offered. These data contradict the general perception that chronic pain patients always derive some emotional secondary gain from their disability. In fact, they indicate that a significant proportion of patients find solicitous responses to be aversive. And yet there are clear benefits in terms of marital satisfaction, as the data generally indicate. This confirms a view of solicitousness as operating bi-directionally, on two different levels: a maladaptive influence in terms of patient functioning and sense of coping with pain; but an adaptive influence in terms of marital satisfaction and the perception of spouse care and concern.

Expressions of understanding, of care, and of concern for wellbeing, are vital ingredients of any relationship. However the operant behavioural model of chronic pain does not recognise these 'secondary' qualities that are inherent in solicitous behaviours, as the emphasis is upon the reinforcement paradigm only. The failure to account for this additional dimension of solicitous behaviours may explain why the treatment studies that have adopted the behavioural approach have not been successful. Suggesting that spouses simply stop attending to pain, and switch their attention onto healthy behaviours, is a gross oversimplification of adult interactions in this context. Pain behaviour is a communication, but responding to pain behaviour is also a communication, and as we have seen these interactions are important in maintaining a healthy marital relationship (see also Ch. 6).

Involving the spouse to promote change

Information

Physiotherapists working with a chronic pain patient on increasing function and independence may find that their efforts are undermined by an excessively solicitous spouse. For example, each time a home exercise programme is prescribed, the spouse intervenes and declares that this is not possible for the patient to manage, it will only make the them worse, and they should be referred back to the doctor for more tests and investigations.

Rather than adopting the unidimensional behavioural approach advocated by the operant conditioning model, a physiotherapist who is concerned about an excessively solicitous spouse should preface intervention with a discussion about goals. This discussion should involve both the patient and spouse. It is important to establish at the outset whether increasing mobility, function, and most importantly independence, is a goal for the couple—such changes should not be assumed. The example of homeostasis given at the beginning of the chapter is also an example of a couple who may be unwilling to accept change in their management of the husband's headaches. It may be that the patient and spouse are quite content to be 'dysfunctional', in which case the evidence suggests that pain management treatment is unlikely to alter this (Roy 1985). If, however, the couple agree that working towards these goals is desirable, the physiotherapist is in a position to initiate some change.

From the outset, the physiotherapist should endeavour to see both the patient and the spouse together. This ensures that information that is given to one is not misunderstood or misrepresented by the other, and also conveys a 'teamwork' approach to chronic pain management. The couple can be thought of as a team, working together to overcome mutual difficulties. The physiotherapist may then explain to the patient and spouse the chronic pain dictum that helping too much is often unhelpful. For example, every time the spouse gets up from the chair to fetch tablets/tea/hot water bottle etc., he or she gets some exercise; however, it is the patient who is in greater need of this movement. Furthermore, the patient is denied the sense of satisfaction that comes from having achieved a small task independently. This 'too much helping is unhelpful' notion can form the framework for the remainder of the intervention.

Before moving forward, the physiotherapist may need to address issues such as the relationship (or its lack) between pain and damage, and the importance of movement in chronic pain, for the spouse as well as the patient. The patient may be quite prepared to begin the physiotherapy programme, but it might be the spouse's anxieties about causing further harm or deterioration which undermines the intervention. An acknowledgment of the difficulties in changing long held habits is also appropriate, as many behaviours can become automatic over time.

Initiating activity

Once this background information has been imparted, the next stage is for the physiotherapist to negotiate a small list of activities which the spouse currently or usually undertakes, but which the patient would be generally capable of managing. Making tea is a good example. Rather than the spouse habitually doing this at breakfast time and in the evenings, it may be decided that this is a task which the patient could perform at these times. The physiotherapist might then encourage the patient to incorporate some of the work that has been done together in the physiotherapy programme into this activity—such as using breaks in sitting according to a pacing plan as prompts to make the tea, or carrying out simple stretching exercises whilst waiting for the water to boil. The physiotherapist should also encourage the spouse to acknowledge the effort that the patient is making in this regard. A genuine word of encouragement from the partner is very important to help the patient feel as though their efforts are being recognised and appreciated.

Once the initial set of small, realistic behavioural targets have been reached, the physiotherapist may then explore increasing the physical demands on the patient. For example, the next stage may be the patient taking over responsibility for preparing the breakfast. As the patient's confidence in their ability to manage tasks gradually builds, the spouse's confidence in 'handing over' such activities will also increase. The patient's activity levels can gradually rise in this systematic, step-by-step manner. Throughout this process, the couple should be encouraged to maintain an open, clear communication about their progress. It is very important that neither feels that the pace of change is too fast or the targets are set too high—it is better to err on the side of slowness and caution than to overextend confidence by pacing up too quickly. For patients who have become very reliant upon their spouse's support, it may take a considerable amount of time before changes become apparent, and this requires consistent encouragement from the physiotherapist and support from the spouse. It is also important to emphasise to the spouse that whilst they may be slowly withdrawing the amount of physical assistance they provide to the patient (called 'instrumental support' in the literature), they must ensure that they do not decrease the amount of care and concern ('emotional support') that they give to the patient. This is conceptualised as redirecting their attention towards their partner as a person, rather than predominantly as a patient. In doing this, the bi-directional influence of solicitous responding is being addressed. The reinforcement of pain behaviour is diminished, whilst the expression of positive relationship communication is enhanced.

Clearly however not all couples will be able to follow this format. One member of the couple may resist making changes to daily routines and plans, as this is threatening to their sense of homeostasis, in family systems terminology. An individual may be too distressed, or unable to give the programme the consistency and commitment that it requires—or there may be long-standing marital problems which surface when the necessary levels of co-operation and collaboration are called for. In such cases, the physiotherapist should consider a referral to local psychology services, or to marriage guidance counselling (such as Relate). It is important that in such instances the couple do not feel as though they have 'failed' in treatment, as it is quite possible to restart the programme once these extraneous problems have been overcome. However it is equally important that physiotherapists recognise their own professional and service limitations, and do not attempt to practice outside their professional boundaries.

Conclusion

Patient-spouse interactions in the context of a chronic illness are complex and multifactorial. The family systems model, although raising a number of important issues for consideration, lacks an empirical basis. The operant conditioning model has extensive empirical support, but has generated very little in terms of successful treatment approaches when involving the spouse or significant other. It has been argued that clinicians cannot simply take a stimulus-response view of chronic pain patients' interactions with their partners, as this underestimates the complexity of relationship dynamics. Physio-therapists may assist chronic pain couples to ease themselves out of a 'solicitous-dominant' interaction pattern by explaining the positive and negative consequences of these behaviours. By giving useful information, and a sensible rationale for change, the physiotherapist may facilitate the couple's transition into more adaptive interactions; small targets are set which gradually shift more responsibility onto the patient. Importantly, this should be achieved without the spouse withdrawing care and concern for the patient's well being. An empirical evaluation of this method is now required.

REFERENCES

Boland JP, Follingstad DR 1987 The relationship between communication and marital satisfaction: a review. Journal of Sex and Marital Therapy 13:286–313

Burman B, Margolin G 1992 Analysis of the association between marital relationships and health problems: an interactional perspective. Psychological Bulletin 112:39–63

Fishbain DA, Rosomoff HL, Cutler BR, Rosomoff SR 1995 Secondary gain concept: a review of the scientific evidence. Clinical Journal of Pain 11:6–21

Flor H, Kerns RD, Turk DC 1987 The role of spouse reinforcement, perceived pain, and activity levels of chronic pain patients. Journal of Psychosomatic Research 31:251–259

Flor H, Turk DC, Rudy TE 1989 Relationship of pain impact and significant other reinforcement of pain behaviors: the mediating role of gender, marital status and marital satisfaction. Pain 38:45–50

Fordyce WE 1976 Behavioral methods in chronic pain and illness. Mosby, St. Louis

Gamsa A 1994 The role of psychological factors in chronic pain. I. A half century of study. Pain 57:5–15

Hanson RW, Gerber KE 1990 Coping with chronic pain: a guide to patient self-management. Guilford Press, New York

Keefe FJ, Caldwell DS, Baucom DH, Salley A, Robinson E, Timmons K, Beaupre P, Weisberg J, Kelms M 1996 Spouse-assisted coping skills training in the management of osteoarthritic knee pain. Arthritis Care and Research 9:279–291

Kerns RD 1995 Family assessment and intervention. In: Nicassio PM, Smith TW (Eds) Managing chronic illness: a biopsychosocial perspective. American Psychological Association, Washington DC, 207–244

Kerns RD, Turk DC, Rudy TE 1985 The West Haven-Yale multidimensional pain inventory (WHYMPI). Pain 23: 345–356

Langelier RP, Gallagher RM 1989 Outpatient treatment of chronic pain groups for couples. Clinical Journal of Pain 5:227–231

Lousberg R, Schmidt AJM, Groenman NH 1992 The relationship between spouse solicitousness and pain behavior: searching for more experimental evidence. Pain 51:75–79

Meissner WW 1966 Family dynamics and psychosomatic processes. Family Process 5:142–161

Moore JE, Chaney EF 1986 Outpatient group treatment of chronic pain: effects of spouse involvement. Journal of Consulting and Clinical Psychology 53:326–334

Newton-John TRO 1998 Reconceptualisating patient-spouse interactions in chronic pain. Unpublished PhD dissertation

Payne B., Norfleet MA 1986 Chronic pain and the family: a review. Pain 26:1–22

Romano JM, Turner JA, Friedman LS, Bulcroft RA, Jensen MP, Hops H, Wright SF 1992 Sequential analysis of chronic pain behaviors and spouse responses. Journal of Consulting and Clinical Psychology 60:777–782

Romano JM, Turner JA, Jensen MP, Friedman LS, Bulcroft RA, Hops H, Wright SF 1995 Chronic pain patient-spouse behavioral interactions predict patient disability. Pain 63:353–360

Roy R 1985 The interactional perspective of pain behavior in marriage. International Journal of Family Therapy 7:271–283

Roy R 1994 Influence of chronic pain on the family relations of older women. Journal of Women and Aging 6:73–88

Sanders SH 1996 Operant conditioning with chronic pain: back to basics. In: Gatchel RJ, Turk DC (Eds) Psychological approaches to pain management: a practitioner's handbook. Guilford Press, New York 112–130

Schwartz L, Slater MA, Birchler GR 1996 The role of pain behaviors in the modulation of marital conflict in chronic pain couples. Pain 65:227–233

Swanson DW, Maruta T 1980 The family's viewpoint of chronic pain. Pain 8:163–166

Turk DC, Flor H, Rudy TE 1987 Pain and families.I. Etiology, maintenance, and psychosocial impact. Pain: 30:3–27

Turk DC, Kerns RD, Rosenberg R 1992 Effects of marital interaction on chronic pain and disability: examining the down side of social support. Rehabilitation Psychology 37:259–274

Wall PD, 1994 Introduction. In: Wall PD, Melzack R (Eds) Textbook of pain. Churchill Livingstone, Edinburgh

Waring EM 1977 The role of the family in symptom selection and perception in chronic illness. Psychotheropeutics Psychosomatics 28:253–259

Watson WL, Bell JM, Wright LM 1992. Osteophytes and marital fights: a single-case clinical research report of chronic pain. Family Systems Medicine 10:423–435

8

Treating sexual dysfunction in chronic pain patients

TOBY NEWTON-JOHN, SUZANNE BROOK

Patients with chronic pain who attend a physiotherapist for treatment will present with a variety of problems and difficulties. However it is fair to say that limitations in movement, joint and muscle stiffness, and loss of fitness will be common to the majority of those seeking help. These difficulties will translate into restrictions in daily activities such as walking, self-care, and domestic chores and become the functional activities that patients and physiotherapists are most likely to target in treatment, as goals to either return to or to improve in quality.

It is also fair to say that an individual with chronic pain who is experiencing these kinds of limitations and restrictions in daily life will also have some difficulty engaging in that most basic of human activities—sexual activity. As we shall see, many of the physical requirements and movements involved in common daily activities are also necessary for sexual activity. However patients rarely make this behavioural link themselves, and this chapter is intended to provide the physiotherapist with sufficient information to facilitate patient understanding of the association, and to generate an appropriate treatment plan with them.

Prevalence of pain-related sexual dysfunction

If one examines the research literature on cognitive behavioural treatment for chronic pain, it would appear that sexual difficulties in this patient population are rare indeed. In treatment outcome studies it is customary for the treatment protocol to be described in order that the various treatment components that were implemented can be reviewed. However it is very rare to see a multidisciplinary, holistic pain management intervention stating that sexual difficulties have been addressed in treatment (Williams et al. 1996; Nicholas et al. 1991). This would suggest one of two possibilities: either there is no call for these issues to be included in pain management treatment, or clinicians are unsure about how to approach the issues within a cognitive behavioural pain management framework.

The research evidence, limited though it is, would certainly discount the first possibility. Maruta and Osborne (1978) published one of the earliest studies documenting sexual dysfunction in patients suffering from chronic pain. Over 60% of their sample reported a deterioration in both frequency of, and satisfaction from, sexual activity. A follow-up study by Maruta, et al (1981) documented dramatic changes in sexual activity in chronic pain couples: 78% of the patients and 84% of the spouses reported significant reductions or complete elimination of their sexual activity. A subsequent study by Coates and Ferroni (1991) found that the frequency of intercourse had 'significantly diminished since the back injury' for 100% of their sample of chronic pain patients, with 36% of couples having ceased sexual activity altogether. This latter figure compares with the study by Flor et al (1987) in finding that 42% of their mixed gender sample had eliminated sexual activity entirely.

Most recently, Monga et al (1998) have confirmed the generally high levels of sexual dysfunction in chronic pain patients, with the majority of patients reporting dissatisfaction with their sexual activities. As Schwartz and Slater (1991) have said, 'Chronic pain often affects the patient's ability to function sexually...in addition to emotional distress, sexual dissatisfaction is a common complaint of chronic pain patients and their spouses' (p.12). Clearly then, issues of sex and sexual functioning are likely to be of considerable importance to the majority of chronic pain patients seen in physiotherapy clinics. Before addressing the more credible explanation for the lack of treatment literature on sexual dysfunction in chronic pain—clinician anxiety—we will explore the various causes of the sexual problems in this population.

Why should sex pose such problems for the chronic pain sufferer?

As we shall demonstrate later, the answer to this question in many ways reflects the complexity of chronic pain, and its multifactorial impact upon an individual's psychosocial functioning. In reviewing the factors which may be relevant to sexual dysfunction in chronic pain, we bear in mind that the incidence of sexual problems in the wider community is also relatively high (Crowe & Ridley 1990). We have therefore chosen to highlight only those issues which are specifically related to those suffering from chronic illness, rather than include all the factors which may interfere with sexual activity in the healthy population. An associated issue is the fact that the majority of chronic pain sufferers are in their late 40s and early 50s, and there may be age-related changes such as menopause which may also play a role in impaired sexual functioning. Again, as these are not pain-specific they have not been included in the list below. However, physiotherapists interested in working in this area should be familiar with the wider literature on sexual dysfunction, and are urged to consult texts such as Spence (1991) or de Silva (1994) for this information.

Factors impairing sexual functioning in the chronic pain patient

There are a range of physical, psychological, and pharmacological reasons why chronic pain patients might experience sexual dysfunction. We will summarise the most common causes of impairment.

1 Joint stiffness, muscle weakness, spasm, and loss of flexibility

These are commonly experienced by patients with low activity levels, and will lead to limitations in movement and consequently function. For example, patients may have difficulty lying for any length of time, and avoid certain positions or postures to avoid getting 'stuck' in an uncomfortable position.

2 Hypersensitivity (allodynia)

Areas of the body which are protected from movement and touch over a prolonged period of time often become highly sensitive. When these areas are then inadvertently moved or touched during sexual activity, it may lead to unexpected increases in pain.

3 Fear of increased pain or damage associated with sexual activity

For many chronic pain patients, sexual activity leads to aversive consequences in terms of increased pain. Tolerances for lying, bending and stretching are insufficient to allow them to adopt certain positions, and a 'flare-up' of pain is the result. This can develop into a conditioned association between pain and sexual activity, which will serve to increase anxiety levels whenever sexual activity is considered.

4 Body image disturbances

Chronic pain patients often put on weight due to their inactivity, which can then impact negatively on their body image. The use of collars and corsets and other aids can also contribute to a decreased perception of self as a sexual being, as can a neglect or loss of interest in self-care.

5 Loss of interest or arousal

For all of the reasons outlined above, chronic pain patients may lose interest in sexual activity. The pain itself is an aversive experience, and as such is not conducive to sexual arousal. Furthermore, problems with sexual arousal may be compounded by mood disturbances, as alterations in libido are frequently found amongst the depressive illnesses. Given that as many as 50% of chronic pain patients are estimated to suffer from a coexisting depressive disorder (Banks & Kerns, 1996), mood disturbances are likely to contribute to many instances of sexual dysfunction in this population.

6 Medication

As the rates of depression in chronic pain problems are so high, many patients will be taking antidepressant medication. The side effects of both tricyclic (e.g. Amitriptyline) and SSRI (e.g. Prozac) classes of antidepressant explicitly include impaired sexual functioning. Other medications that are commonly prescribed for individuals with chronic pain, such as opioid analgesics and anxiolytics, may also produce side effects, such as drowsiness, nausea and gastro-intestinal problems, which will impact negatively upon sexual arousal.

7 Partner anxiety

Just as the patient may fear increased pain as a result of engaging in sexual activity, the patient's partner may also be fearful of this outcome. Most partners are very reluctant to engage in any activity which is likely to precipitate more pain, and therefore they may encourage a reduction in sexual activity. Unless there is good communication within the couple, this anxiety on the partner's behalf can be transformed over time into a patient belief that the partner 'is not interested any more'. A sense of rejection can then compound the problems for the patient.

For any individual with chronic pain, one, several or conceivably all of the above factors may contribute to their sexual dysfunction. The ways in which these factors can interact is depicted in Figure 8.1. The sheer breadth of potential factors suggests that treating the problem is unlikely to be straightforward, particularly given that patients themselves may not be clear about why they are experiencing difficulties. However, before going on to address these issues in terms of treatment, we will reflect briefly on the issues facing the physiotherapist in this context.

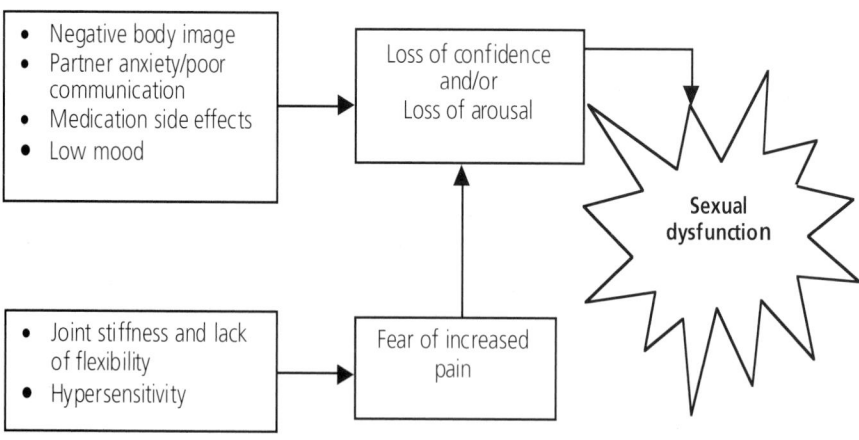

Fig. 8.1 Interaction patterns to produce sexual dysfunction in chronic pain paients.

Why should sex in chronic pain sufferers pose such problems for the health professional?

It was noted above that there is a paucity of clinical research on the issue of sexual functioning in chronic pain, despite evidence that it is a widespread and significant problem. Nor is there much evidence that it is customarily included as a topic for treatment in multidisciplinary pain management programmes. It would seem reasonable then to assume that practitioners working in outpatient settings are equally likely to be avoidant of the issue when carrying out an assessment of their patient's physical functioning and overall quality of life. A number of reasons for this reluctance are possible:

- The patient will get embarrassed
- I (the physiotherapist) will get embarrassed
- The patient will think that I am being intrusive, and I will lose rapport
- I don't know what to do with the information when given it.

Each will be discussed below:

Patient embarrassment

The degree to which the patient is embarrassed by an enquiry about sexual difficulties is very much related to how the question is put and then followed up. At one level, discussion of sex and sexuality remain cultural taboos in Western society and therefore will cause embarrassment; at another level, the patient is being questioned in a (hopefully) confidential context in which the information is being sought in order to improve the treatment delivered to them. Taken in this sense, asking about sexual functioning is as reasonable as asking about occupational or social functioning—they are all areas in which pain may have an impact, and for which there are useful methods for improving coping.

Therapist embarrassment

Given that discussing sexual behaviour is a cultural taboo, it is likely that the physiotherapist who is new to this area may experience some embarrassment carrying out the assessment. During moments of embarrassment, and particularly in relation to sexual behaviours, we often resort to humour to feel more at ease. However, experience indicates that an easygoing, but non-jocular manner is much more productive when assessing and treating sexual dysfunction.

Furthermore, for reasons of both embarrassment and the preservation of professional boundaries, it is important to consider whether engaging a patient of the opposite sex in treatment is appropriate. It may be advisable to refer to a same-sex physiotherapist if sexual problems have been identified and agreed upon as a treatment goal.

Therapist Intrusiveness

Rapport, or patient trust in the therapist's integrity and competence, grows as the therapeutic interaction continues. For this reason, asking about potentially embarrassing or threatening issues is best left towards the end (but not the absolute end) of an assessment session. Provided that the assessment has been carried out in a sensitive and thoughtful manner to that point, very few patients take offence at a question phrased such as: 'And has the pain had any impact upon your physical relationship?' The patient may be reluctant to discuss the issue further, as is his or her prerogative. However, the therapist is unlikely to lose rapport from inquiring in this way.

Therapist lack of confidence

Perhaps the most common reason for sexual dysfunction being under-treated in chronic pain patients is a lack of physiotherapist knowledge about how to proceed with a treatment plan once the information has been obtained. In other words, having carried out an assessment and determined that a patient's chronic pain problem is having a significant negative effect upon his or her sexual activity - what does the physiotherapist do next? It is hoped that the present chapter will at least offer some ideas in this regard.

Treating sexual dysfunction in the context of chronic pain

The cognitive behavioural treatment of chronic pain is based primarily on a self-management model (Hanson & Gerber 1990). One of the central aims of this approach is to teach specific skills and strategies, which allow individuals suffering from chronic pain to gradually resume physical activities which their pain has previously denied them. The treatment philosophy in relation to sexual dysfunction is to extrapolate those skills which are taught to patients as a means of improving function in everyday activities—and apply them to sexual activity. The core skills which make up the standard cognitive behavioural pain management intervention are equally applicable to sexual activity, however this often comes as something of a revelation to chronic pain patients. The extrapolation of skills involves a number of planning stages: groundwork, pre-sexual activity, during sexual activity, and post-sexual activity. Although they are described as discrete sections for the purposes of clarity, there will obviously be carry over of individual components from one section to another.

Groundwork

Communication. Before commencing any treatment intervention concerning mutual sexual behaviour, it is essential that the patient's partner is aware of the treatment goal and is in agreement with it. Co-operation, understanding, and considerable patience on behalf of the partner are essential ingredients in the successful outcome of this intervention.

Planning. In order to ensure that the experience is as anxiety-free as possible, it is important that the patient does some planning. Negotiating with the partner to find a mutually suitable time, when disturbance is unlikely and fatigue levels are not too high, is crucial.

Desensitising. If lying on certain parts of the body are too uncomfortable for the patient to even initiate sexual activity, these areas should be desensitised first. Setting a manageable baseline for touch, and slowly but systematically increasing the amount of touch that is tolerated will build towards a sufficient tolerance to engage in sexual activity. This can be incorporated into sensate focus exercises (see Spence 1991) in order to improve confidence or arousal difficulties.

Before commencing sexual activity

Stretches. Patients may benefit from beginning with a warm-up which involves stretching all areas of their body.

Relaxation. As anxiety is likely to be high when confronting an activity that has been avoided (in some cases for many years), using relaxation strategies as a preparation for sex is useful. A warm bath, aromatherapy oils, and soothing music can complement the use of mental relaxation strategies.

Cognitive therapy. To help reduce anxieties as well as to prevent 'catastrophising' about possible negative outcomes, patients can be encouraged to employ their cognitive therapy skills prior to initiating sex. Having been taught the principles of identifying and challenging maladaptive beliefs and assumptions, patients may use these skills to challenge unhelpful thoughts such as 'I won't be able to cope with the flare-up', 'I haven't done this for so long, I'm bound to let my partner down', and 'I didn't enjoy it the last time; this won't be any different'.

During sexual activity

Pacing. Patients often find this suggestion ludicrous at the outset, and feel that they could not possibly keep to any tolerances or times whilst engaging in sexual behaviour. However once it is explained that sexual positions have tolerances, just as the more common activities of sitting, standing and walking, this makes more sense. If they ignore these tolerances, it is very likely that they will experience a flare-up of pain as a result. It is important that patients are aware of changing their posture regularly during sexual activity, if not necessarily by the clock as in strict pacing practice. The partner's awareness of the need to pace during sex is also very important, as they can facilitate regular changes of position.

Humour. Not strictly a cognitive behavioural treatment component, but we have found it useful to remind patients that they are supposed to be enjoying this treatment activity, and taking it too seriously can undermine its efficacy. Being relaxed with their partners, and incorporating a degree of lightheartedness into pacing, for example, can be very useful.

183

Following sexual activity

Stretching. As with concluding any demanding physical activity, patients should be encouraged to stretch once they have stopped in order to prevent stiffening and subsequent increases in pain. This 'warm down' approach mirrors the preparation phase described prior to engaging in sexual activity.

Communication. Underpinning the success of a shared enterprise such as sex is clear, open communication between the partners. Given that the approach outlined above is very different from most people's experience of sexual activity, it is important that both patient and partner are encouraged to discuss their feelings about the activity that they have just engaged in. Building confidence for future sexual intimacy will depend to a large degree on how well the couple can discuss their needs and preferences in relation to sex, and are able to negotiate these in a non-threatening manner.

This then is a cognitive behavioural treatment outline for sexual dysfunction in chronic pain patients. However there are always instances where treatment does not adhere strictly to textbook guidelines, and we have therefore included some of the more common reasons why problems may arise.

Obstacles to treatment

Treating sexual problems, as with all pain management strategies, requires persistence and perseverance. Patients (and clinicians) should not be overly discouraged if the first attempt to restart their sexual life was not successful. Problem-solving with the patient will usually pinpoint the reason for the problems—overestimating physical tolerances, inadequate prior com-munication with the partner, and poor timing are often the cause of an unsatisfactory outcome.

Many patients complain that adopting the approach described above takes all the spontaneity out of their sexual activity, and that it is too 'mechanical' and 'ruins the mood'. To an extent, they are quite right—at the outset, it is a very planned and orchestrated activity. However this is to build confidence in the initial stages of treatment, when various tolerances have yet to be determined and anxieties in both patient and partner may be high. This does not mean that the treatment programme need be unromantic—the use of music, candles, massage and so on can be incorporated into the programme to provide a more romantic environment. Once confidence and skills have been developed, adopting a more spontaneous approach to sex becomes more feasible.

It is generally advisable to begin this form of intervention once the patient has a good grasp of the various pain management skills as they are customarily taught. For example, a patient who has already experienced the benefit of pacing in relation to shopping or work activities will be more likely to accept the rationale in relation to sexual activity.

Partner understanding of the rationale of the pain management strategies is also important for compliance. If the partner does not understand or accept what is being suggested in treatment they may be less willing to cooperate, and it is therefore important to try and include them in the treatment process from the outset.

It should be recognised finally that sexual difficulties can often reflect more enduring relationship problems, and that issues beyond those related to pain and pain management may be causing the difficulties. It may be the case that marital counselling is necessary as a prelude to beginning work on the specific issues addressed above.

Conclusion

The evidence presented in this chapter indicates that problems with sexual activity are widespread amongst the chronic pain population. However, the treatment literature rarely addresses sexual functioning as a treatment goal, perhaps because of continuing cultural taboos about sex and sexuality. An argument was proposed that the cognitive behavioural approach to pain management has a great deal to offer in relation to treating sexual dysfunction in chronic pain, because of fundamental commonalties between sexual activity and other forms of activity. By extrapolating general pain management methods as they are traditionally taught, and applying them to the particular domain of sexual activity, patients can learn to increase their confidence and abilities in this area also. The requirement now is to demonstrate the efficacy of this approach in a research context.

REFERENCES

Banks SM, Kerns RD 1996 Explaining high rates of depression in chronic pain: a diathesis-stress framework. Psychological Bulletin 119:95–110

Coates R, Ferroni PA 1991 Sexual dysfunction and marital disharmony as a consequence of chronic lumbar spinal pain. Sexual and Marital Therapy 6:65–69

Crowe M, Ridley J 1990 Communication training. In: Crowe M, Ridley J (Eds) Therapy with couples: a behavioural-systems approach to marital and sexual problems. Blackwell Scientific Publications, Oxford 125–151

de Silva 1994 Sexual dysfunction. In: Lindsay SJE, Powell GE (Eds) Clinical adult psychology 2nd edn. Blackwell Press, London 199–213

Flor H, Turk DC, Scholz OB 1987 Impact of chronic pain on the spouse: marital, emotional and physical consequences. Journal of Psychosomatic Research 31:63–71

Hanson RW, Gerber KE 1990 Coping with chronic pain: a guide to patient self-management. Guilford Press, New York

Maruta T, Osborne D 1978 Sexual activity in chronic pain patients. Psychosomatics 19:531–537

Maruta T, Osborne D, Swanson D, Halling JM 1981 Chronic pain patients and spouses: marital and sexual adjustment. Mayo Clinic Proceedings 51:307–310

Monga TN, Tan G, Ostermann HJ, Monga U, Grabois M 1998 Sexuality and sexual adjustment of patients with chronic pain. Disability and Rehabiliation 20:317–329

Nicholas MK, Wilson PW, Goyen J 1991 Operant–behavioural and cognitive-behavioural treatment for chronic low back pain. Behaviour, Research and Therapy 29:225–238

Schwartz L, Slater MA 1991 The impact of chronic pain on the spouse: research and clinical implications. Holistic Nursing Practice 6:9–16

Spence SH 1991 Psychosexual therapy: a cognitive behavioural approach. Chapman and Hall, London

Williams AC de C, Richardson PH, Nicholas MK, Pither CE, Harding VR, Ridout KL et al 1996 Inpatient vs outpatient pain management: results of a randomised controlled trial. Pain 66:13–22

Chronic pain, pregnancy and child rearing

CHRISTINA PAPADOPOULOS, VICKI HARDING

The mean age of chronic pain patient populations reported in a meta-analysis of 65 studies is 45 years (Flor et al 1992). However, there is still a considerable proportion of younger women with chronic pain who would like to start a family, or to add to their family. The most common area of pain reported by chronic pain patients appears to be in the lower back (e.g. Williams 1993). A significant group, however, present with abdominal, pelvic, or perineal pain as their main pain, or as a secondary but significant pain. It is therefore not surprising that many younger female patients have concerns about pregnancy, labour and child-rearing. Some women report that their chronic pain began during pregnancy, labour or in the post partum period, so they quite naturally have concerns about having another baby. It is possible that friends and relatives may heighten these concerns. A few patients with back pain and/or pelvic pain also report that their doctor has advised them not to have children.

This chapter describes various concerns that this group of women have, and how their concerns arise and develop. It then illustrates how physiotherapists who use a cognitive behavioural approach can help women learn to plan for pregnancy despite chronic pain.

Concerns about having a baby

Advice that pregnancy is unwise

Many women feel they have been told, explicitly or otherwise, by their doctor that they should not have children due, for example, to their:

- Spinal fusion
- Spondylolisthesis
- Scoliosis
- Hip arthrodesis
- Inability to cope with the pain
- Inability to come off medication.

This may indicate an insufficient explanation on the doctor's part. The doctor may have past experience of poor coping by this or another patient, and feel that with the additional handicap of chronic pain having a baby would be very burdensome. The doctor may feel quite daunted by the prospect of supporting the woman through pregnancy and child rearing. However none of these conditions, in themselves, makes pregnancy and child rearing impossible.

It is often not only doctors that advise against having a baby. Sometimes friends and relatives can add to a woman's apprehension by describing their own, or friends' horror stories which, when coupled with catastrophising and general poor coping skills, make pregnancy seem like an impossible prospect.

Hearing about other women who have coped with spinal fusion, severe scoliosis etc., and have been able to have a successful pregnancy, will contribute to helping a woman reconsider her position. It is important not to state that the patient's doctor or relative was wrong, but to discuss his/her position or concerns, and show that these are not insurmountable with further guidance, thought, planning and practical strategies.

Fear of increased pain

Most patients fear increased pain and being unable to cope during pregnancy. Whether a woman will have more or less pain during pregnancy really is unknown. Patients may report either and it is not possible to predict what they will have. Discussing the coping skills she has or may learn on a pain management programme, and how these may help her cope with increased pain in pregnancy, will be useful.

Maintaining and working on the physical aspects of a pain management programme will be helpful in preventing flare-ups of pain. These include:

- Pacing, with regular movement and regular rests to avoid over and underactivity.
- Building up and maintaining fitness, including general fitness needed for the day to day care of a baby, as well as more specific fitness such as upper and lower limb strength, and trunk strength for activities such as carrying, pushing a pram, or lifting a baby out of a cot.
- Building up specific tolerances to the tasks involved in child rearing, such as carrying, lifting and standing.
- The practice of relaxation techniques, to be used not only during rest periods but also during activities such as feeding and changing.

Fear of further or new damage

Emphasising the naturalness of pregnancy (the body is designed for it) rather than a disease model of pregnancy can contribute to overcoming unhelpful beliefs. Some useful issues to discuss include:

- Allaying fear about pain from the traumas of pregnancy and childbirth, such as episiotomy, by explaining the healing process. This should include the nature of scar formation, how to optimise healing, and its likely time span.

- If a patient's pain originally began in association with pregnancy, it is worth discussing the event with her. Pregnancies can vary. If she thinks of someone she knows who has had several pregnancies, she may recognise how each pregnancy and birth was different for that same person, and that damage does not generally occur as a result of pregnancy.
- Some backache is inevitable for some people, but pacing and various supports found in mother and baby stores can help.

Some women have found that delivery or examination positions cause pain. Helpful pain relieving strategies include:

- Practising and pacing up positions such as four point kneeling, lying supine with hips flexed and abducted.
- Doing regular stretches particularly for the hips, knees and lumbar spine.
- Using a good birth plan (an example can be found on page 193).
- The practice of assertiveness skills.

Weakened muscles and ligaments can find it hard to cope if too many lifting demands are put on them after the birth. Learning about the various options of positions for core activities such as feeding, dressing, changing and carrying, good planning, adaptation of furniture and organising appropriate assistance is vital.

Fear of labour

It is important to normalise and demedicalise the process of giving birth as much as possible; the woman needs to realise that we are designed to carry and deliver babies. It is also useful to recognise that most women will hold some apprehension or fears regarding the birth of their baby and that this is quite normal. Some of the fearful factors associated with labour are:

- The prospect of long hours in one position.
- Not being able to lie on their back, squat, kneel, abduct the hips etc.
- Fear of epidural anaesthesia as a consequence of previous bad experiences with epidurals for spinal pain.
- Fear of forceps.
- Fear of the uterus bursting, adhesions splitting, pelvic floor damage etc.
- Fear of not being in control. Previous experience may include not feeling in control when decisions were made for them by medical staff with little regard for their opinion or wishes.

Clearly the physiotherapist's experience, confidence and knowledge is vital if they are going to allay a woman's fears. Some women find it helpful to meet patients that have experienced a successful labour. By talking to other women, a patient may see that there are practical strategies or ways of dealing with situations she may find fearful.

Fear of child rearing

A patient with chronic pain may fear not being a 'good mother' to the child, who will make physical demands upon her, for example not being able to:

- Carry baby long distances
- Pick baby up, hold, and give him/her cuddles e.g. after a fall
- Restrain the baby in potentially dangerous situations
- Carry baby up and down stairs.

A woman's expectations need assessing here: she may need to challenge her concept of being a 'good mother' and learn to be satisfied with being a 'good enough mother'. It can help to think of those qualities she sees in a friend that she considers to be a good mother, or to list the important attributes she has to balance against her perceived physical shortcomings. Encouraging her to appreciate the 'goodness' of a less physically able mother e.g. paraplegic or amputee, may help her challenge her judgements of herself. It is important to help her recognise the qualities she possesses and to set her expectations at a realistic level.

Physical abilities should be discussed, recognising that her physical fitness will continue to improve with pacing and maintaining a regular fitness programme. This means she will be fitter by the time she has the baby, and her strength and stamina will have a better chance to further increase as the baby gets bigger.

Other practical issues

A checklist of essentials for pregnancy preparation appears as Box 1. Physiotherapists may wish to add to this basic list for each client.

Box 1 Essentials for pregnancy preparation

- Planning.
- Practice and experimentation with basic activities: sitting, right and left side lying, squatting, kneeling, carrying, reclining, walking, standing, pushing.
- Setting achievable goals to encourage self-efficacy.
- Communicating: asking/planning for help.
- Improving fitness/health.
- Becoming familiar with the changes that occur in pregnancy and labour; what to expect.
- Learning to say 'No'.

Breastfeeding

Breastfeeding can be a wonderfully relaxing and reinforcing activity for the mother. Physiologically, breastfeeding stimulates the release of oxytocin which gives a feeling of relaxation and sleepiness. Emotionally, it is a time of great intimacy and bonding with the child. To make breastfeeding as reinforcing and as comfortable as possible, it is useful to discuss feeding positions, sitting/ lying tolerances, and the use of pillows and cushions. Alternating feeding positions throughout the day will help prevent prolonged sitting in one position. It will also help prevent sore breasts and encourage the stimulation of all the mammary ducts. Side lying while feeding can be a good opportunity for the mother to rest. Working on pacing up the time she can sit or lie on the right/ left side comfortably will help in preparation of feeding. Some mothers find that using a low chair, such as the old Victorian type of nursing chair, or a rocking chair, can provide a comfortable feeding position. Pillows and cushions placed under the baby to lift them up to the breast can help prevent a stooping forwards posture, as well as producing a more restful position for the mother's shoulders and arms.

Physical demands of caring for a baby

Patients can be quite worried about being able to look after their baby. They may worry about whether they can carry or lift the baby out of a cot or off the floor. Some women might be frightened about dropping their baby. Goal setting can be a useful way of tackling these issues. First, ask the patient to identify and list all the activities she finds worrisome. This will help her focus and be methodical about solving the problems raised. She can then take one activity at a time and look at what is required to achieve this activity/goal.

An example may be giving the baby a bath, where the tasks involved may include:

- Undressing the baby
- Carrying the baby into the bathroom
- Kneeling on the floor while holding the baby
- Bending over the bath whilst kneeling
- Holding the baby with one arm and washing with the other arm
- Lifting the baby out of the bath
- Standing up whilst holding the baby
- Drying and dressing the baby.

From this list, the patient and physiotherapist can look at what is required to achieve each component of the goal. For example, kneeling on the floor while holding baby. This will require good leg strength, balance, knee and hip flexibility and arm strength. From this, a daily graded exercise programme can be worked out, as well as a graded functional programme. Eventually the patient will be physically able and confident in getting into a kneeling position, maintaining it for sufficient time whilst holding a weight of around 8 pounds, and then returning to a standing position.

It is important that the patient avoids over-strain wherever possible, e.g., stooping over a low bed while changing a nappy—an activity performed 6-10 times a day. Planning and organising the home environment so that furniture such as cots, changing mats and push chairs are at a desirable height and position is vital. Discussing better and more natural ways of performing activities will reduce the stress and strain of doing things. This way of thinking should become habitual.

Patients can be quite fearful of dropping their baby or of not being able to carry the weight. Describing the use of a front sling, then later the back pack type carrier, is helpful. Patients will also come to recognise that babies start off small and light, and allow their mothers to pace up their upper body strength as they grow. A discussion about the need for carrying can highlight the fact that toddlers can learn to climb up onto the mother, rather than mother bending forwards to pick them up.

Asking for help

Mothers need to plan in advance what regular help is needed and can be requested for the baby, the house, and the family. Help can be given by their partner, parents and other relatives or friends and may also come from Social Services in certain circumstances. They may need to learn to accept 'good enough' in their role as wife and mother, and for the house.

Handouts

The physiotherapists from the pain management unit at St Thomas' Hospital in London (INPUT) have produced a handout on pregnancy (see Appendix 1) for those who request it while on the pain management programme. Rather than merely giving out the handout, we always discuss it with the patient. It has also been found to be useful for impending grandmothers, partners, and aunts with pain problems. The handout is printed at the end of this chapter and INPUT is happy for it to be used or adapted by a physiotherapist for their patients, as long as they go over it carefully with their patients.

Birth plan

A birth plan (see Box 2) can be very helpful for certain women, particularly those who have had unhelpful past experiences or have particular fears about labour. It will offer a woman the opportunity to discuss her wishes and preferences with the midwives. Recently, a maternity record book has been produced nationally (UK) and within this is a large section for a birth plan to be created. It's title *Your Preferences For Your Baby's Birth* shows the increasing importance placed on finding out what women want during labour.

Box 2 Birth Plan

I am writing a Birth Plan so that any medical professional involved in my care is completely aware of my special needs and wishes regarding the birth of my child.

You may be aware that I suffer with chronic low back pain radiating into my left leg. This started following the delivery of my first child and was exacerbated by my second pregnancy. My chronic pain has caused considerable distress and impairment which I have worked hard to manage with the help of a pain management programme I attended last year in London.

As you can appreciate, I am keen not to increase my already constant pain any further. Hence a birth plan, which I hope we can discuss and work with together.

Positions

I would like flexibility in the positions I use and a bed that I can get on and off from independently i.e. one that raises and lowers, and is of reasonable comfort. The availability of several pillows/bean bags would help me become supported and comfortable which in turn would put less strain on my back. If, for whatever reason, I need to change position—turn over, get up etc—please allow me the time to try and do it independently as I am a better judge of how I can move and change position, and it is less likely that I will strain my back this way. I will ask if I need assistance. Obviously, simple guidance will be most helpful.

Pain relief

I would like to discuss my options regarding this matter. My main concern is the exacerbation of my low back pain. A birthing pool would be a very attractive option, but I gather not feasible. I have considered the option of a spinal block and would like to discuss this further, as it may actually place my back under undue strain without me being aware, but at the same time, may help me mange the immediate postpartum back pain better.

Method of delivery

I am keen to have a natural birth with as little intervention as is safe. If there is a need for assistance and there is an option between a ventouse or forceps, I would prefer a ventouse. If I have to have a section, I would prefer this under a spinal block rather than general anaesthetic.

Pain relief

Sometimes women who have had an epidural for sciatic pain report that it made their pain worse. This can make them anxious about the possibility of having an epidural anaesthetic during labour. These fears can be ameliorated by explaining the differences, for example, in volume between an epidural used for sciatic pain and one used during labour. Some women have reported an increase in their back pain following an epidural during a previous birth, or have heard of this from another person.

There are two considerations here:

1 Was the epidural the cause of the pain, or was it a combination of the process of labour, lax ligaments and being in positions that they are not used to?
2 While the epidural is effective the woman feels no pain and may stay in one position for too long or get into positions she would not normally assume.

It is important that the patient problem-solves how she can make her midwife aware of what she can and can't do before the epidural is inserted, and that her needs and concerns are heard.

Other methods of pain relief should be discussed so the patient can make an informed choice. These may include: TENS (transcutaneous electrical nerve stimulation), birthing pool, relaxation, and breathing exercises, as well as alternative pharmacological options such as pethidine and 'gas'.

Pelvic floor muscles

The importance of pelvic floor exercise both before and after delivery needs to be emphasised for the prevention of stress incontinence. Sometimes, episiotomies are necessary and it is helpful to let the woman know that repairs are OK and that patients who start their pelvic floor exercises early will recover more quickly. Discussing the healing process and the importance of movement, will help her put this into context. There are many ways of teaching pelvic floor exercises. One is to describe the muscle as a sling that holds the pelvic contents in position and attaches from the pubic bone at the front through to the coccyx behind. Describe the two main types of muscle (slow and fast twitch) and emphasise the importance of exercising both. For the slow twitch muscle, contractions should be slow. Ask the woman to focus on her perineal area, imagining it as an elevator: the doors close, the lift goes to the first, second, third, and fourth floor. It then comes back down, floor by floor, to ground floor where the door opens and the perineum relaxes. This is all done to a slow count.

For the fast twitch muscles, ask the patient to see how many short and fast clenches she can do in one go. Once she has found a baseline for each type of exercise, she can gradually pace up the amount. It is important to give guidance however, as often incorrect muscles are used. Guidance may be obtained through self-examination, internal examination by the physiotherapist, or the use of a periniometer, however the therapist must be well trained before using the two latter techniques. A useful book for both therapist and patient is *Women's Waterworks* by Pauline Chiarelli.

Hypermobility

Many chronic pain sufferers who are hypermobile find pregnancy a good time, with less pain than usual. A few have more pain, so patients need to be ready to deal with this by pacing and getting the family to help.

Hypermobile women do seem to be more likely to need braces or binders. It is worth mentioning the various kinds available and indicating that different supports suit different people. If support appears to be necessary she may need to seek the advice of a physiotherapist who specialises in obstetrics.

Conclusion

Chronic pain does not prevent a woman from having a child. The physiotherapists at INPUT come across about half a dozen women per year who have a baby after attending the programme. Some ring to ask advice while they are pregnant and some write after the happy event, often to thank the team for all their help and support. We have found it useful to ask these patients how they have dealt with their pregnancy and labour, and for advice they would give other women with chronic pain wanting a baby. An example of one woman's experiences appears as Appendix 2.

If a patient is keen to become pregnant, we usually advise her to continue practising and using the principles she has learnt for 6-12 months after finishing the programme. She will then be versed in all the essential skills, not only for pain management but for pregnancy and child rearing. Good pacing, a graded fitness programme, relaxation techniques, communication skills, and coping skills are helpful to any pregnant woman with or without pain. One of the most helpful things the INPUT team, and other patients that have had a baby, can do for women who fear pain in pregnancy is to help them gain the control and self-confidence they need to manage their pain.

There is nothing more satisfying than seeing a patient's face light up when the possibility of pregnancy is first raised, and then later to receive a letter or phone call letting us know that all is well with mother and baby. More importantly, being a chronic pain sufferer and yet still having a child successfully can give encouragement to other women with chronic pain who would dearly like to have a child.

REFERENCES

Flor H, Fydrich T, Turk DC 1992 Efficacy of multidisciplinary pain treatment centers: a meta-analytic review. Pain 49:221–230

Williams AC de C 1993 In-patient management of chronic pain. In: Hodes M and Moorey S (Eds) Psychological treatment in disease and illness, Gaskell Press, London.

Appendix 1   Patient Handout

CHRONIC PAIN AND PREGNANCY

Women who have been on the INPUT programme usually find they are managing their chronic pain better, feel fitter and able to do more, and are achieving some of the goals they have set. At this point they may start to think about more long term, life goals, like having a baby. Once the thought 'Could I have a baby?' crosses your mind, several questions and worries may also come up.

WHAT OTHER INPUT WOMEN HAVE ASKED ABOUT HAVING A BABY

- Will pregnancy cause further damage to my spine? Will I be able to carry a baby?

- Will pregnancy make my pain worse—and what about delivery?

- I can only just manage my own pain problem/look after myself and my partner—how can I manage with a baby as well?

- Surely I won't be able to do pacing when I have a baby, but pacing helps me get through the day. I'm frightened of not being able to do it. How can I manage both the pain and the baby?

- What about medication when I'm pregnant. Will I be able to manage without pain killers, or will they harm the baby?

- Can I continue with my exercises and stretch through pregnancy and are there any special exercises I need to do?

- When the baby is born, how will I manage to lift it and carry it? How will I carry the pushchair when I can't lift much now?

- How can I breast feed when sitting is so painful and difficult?

- I don't like to ask for help, people must be so sick of my pain; how can I ask for more help?

    This handout will, we hope, answer some of these questions.

PREGNANCY AND YOUR BODY

Being pregnant and having a baby is a very natural process that your body has been designed to do. Your womb is prepared and waiting, your bones and muscles and your whole body have been made in such a way that they expect pregnancy and childbirth. Having chronic pain, of itself does not alter this. There are some conditions where doctors categorically advise patients that they must not have children. **This is extremely rare**. Many women with heart defects, extremely deformed spines and hips, or damaged organs such as lungs, liver, or kidneys, have had a family. Some women with no arms (thalidomide victims) some with no legs, and many who are paralysed from a broken back have still been able to have and bring up a family. Obviously they need more advice, may need more tests and care from their doctor during pregnancy and labour, and may need more support than average from their families with bringing up the children.

PREVIOUS DAMAGE

You may have had a quite severe injury or major surgery in the past and wonder if this will affect being pregnant. At INPUT you will have learnt about the process of healing. You will thus know that healing has finished and you now have scar tissue. Scar tissue needs to stretch and can be helped to remodel back to normal tissue as much as possible by *using* that part of the body. The exercise and activity programme at INPUT will have taught you how to do this, so keeping these up **will** make a difference. Spinal fusions, for example, do not pose any problems for pregnancy of themselves. In fact, many women with severe scoliosis (twisted deformed spine) who have had their spines totally fused from shoulder level down to the back have still had families.

Being pregnant will bring changes to the spine—these are discussed later—but these changes occur gradually. You can learn to adapt and with pacing avoid extra difficulties.

PREPARATION AND PLANNING FOR PREGNANCY

General health

There are many books which will advise you about preparing for pregnancy. A list of some easily available books is at the end of this handout.

Whether you have chronic pain or not, it is essential that you look carefully at your diet and your alcohol intake, and give up smoking. If you want to become pregnant, see your doctor about advice for what to do about your present medication, with a view to decreasing and perhaps stopping your pain medication if you have not already done so.

Muscles and joints, heart and lungs

Everyone should plan to get fit before pregnancy. When you have a back problem it is worth making the spine, muscles and all joints as healthy as possible, building up fitness in preparation for pregnancy and labour, and looking after the baby. Pacing up the INPUT exercises and gradually getting back to some sport will do this, as the handout *Joints* will remind you. You may also need to remember that **feelings** of weakness in the back or joints, or a sensation that they might break if they are moved too far, are just that—**only** feelings. Feelings of weakness get worse with the less you do, and improve with the more you do—provided you pace it up. Bones and joints toughen up and strengthen in response to the physical movement and stresses you give to them. Feeling tired can come from overdoing and not taking sufficient regular breaks/rests, as well as from being unfit.

Building blocks

In addition to general fitness, it will also be necessary to look at your activity building blocks before becoming pregnant. To cope with being pregnant and looking after a baby/toddler you will need to check that you have built up the following activities sufficiently.

Activity	Time	Use
Sitting straight	20 mins	— resting with the weight off the feet — breast feeding
Lying on right side and on left side	15-30 mins	— rest positions when pregnant — breast feeding (alternate with sitting)
Lying on the tummy	15 mins	— after the baby is born to help the womb go back into place
Squatting	2 mins	— stretch ligaments etc ready for labour — may be used during labour (10 mins+ tolerance needed) — getting down to toddler's level /playing with toddler
Kneeling on kneeler	10 mins	— during labour, especially last stage — changing baby's nappy on a bed or floor — bathing baby — playing with toddler on the floor
Carrying 20 lb	10 lb	— holding the baby — carrying baby + pushchair (approx) or small toddler
Lifting 20 lb	10 lb	— lifting baby out of bath/cot/car seat — lifting small toddler
Walking with no aids	15 mins	— help pain in the 1st stage of labour — manage shopping, going to parks with toddlers
Pushing	50 lb	— push toddler + shopping in pushchair/supermarket trolley

These times and weights are merely a guide. It is possible to manage with a bit less on some if you have sufficient help, but it is best to build up your tolerances so that you can easily manage things rather than struggling at your limits.

Negotiation with relatives and friends

You will have already discussed managing your pain problem with your partners and will need to involve them with your plans for having the baby. They will have to help you a lot during pregnancy and in the years after the baby is born. It is always useful to find out from relatives and friends whether they would be prepared to offer any help during and after the pregnancy. It is often the case that you can't keep the 'to be' grannies away when the prospect of a grandchild is afoot! It may be that you would rather not ask for help, but with any pregnancy there may be times when you are unable to do the shopping, do the hoovering, or take the bus to the antenatal clinic and regular help (such as a weekly visit to the supermarket with a relative) may make all the difference. During the early days and weeks after the birth most mothers will say 'Get as much help as you can'. The first few weeks are very special and you may prefer to spend this time alone with your partner. He can help and support you, but sooner or later will probably have to go back to work, so that you are left with a small baby alone at home. Health visitors will visit and advise you on queries you have, but some regular help with the shopping, washing or housework will be necessary until you have become accustomed to the change in routine.

When thinking about asking your friends and relatives how much help they can give you, you may like to read the handout on good communication. A simple way may be to ask your friend/relative if they would like to go over your plan for pregnancy with you. They may well have had first hand experience of this and feel very good about being asked for their advice. Once you have a workable plan, you will find it easier to ask for help, and will probably find that help is offered anyway.

Planning for pregnancy at work

If you are working and trying to be or are pregnant you will need to plan to pace your work more carefully, as you will feel more tired while you are pregnant. Simple measures, such as alternating between jobs done standing and sitting, using your breaks to rest or do some relaxation, allowing more time to get to work so you are not rushing, and negotiating with colleagues for help with heavier work-loads, will all be necessary. Making a timetable of how you spend your day/week may be a good way to look at what you are doing and how you could change it. It is your right that your employer should offer you alternative jobs to do if your job becomes too heavy during pregnancy. It is important to remember that you cannot be made redundant because you are pregnant. If you want further information regarding yours rights as a pregnant women contact Maternity Alliance (address at the end of handout).

CONCEPTION

The peak fertile period, when the egg is released from the ovary, comes about 14 days before the end of the cycle. If you are irregular and don't really know when you are fertile you can buy a urine testing kit from your pharmacy. This will help you determine your fertile period. Among couples having intercourse without contraception, 25% of the women will conceive within the first month, 60% within 6 months, 75% within 9 months, 80% within a year, and 90% within 18 months, so the large majority of women will conceive within 18 months if they are not using contraception. The handout on sex includes some positions that can be more comfortable for people with back pain, which you may find helpful. Do remember to remain lying down for some time after sex rather than standing up. If you need to move, just turn onto your side. So on a final note why not relax and enjoy this special time with your partner.

If you are having problems or worries about conception go and have a chat with your GP. S/he may be able to give you some simple advice that makes all the difference.

PREGNANCY

The first 3 months (the first trimester)

Common problems and how to cope

Tiredness. Sometimes during the early stages of pregnancy you may feel more tired than normal. This is due to hormonal changes and tends to settle after the first 3 months. During this period if you do feel tired it is important that you are doubly aware about pacing your activities and try not to overdo any one thing. Regular short rests incorporating some of the relaxation techniques you have learnt at INPUT can be very helpful.

Nausea. This is a complaint that some may never experience and others do to varying degrees. Hormonal changes again are said to be responsible for this. A useful tip includes having some plain dry biscuits with you at all times as they can often help alleviate this unpleasant feeling. A useful point to remember is that often you feel more nauseous when you are tired, so pacing your activities and taking time out to relax should help feelings of nausea.

Varicose veins. 'Varicose' veins are swollen veins just below the skin, and occur most commonly in the legs. As your pregnancy develops in the first three months, your blood volume increases by about one-third. In addition to this, your veins and arteries are more relaxed due to changes in your hormone levels. This, plus an increase in weight, can lead to the development of varicose veins. Helpful tips to minimise varicose veins:

- avoid standing still for long periods

- do some of your relaxation lying down with your feet up

- squat regularly as this helps push the blood up the legs

- high factor support tights or stockings may help

- prevent constipation wherever possible (see below).

Constipation. This often occurs in the early months of your pregnancy, and is due to the hormone progesterone. This makes the bowels more relaxed and sluggish, so more water than usual is absorbed from the stool, making it hard and dry. Helpful tips:

- drink plenty of water

- eat lots of fruit, vegetables and high fibre foods such as wholemeal bread

- take regular exercise to help the bowels move.

Laxatives are not recommended by doctors—dried figs and prunes in combination with a high fibre diet will do the same job and are safer.

If you are still having difficulties, pass your stool while squatting rather than sitting on the loo. Sitting on the loo does not allow the bowels to open up properly, whereas squatting does, is more natural, and minimises straining. You can 'go' over a child's potty or put some paper/newspaper on the floor.

Third to sixth month (the second trimester)

The second trimester could be called the 'blooming phase'. Your energy levels should start to improve, feelings of nausea will settle, and you will probably have rosy cheeks from the increase in your blood circulation. During this period you should expect to gain about 6kg (13lb), though this can be variable and should only be used as a rough guide. It is best to stick to a sensible healthy diet and keep up physical activities and hobbies as much as you are able. Swimming is a very pleasant and beneficial activity as the water takes your weight while you exercise, and they say the baby enjoys it as well! With all activity it is important to remember to pace it and if you haven't done the activity before, to set a low baseline and gradually build up.

You will probably start attending antenatal clinics at the beginning of your second trimester. You will meet a midwife who will ask questions regarding your general health, as well as do some general checks such as take your weight, and blood and urine tests. It will be a good time to mention to her that you have a pain problem and introduce her to your plan for pregnancy. You will probably have an ultrasound scan as some point between 18 and 20 weeks to check that all is well with baby.

Last three months (third trimester)

You will probably be invited to attend parent-craft classes at your local hospital or health centre. These are usually a course of six sessions where advice on gentle exercise, breathing exercises, available pain control for labour, and basic baby care such as how to bath a newborn is taught. A visit to the labour ward is also often available if you wish to go. Partners or significant others are usually invited to at least one of these sessions so they are able to offer help and support if you wish during labour. Sessions are taught by a midwife, health visitor and physiotherapist, and it is a good opportunity for you to ask questions and allay any fears you may have regarding the birth. It is also worth mentioning that the National Child Birth Trust runs private antenatal classes. A course of six sessions can cost anything from £30 to £60. Other NCT classes, such as yoga for pregnancy, postnatal support groups, breast care advisory service, and exercise groups, are available in different areas. It is best to contact headquarters (telephone number below) to find out what is available in your area early on as these classes get booked up very early.

During the last 3 months you will probably gain a further 5 kg (11lb) in weight, though this is only a rough guide and varies from person to person. The extra weight carried in front will make you lean back more, changing your posture, so you will need to pace more when standing and walking. The changes in posture can be helped if you have continued to do gentle exercise throughout your pregnancy to maintain and strengthen the muscles around the lower back and tummy area. If you are unsure about what exercises to do ask the physiotherapist at your parent-craft classes.

At this time the hormones will be softening your ligaments. This is preparing for the birth, when the pelvic bones will separate slightly to allow the baby through. The softening may be more pronounced in women who are double jointed or naturally very supple. It can make the back feel less supported and ache more. It is important for these reasons that you pace your activities as much as possible, allowing time to lie or sit down and practice the relaxation techniques you have found to work for you. It is also a time to ask for help as daily chores may become too tiring. If you have a particular problem at this stage, there are elasticised supports that should be available from the physiotherapist at parent-craft classes.

Relaxation/breathing exercises

Relaxation and breathing exercises are often taught in parent-craft classes, usually by a physiotherapist. There are a lot of books available that talk about the different relaxation techniques that can be used during pregnancy and labour. If you have attended INPUT then you will have an added advantage as you will already know how effective relaxation can be and also have a first hand working knowledge of some of the techniques. You will be taught various breathing exercises at your parent-craft classes to be used during labour, the tummy breathing you were taught at INPUT will come in useful.

LABOUR

Pain control during labour

There are many options for pain relief during labour, and it is advisable that you think about this beforehand so you have some control over what happens during that special time. You can always change your mind if you want to. You will find out about what is available at your hospital from the parent-craft classes, or you can discuss any queries you have with your midwife, GP or obstetrician. We know from INPUT patients that pain control that does not work for chronic pain, still works for acute pain in the same person. If your pain control is not working, or not working enough, do ask for more or something else.

If you are using TENS during labour and feel it isn't working, don't switch it off. It is best to add something else, as the TENS will be working to a degree and you may get a lot more pain when it is turned off. You may have been disappointed by epidurals for your back pain or sciatica, or even found it very painful, and are frightened of having another. The epidural for labour is different and the pain is different. It is acute and will not last. There are still other options than epidurals. These include entonox, pethidine, TENS, massage and the support of your partner.

Positions and pacing

Over the years doctors have expected mothers to lie on their backs during labour and the birth, as it was convenient and comfortable for them. It is now known that lying on your back slows the progress of labour, and during the birth the baby has to be pushed uphill! It also prevents the pelvic bones from opening naturally, so it is harder for the baby to get out. Thankfully things are changing and maternity units are much more open to supporting the wishes of the mother. During the early stages of labour many women find moving around, getting into different positions, and gentle massage can be very helpful. Later, walking around between contractions helps pain relief and speeds up the labour. It is possible to still walk around and have the baby fully monitored though you may need a little help from the midwife or your partner if you need to have leads attached.

Usually you can give birth in any position you feel comfortable in. You can take extra pillows, bean bags etc if you wish to. Some hospitals have birthing stools, and some even have birthing pools. You will be able to find out what is available when you visit the maternity unit. What is important is that you choose, have the flexibility of several options, and have control over the situation. Pacing up squatting, crouching, and kneeling will have been essential to allow you to use the delivery positions and change to another when you feel you need to. An important thing to remember as well is to relax between contractions. Some relaxation techniques, or some of your favourite music may be helpful; yes, you can even pace the birth! Often expectant mothers write out a birth plan so the staff know what you do and don't want during labour. Remember you can always change your mind— you are not bound by the plan.

EARLY DAYS

Asking for help on the ward

If it is your first baby you will probably stay in hospital overnight, just to get you settled with the newborn. This is often an ideal opportunity to ask for help, and support. The midwives will give advice and practical help, but if you don't ask they might assume you don't need help, so remember your communication skills. The Domino practice is used in a few hospitals, where you come into hospital with your community midwife when you are ready to give birth. Your midwife helps you deliver the baby, you have 4 hours to rest, and then you go home.

Help at home—family, friends and professionals

Once you go home you will find your routine quite disrupted, particularly during the first six weeks. You and the baby will both gradually settle once you get to know each other. This time can be very tiring for you. The one thing that all mums say regarding the first few days and weeks, is to get as much help as you can during this period. This is why it is advisable to negotiate with relatives and friends well in advance. The community midwife will visit you at home soon after the birth to check you and the baby are OK. After about 11 days the health visitor will start visiting to check the wellbeing of the baby and you.

Body mechanics

For an average of 6 weeks after birth, your ligaments will still be quite stretchy from the hormone Relaxin that your body produced to enable the baby to come out easily. During this time, when your tummy muscles will also not be as strong as usual, your back could be more easily damaged by incorrect lifting or bad posture. It is therefore important that you prepare for this in advance, making sure things are at the correct height, and plan a routine with your partner so that you cut out unnecessary lifting.

Cots. You should be able to touch the cot mattress when the cot sides are down without leaning over or bending over. Modern cots are usually high enough for this, but if you are very tall or are using an older family cot or crib, you may find it lower than this. To raise a cot you will need to place a platform or blocks under the legs. Blocks can easily be made by a friend who is handy with a saw and a screwdriver.

Changing area. You may be able to afford a changing table, but check that it is high enough for you. Otherwise you may need to change baby on your bed and kneel while you do it, or adapt another piece of furniture. Some people have used the top of a chest of drawers, putting plastic and some towelling on top, and getting a friend to make sides to it that go up and down so baby cannot roll off. Remember however, that you should never leave the baby alone on a changing table.

Breast feeding. You will need to plan how and where you are going to do this so your back is comfortably supported and your arms relaxed. Old fashioned nursing chairs were ideal. They were on rockers so you could easily calm baby down, and were low so that with your feet on the ground your knees were slightly up to hold baby to you, and your arms did not get tired. You did of course need strong leg muscles to get up from a low chair! Nowadays you can adapt the chairs you have. Choose one that is not too long in the seat, so that your bottom goes right back and your back is fully supported. Chair arms with a pillow over them helps support your arms and relax them. A foot rest will bring your knees up, then a pillow on your lap will bring the baby up to you so you don't have to lean over and your arms don't have to hold the baby up. Several times a day you will be able to breastfeed lying down on your side with the baby supported on pillows. It is important you do this, as there are few times when you have the opportunity to have a rest and you need to make as many as possible.

Bath time. Provided you are careful of the taps, a sink or basin can be used to bath small babies. It is an idea to have a chair nearby so that when baby is clean you can sit down, just supporting under his/her head, and let baby splash about in the water while you have a break. Most people want a baby bath however, and the sort that fit over a real bath are ideal. You can fill it direct from the taps so don't have to carry water about, and there is a plug in the bottom so the water just runs away into the bath. Being over the bath raises it so you should be able to reach baby easily by kneeling next to the bath. Using a kneeler (that doesn't mind getting wet!) is probably a good idea. If you only have a conventional plastic bath, don't put it on the floor or the bottom of the bath, put it up on a table or draining board and fill **and** empty it with a plastic jug so you can pace your carrying.

Carrying the baby. As you will have paced up carrying, holding the baby in your arms and walking will be fine for short distances. For outdoors you may decide to use a sling while baby is small or go straight to a push chair. Crying babies often calm down if you walk about rocking them. However, if they 'train you' to do this you will soon wear yourself out, and get aching arms and round shoulders. Try to find ways to comfort them other than carrying. A rocking chair is good for this as they lie on your lap or over your shoulder and all you do is rock to and fro pushing with your feet. Many babies still persist in crying, even if when they have had plenty of attention, when they are well fed, are the right temperature and have a clean nappy. This is often very frustrating and a source of tension for you. It is important to try to not get worked up or to blame yourself. Sometimes the only thing is to continue to use calming words or even leave them to cry it out.

205

Some toddlers 'train' their parents to pick them up a lot, always asking for it and getting angry/crying if they are not carried. Try to start as you intend to continue and don't teach your child the habit. If they want a cuddle they will learn to ask for one then wait for you to sit down when *they* climb onto your lap and get a cuddle (a much better one than if you are struggling to carry them as well). If they are tired of walking, you both stop to pace the walk and have a rest, or *they* get into their push chair. You will, we hope, be able to carry a small toddler a short way after you have practised and paced it up. To help lifting and save you bending so much, try teaching them to climb onto a chair first. Be careful doing this when you are tired and be careful not to allow them to come to expect to be carried all the time.

We hope this has given you some ideas in the planning that is required when considering having children if you are a chronic pain sufferer. If you have any further concerns that you, your partner and your doctor cannot seem to get to the bottom of, it may be helpful to ring someone at INPUT to discuss them.

USEFUL BOOKS

Conception, Pregnancy and Birth Miriam Stoppard. Dorling Kindersley 1993

Natural Pregnancy Janet Balaskas. Sidgwick & Jackson 1990
This book has good sections on relaxation, and natural remedies for common complaints of pregnancy.

Womens Waterworks Pauline Chiarelli. NEEN Health Care 1988, East Dereham

USEFUL ADDRESSES

British Pregnancy Advisory Service (BPAS)
Austy Manor
Wooton Wawen
Solihull
West Midlands B95 6BX

Provides many services, including pregnancy testing, counselling, fertility investigation and artificial insemination

Family Planning Information Service
27-35 Mortimer Street
London W1N 7RJ
0171-636 7866

Provides free leaflets including booklist and advice on all family planning matters

Disabled Mothers Group, Disability Resources Centre
11 Warner Road
Walthamstow
London E17

Maternity Alliance
12 Britannia Street
London WC1X 9JP

Pressure group & information service on maternity rights & services

The National Childbirth Trust (NCT)
9 Queensborough Terrace
London W2 3TB
0171-221 3833

Provides useful information and a national contact register for both able-bodied and disabled parents.

National Contact Register for Parents with Disabilities

6 Forest Road
Crowthorne
Berkshire RG11 7EG
01344 773366

A register of parents with a disability.

Association to Aid the Sexual and Personal Relationships of Disabled People (SPROD)
286 Camden Road

London N7 0BJ
0171-607 8851

Can provide information on sexual matters as well as contact with an individual counsellor

Appendix 2   Patient Handout

PATIENT REPORT

The patient report overleaf is included because it provides a personal perspective on the difficulties of motherhood and child-rearing when there is the additional burden of chronic pain. Patient reports like this one serve to expose the reality of the chronic pain experience and the many obstacles that can occur. Even so, tackled in the right way using appropriate management skills, many obstacles are surmountable. It is hoped that this report provides a positive message for other patients in similar situations. It may be copied for distribution to patients.

Therapists' background information

Age 19:   hurt back lifting a patient as a student nurse.

Age 20:   myodil myelogram and laminectomy for L4/5 herniated disc— helped for 1 year.

Age 24:   2nd myodil myelogram and laminectomy—'mopping up'.

Diagnosis: Severe adhesive arachnoiditis from the upper portion of L4 to the end of the sacrum.

Pain distribution: Low back, buttocks and vagina, lateral lower leg and calves, interscapular area and sternum, up either side of neck, sub-occipital round to right eye, permanent headache with migraine type every 6 weeks.

Numbness: Lateral right thigh, anterior lower legs and feet from 4" above the knees except both great toes, and ulnar distribution both arms.

Intermittent urinary retention when numbness in the legs is worse.

O/E some fair lumbar spine movement all directions—only about a quarter reduced, but only 10° of neck flexion, 90° of shoulder flexion (pulls in face), very tight SLR/Slump and hip flexion to 105° (pulls in face/top of head).

Summary: Major loss of range of tests that mechanically stress the nervous system. Tethering and constriction of dural tissue in the lumbar region and even elsewhere in the spinal canal is a possibility. Marked extrasegmental referral of symptoms (hip flexion and shoulder flexion causing facial symptoms) most likely indicates altered central processing, but could also relate to adverse neural mobility factors too. She has maintained a degree of muscle fitness, and areas of avoided activity generally relate to movements and postures that physically stress neural tissue.

Motherhood and chronic pain

When my son was 14 months old, I was diagnosed with arachnoiditis. The pain was so bad that they thought I had a spinal tumour. No further information was given and I was told to learn to live with the chronic pain.

I had, through desperation, developed various methods of looking after a small baby, mostly alone, as my husband travelled a lot. I had great difficulty picking the baby up and always had to move in stages: first the baby, then the carry-cot, then the wheels of the pram etc. When he started to crawl, I took him to the top of the stairs and placed him on his tummy. I then pulled him down one step at a time, backwards, and he soon caught on! As soon as he could stand, I taught him to climb up onto a chair. I could then either pick him up, or get him to climb up onto his changing mat. These activities were always supervised and neither of my sons ever fell down the stairs (as did many of my friends' children, because they had stair gates.) This used to make some peoples' hair stand on end, but as anyone will tell you, these children have a built in sense of responsibility that does not adversely affect their childhood but makes them very caring individuals.

As I was unaware of the progressive nature of arachnoiditis, we decided to have a second baby, when Daniel was 18 months old. I suffered an immediate increase in pain and could take no pain relief. I was housebound for nearly 9 weeks. After that I was almost completely pain free for 12 weeks, during which time I learned to drive. I lived in a village and realised how isolated I would become with a second baby. Then disaster struck. I went into labour at 24 weeks and was rushed to hospital with our son. I had contractions every two minutes and they tried to give me pethidine, but I implored the young houseman to help me save my baby and so against their better judgement, they put up a special drip, but the contractions started again, so I was sent home with the oral version of the medicine, and told not to be too hopeful.

I continued to look after my baby son and to rest and suffered the side effects of the tablets. It raised your heartbeat until you felt like you were having a panic attack and your hands would have the shakes! I sat my driving test when I was 30 weeks pregnant and failed. So, back home, back to bed; but 4 weeks and one day later, I was back. I knew that if I didn't pass my test before the baby was born, I would be housebound. I got the manager of the centre and when he told me to reverse around the corner, I twice ended up on the wrong side of the white line. He said: 'I think we'll give you the benefit of the doubt on that one, because of your bump. Pull over and get your breath back.' Little did he know! To this day I still cannot turn to reverse. I did pass but we were gone so long my driving instructor telephoned the maternity hospital!

My second son, Tom, was born at 36 weeks, by Caesarian section. He was not only premature, but born in November—my worst time of the year, pain wise. When he was two weeks old, I had to stop breast feeding him, so that I could take pain medication. There were times when the pain was so bad that I had to bottle feed him through the bars of his cot at night. When he was a little older, his brother used to climb into his cot and lift him up, just enough, so that I could pick him up. He was a fighter and is now nearly fourteen years old and almost six feet tall, like his brother.

I have been a single parent for the last eighteen months. I have had a home help for the last 5 years, who now also does my shopping and housework and, since December 1997, I have been able to drive a car, adapted by Motability, which has given me a greater degree of independence. I attended the INPUT pain management programme, for four weeks, in July 1997 and I wish that I had had those management techniques all those years ago!

Eight years ago, as my health deteriorated, we moved into a town. I had been relying on school transport, but I realised that as the boys got older, there would be periods, sometimes for weeks at a time, when I could not drive and they would need to be independent. During flare-ups, I had a sixteen year old student to take them to the park or swimming. I also found a female taxi driver who used to ferry them to and from a wide selection of council run sporting activities during the school holidays. I used my disability benefit to pay for these times. I had to arrange it so that life could continue as well as possible without me. I used to feel guilty about this, until I realised that the most important thing was, that no matter how ill I was, I was always there. That still counts today.

My sons are my reason for getting out of bed in the morning. They say they do not feel that they have missed out on too much through having a mum with a disability. Indeed, they have often said that we did more things than some of their friends. When I was housebound, they were too, so we had more contact and tried that little bit harder. A good sense of humour is an absolute must, and we've had many occasions where if we hadn't laughed, we would have cried! They still talk about the day, three years ago, when mum went body surfing with them and then had to sit on the waters' edge for twenty minutes, in front of the life guards, hoping that the tide was going out and not in, while she got some feeling back in her legs. Did you say irresponsible? No, fun in safety, with help on hand, if needed.

Of course they would rather their mum did not have chronic pain, but things have been so much better, since INPUT, for all of us. The boys are a constant source of fun and encouragement, as well as the usual painful teenage bits! (and they say, the usual embarrassing mum bits!) Daniel is a talented musician and plays in a band. He has just completed his GCSE exams, and will be going on to college to study music in September. Tom is very sporty and is bright enough to be taking his GCSE exams a year early. He wants to be a solicitor. I am very proud of my sons and how they have coped with the changing circumstances over the years.

They can also both cook and have been doing so, with supervision, since they were twelve. They also know their way round the ironing board! They cut the grass and do the heavier garden work and have been known to shout, 'I thought you were meant to stop, when your timer goes' if I get carried away with the dead heading!.

We are looking forward to going on holiday to Dorset, this summer, something I would never have believed possible this time last year. And when they were with their father at Easter, I flew to Dublin by myself. That was my first long-term goal since leaving INPUT. Now I have been invited to Hong Kong in October. And the boys? They said, 'Go for it, Mum!'

I am not a failure if I don't succeed, I'm a success because I tried.
Feel the fear and do it anyway.

Index

CNS Press is owned by physiotherapists, and specialises in publishing books by physiotherapists for physiotherapists. We understand the needs of the profession, and we aim to publish quality books at an affordable price.

We offer a 30 day money back guarantee if you are not completely satisfied with your purchase, so you can order our books with confidence.

Contact CNS Press for a list of our new and forthcoming titles and for details of achesandpainsonline courses.

CNS PRESS
Kestrel
Swanpool
Falmouth
Cornwall
TR11 5BD
UK

Ph: +44 0 1326 312156
Fax: +44 0 1326 211149

Email: info@cnspress.co.uk

WWW: www.achesandpainsonline.com

Now Available...

Editor: Louis Gifford

Topical Issues In Pain 1

Introductory essay
**Integrating pain awareness into physiotherapy –
wise action for the future.** David Butler

Part 1: Whiplash – science and management

Whiplash – is there a lesion. Michael Thacker

The mature organism model. Louis Gifford

Tissue and input related mechanisms. Louis Gifford

The 'central' mechanisms. Louis Gifford

Output mechanisms. Louis Gifford

Physiotherapy management of whiplash injuries: review. Michael Thacker

Minimising chronicity after whiplash injury. Vicki Harding

Management of chronic pain following whiplash injuries.
Suzanne Shorland

Patient assessment – case history. Suzanne Shorland

**Understanding people with chronic pain following whiplash –
a psychological perspective.** Kate Treves

Part 2: Fear – avoidance beliefs and behaviour

Fear – avoidance theory. Patrick Hill

Iatrogenic disability and back pain rehabilitation. Michael Rose

Cognitive – behavioural approach to fear and avoidance. Vicki Harding

Are we being patientist? Vicki Harding

Structure orientated beliefs and disability due to back pain. Max Zusman

Announcing...

Editor: Louis Gifford

Topical Issues In Pain 3

Part 1: Placebo

The placebo response. Nigel Lawes

The neurobiology of the placebo response. Nigel Lawes

Placebo mechanisms of pain relief . Patricia Roche

Part 2: Muscles and Pain

The psychophysiology of muscle pain. Paul Watson

The epidemiology of chronic muscluoskeletal pain. Ann Papageorgiou

The role of the back muscles in low back pain. Patricia Dolan

Muscle injury, healing and health. Louis Gifford

Part 3: Sympathetic Nervous System and Pain

The sympathetic nervous system: a biological perspective. Louis Gifford

Perspectives on the pathobiology of complex regional pain syndromes. Michael Thacker

Assessment: the change of focus in chronic management. Case History. Suzanne Brook

Pain mechanisms: sympathetically maintained pain vs sympathetically independent pain. Michael Thacker

Mental stress and tissue health. Louis Gifford

How to introduce exercise into a treatment plan. Suzanne Brook

A critical review of the management of complex regional pain syndromes. Michael Thacker

Management case histories. Suzanne Brook

Publication 2001

Topical Issues in Pain 4

Publication 2001

To order additional copies of Topical Issues in Pain 1 and 2, or to register your interest in receiving information about new titles as they become available, simply complete this form and the payment details overleaf and return it to us, or contact us via our web site or email address.

CNS Press,

Kestrel, Swanpool, Falmouth, Cornwall TR11 5BD, UK

ph: (+44) 01326 312156 · fax: (+44) 01326 211149

email: info@cnspress.co.uk · www.achesandpainsonline.com

❏ Mr ❏ Mrs ❏ Ms ❏ Miss ❏ Other

First Name	
Last Name	
Street Address	
City/Suburb	
County/State	
Postcode	
Country	
Ph (wk)	
Fax (wk)	
E-mail Address	

❏ *Please place me on your mailing list and notify me when other titles are published*

Topical Issues in Pain 1

❏ *Please rush me* .... *copy/ies of* Topical Issues in Pain 1 @:		
❏ UK - £23.50 per copy inc. p&p	£	
❏ PPA members £20.00 inc. p&p (UK)	£	
❏ Europe - £23.50 per copy + £2.50 p&p	£	
❏ Worldwide - £23.50 per copy + £3.50 p&p	£	
Please indicate clearly number of books required, tick applicable boxes and complete total column. (Postage for Europe and Worldwide, air-mail) £	Total	

Topical Issues in Pain 2

❏ *Please rush me* .... *copy/ies of* Topical Issues in Pain 2 @:		
❏ UK - £25.00 per copy inc. p&p	£	
❏ PPA members £21.50 inc. p&p (UK)	£	
❏ Europe - £25.00 per copy + £2.50 p&p	£	
❏ Worldwide - £25.00 per copy + £3.50 p&p	£	
Please indicate clearly number of books required, tick applicable boxes and complete total column. (Postage for Europe and Worldwide, air-mail) £	Total	
Total from Topical Issues in Pain 1 Orders £		
Total £		

I am paying by: ❏ credit card   ❏ cheque / money order
(made out to CNS PRESS and in £UK currency only)

❏ MasterCard   ❏ Visa   ❏ Switch   Expiry date: ❏❏/❏❏

Credit card number: ❏❏❏❏ ❏❏❏❏ ❏❏❏❏ ❏❏❏❏

Cardholder's name
(Please print)

Cardholder's signature